ROMAN PASSIONS
A HISTORY OF PLEASURE IN IMPERIAL ROME

Roman Passions

A History of Pleasure in Imperial Rome

Ray Laurence

continuum

Continuum UK, The Tower Building, 11 York Road, London SE1 7NX
Continuum US, 80 Maiden Lane, Suite 704, New York, NY 10038

www.continuumbooks.com

First published 2009

British Library Cataloguing-in-Publication Data
A catalogue record for this book is available from the British Library.

ISBN 978 1 84725 032 2

Typeset by Pindar NZ, Auckland, New Zealand
Printed and bound by MPG Books Ltd, Cornwall, Great Britain

Contents

Illustrations

Introduction: Roman Passions

PLEASURE AND HISTORY

As a student working on a fairly impenetrable PhD thesis, I attended a lecture by Oswyn Murray at the British School at Rome. His delivery was emphatic, well argued and slightly evangelical: historians needed to be involved in the definition and writing of a history of pleasure. It was a subject that in 1990 simply did not exist, although Michel Foucault had done much to demonstrate the possibilities. Oswyn was adamant though that we were faced with a choice, which he explained with an interesting metaphor. At breakfast in a bar in Rome, there is a choice between a *panino* (a bread roll) and a *cornetto* (a croissant – perhaps filled with jam or cream); he suggested that he would choose the *cornetto* every time.[1] There was a fierce debate – famous Italian professors made the case for panini on nutritional grounds, yet Oswyn stuck firm. This was for the simple reason that a history of pleasure was not about utility, but individual choice and enjoyment, which he equated with the qualities of a *cornetto*. His vision for a history of pleasure displeased some academics as it detached the explanation of human action from a functional basis centred on the utility of pleasure.

The lecture shifted my own thinking about what made good history, but I was unable to do much about this until I had written my thesis. It was only many years later that I found myself in a position to return to the issues Oswyn raised and was surprised that little had been published on Roman pleasure. There were, it is true, many more books on the Roman concept of immorality, and the Roman thinking about sex, food and its consumption was to have far more written about it; music and song were even taken seriously; yet I had a feeling that much of the modern writing on the subject did not engage with what Oswyn had set out as a history of pleasure (there were far too many *panini* and far too few *cornetti*). These concepts of a history of pleasure need to be revisited before we can set forth on an investigation of what the Romans saw as their passions. At the heart of the history of pleasure lie two assumptions: the first that pleasure is engaged with not so much from the point of view of its usefulness to society, but for enjoyment; and, second, that pleasure has a close relationship to the definition of a culture.[2] What we are looking at in this book are the passions that the Romans collectively felt defined themselves as a culture and from which they derived pleasure. Yet a history of pleasure needs to do more than simply describe what the Romans did.[3] For this book, I have inserted an underlying argument, familiar to many writers of the time, that the Romans of the first century CE had a greater range of goods, tastes, smells, vistas, colours, and perhaps also sounds at their disposal than their predecessors of the previous century. Engagement with these new items and their display or use in front of or with others institutionalized these novelties into what might be described as a repertoire of pleasure.[4] Equally, there is a sense that these new or more developed passions of the first century CE depended for their novelty value in their potential for denunciation by others. To enjoy an activity in the first century CE, you needed a moralist, often an older man, to denounce the activities of the young or older men adopting the novelties that appealed to the young. Hence, the use of pleasure created a rhetorical means for the denunciation of another person's character, and in a society in which rhetoric ruled supreme, new pleasures were grist to the mill. What we have here is a classic case of a society creating a new set of rules to problematize the very nature of pleasure familiar to us from the work of Michel Foucault on sexuality. Oswyn Murray interestingly pointed out that pleasure in antiquity, for example in the Greek *symposium*, was ritualized to enhance pleasure and socialization rather than problematization.[5] This is true certainly of the basic structure of pleasure, but there is a difference in context. Murray was dealing with the *symposium* in Classical Greece, a very different context to the focus of this book on Rome in the first century CE. I will be looking at a culture whose variety of goods had increased, whose access to, for example, wine had increased in terms of availability, and whose engagement with pleasure was of a different nature. All of these factors led to the limitation, critique and ultimately the problematization of pleasure to restrain an individual's autonomous passions. In short, Rome in the first century CE is a very different context to that of earlier periods of classical history, and what made it different was its engagement with pleasure. We need simply think of the expansion of the vine into southern Gaul and Spain with a view to the mass export of cheap wine to the inhabitants of the city of Rome. At the same time, the elite (often owners of these provincial vineyards) found new products and new ways to develop their own culture of pleasure, distinguished in the case of wine by its quality from that of the wine drunk by the plebs. This society was rather different to that of its predecessors, and perhaps should also be distanced from later imperial societies experiencing an increase in the variety of goods available to it. The passions set out in this book are those of a particular culture: that of Rome and Italy in the first century CE.

PLAN OF THE BOOK

Rome in the first century CE appears at the outset to be dominated by those who enjoyed pleasure and those who set out to denounce it. The chapter that follows this introduction seeks to put pleasure in its rightful place in Roman culture via a study of gifts (real and imagined) that were exchanged at Rome's winter festival: the Saturnalia. Gifts had a significance for all, from emperor down to the most humble citizen – giving was a pleasure that all sought to excel at. At the same time, the act of giving was an action by which wealth, social status, morality, wit and other social qualities associated with the giver could be communicated. Chapter 2 examines the role of pleasure in the lives of the emperors. Pleasure did not just define an emperor's free time away from the affairs of state, but can be seen as having a central role in the construction of power at Rome. Even the most austere emperor, Augustus, used pleasure to define his power – whether in distributing money to gamble with or the power to coerce others (or their wives or children) to have sex with him. What gives the emperors a distinctive personality or character was their use of pleasure as much as their actions in the political realm. Hence what we find in this chapter, as in the previous one, is that pleasure takes centre stage. The emperor and his people needed a new setting for pleasure that would eclipse that found in any other city in the world. There was a new urban aesthetic developed at Rome, which is examined and discussed in Chapter 3. Matching these changes to the urban landscape was the development of the pleasure villa or garden (*hortus*) that is the subject of Chapter 4. By the end of the century, we can identify in the representation of these landscapes of pleasure a new attitude not found at the beginning of the century. These are landscapes to delight the senses. What these pleasure palaces do is extend the aesthetics of urbanism into the private realm and in a rural setting. In turn, the private palace was made available to the plebs in Rome with vast palaces with adjoining parkland constructed in the city for their pleasure – a sensual feast at the centre of which stood the emperor. The ultimate pleasure palace was of course Nero's Golden House – a public place in which the emperor could display his own engagement with pleasure and in which his people could have access to new sensory delights.

The next two chapters move towards an understanding of how the human body engaged with pleasure in the first century CE, beginning with the sensations that were associated with bathing and moving onto what we regard as the erotic. The baths were the public place where the Romans were naked, whereas the bedroom was the private room in which sex took place. The former had been subject to quite a number of changes over the course of the first century CE. There continued to be an emphasis on rooms of different temperature, but what was so different was the lighting of the baths via large windows to light up clear water and marble surfaces within which the bathers could experience sensations and also observe the bodies of others. The new environments for bathing developed a sensory experience that defined a person as Roman. It is something of a disappointment to discover that the Romans did not have orgies. Much has been written about Roman sex, mostly derived from literature with a selection of illustrations carefully chosen from wall paintings. In Chapter 6, I want to put Roman sex into an archaeological context. Hence, for the most part, the evidence used in this chapter derives from the graffiti, wall decoration and objects found in Pompeii. This allows us to understand what pleasures might have been considered normative and what were seen as fantasy or unusual experiences. The gentle art of insult in Pompeian graffiti creates categories of deviants (not all may have existed in reality). Straying away from Pompeii, the chapter ends with discussion of the normalization of child abuse via the institution of slavery, the representation of orgasms and recent discussion of Roman homosexuality.

The following two chapters take us into a different area and a wider range of sensations: smell, sight, sound and touch. Dining, the formal setting for the consumption of food and wine, expands the range of pleasures experienced. Yet, at the same time, through engagement with these sensations, distinctions of status and deference were reinforced; even though the ideals of conviviality defined all as equal – evidently some were more equal than others. Importantly, as we shall see, it was the pleasure of dining in association with the drinking of wine that defined people as civilized rather than as barbarians. Like the pleasures of bathing, those of consuming food and drink established the identity of the Romans. What we find in the examination of food is a fundamental change in taste across the first century CE with a massive increase in the importation of spices from the Indian subcontinent via Rome's ports on the Red Sea. Moreover, there were also concomitant changes in the production of wine – not least the creation of a mass market for cheap wine imported from the provinces to Rome on the one hand; and at the same time the development of high quality and higher-priced wines produced within Italy. Hence, although food and wine might define a person as Roman or civilized, the produce that provided that definition was subject to considerable change over the course of the first century CE.

The first Roman Emperor, Augustus, continues to provide modern scholars with surprises. Not least was his addiction to pantomime, a new art form that the Romans of the first century CE (apart from the emperor Tiberius) took to their hearts, joining in with the singing and dancing on stage. The audience was not averse to expressing its feelings with a full-blown riot. This was the century that would see Rome's emperor perform on stage, the culmination of a cultural process of evolution derived from Augustus' passionate approval of the new art form. What defines Roman culture in the first century CE is in some ways a new-found passion for song and dance – something that modern scholars are only beginning to appreciate fully and which is investigated in Chapter 9 of this book. The impact of this cultural change cannot be overestimated and is seen today when we visit Italy; most Roman towns of the first century CE had their theatre – an acoustically designed space in which to listen to music and song, while being visually stimulated by the dancing of performers and the chorus. Alongside the building of theatres, the first century CE saw the spread of the amphitheatre across not just Italy but also into the provinces; while in

Rome the new Flavian dynasty of emperors built the Colosseum – the largest amphitheatre and a lasting monument to the Roman love of entertainment. Within these structures, executions, gladiatorial combats and beast hunts took place. These were venues for seeing violence and killing at first hand. So much of our understanding of Roman society is dictated via a frame of violence, whether seen in the actions of soldiers, the audience watching the gladiators in the arena or in the intentions of some emperors. Chapter 10 sets out to place violence in its cultural context and to examine the elements of violence done to others that were enjoyed by the Romans in the first century CE. Opening with violence inflicted on slaves in the domestic sphere, the discussion shifts onto the public humiliations of criminals and the pleasure gained from watching such events. It is argued here that there is a human fascination with the infliction of pain and humiliation on others. A feature of the modern world as much as the ancient, it is seen today across the world as enemies of all modern states are ritually humiliated (for example Saddam Hussein's capture and execution), and it forms the foundation for much of our fascination with the more extreme forms of violence found in Roman society – many of which formed the bedrock of Ridley Scott's film *Gladiator*. Disturbingly, human beings gain pleasure from violence (even if today they choose not to participate, individuals can be drawn to representations of violence in fiction or non-fiction), and the Romans used violence to humiliate society's enemies – actions that were viewed publicly and seen to have brought collective pleasure.

Chapter 11 shifts focus towards another pleasure, the human passion for collecting objects. The Romans of the first century CE had greater access to public collections of sculpture and painting than at any other time in their history. The need to display collections of objects influenced the design of spaces – creating a new, well-lit temple design. However, the real passion was for the acquisition of curiosities for private collections that might be displayed to others in private or in public. The enthusiasm for the acquisition of such objects exists today and has been most clearly articulated by John Paul Getty in the twentieth century, who described his passion for the purchase of art objects to be similar to the addictions of drug abusers and alcoholics. Hence, collecting has to be included in this book. Alongside objects, Romans also collected human oddities. These humans, today, would be described as those with 'birth abnormalities', whose life expectancy, in the absence of modern medical intervention, would have been low. The survival of these human beings beyond infancy was a rare occurrence, but their rarity was a phenomenon that made them a collectible item. Sold in the slave market, these 'different' humans provided a source of pleasure to others in the first century CE. In fact we see a shift in attitude to them from being monsters to be destroyed in earlier times to becoming items of value by the end of the first century CE.

In writing the chapters of this book, I became acutely aware that Roman culture in the first century CE was subject to so many fundamental changes. In fact, seen historically, there was probably greater change after the death of Rome's first emperor than in the period of transition from the Republic of Cato and Cicero to the monarchy established by the emperor Augustus. It is this sense of change that forms the basis for the final chapter of the book. What is argued here is that the emperors became the central figures for the definition of pleasure and could create fashions that would survive long after their deaths. However much rhetoric was devoted to the restoration of traditional values with the advent of each new emperor, what was actually occurring was change. New emperors defined new forms of pleasure, and the focus on the emperor in both public and private created models of behaviour for the Roman elite to emulate. In short, nothing remained the same over the course of the first century apart from a moral rhetoric that pleasure was to be held at a distance and that feature demonstrates the importance of pleasure in the definition of individual identity and a society that was seen as Roman, rather than Greek or barbarian.

THANK YOU

This book was written while holding a Birmingham Research Fellowship. I am grateful to the University of Birmingham for providing both financial and intellectual support for my work. While working on *Roman Passions*, I was also involved in two other major research projects at Birmingham: *The City in the Roman West* with Simon Esmonde Cleary and Gareth Sears and *The Roman Life Course* with Mary Harlow. In discussion of these subjects, at something of a tangent to *Roman Passions*, my colleagues have revealed new ideas and thoughts on the structure and constitution of Roman society. I acknowledge the help of Gareth, Mary and Simon along with other members of the Institute of

Archaeology and Antiquity who have stimulated ideas based on their dazzlingly wide range of knowledge of societies in the past. They all have my very warmest thanks – the last three years have been a pleasure and a rare treat. Some of the themes pursued in this volume have their origins in another book: *Pompeii: The Living City*. Hence, I acknowledge Alex Butterworth's unspoken contribution, working with him shifted my focus and he revealed new ways to frame Roman social history. *Roman Passions* was researched and written in two libraries, the British Library (Social Sciences Section) and the Library of the Institute of Classical Studies, both pleasant and agreeable environments (regardless of the internal politics of the future location of the latter); hence I wish to thank all the library staff for their aid and work in maintaining their fine collections of books and journals. Michael Greenwood at Continuum initiated the idea for this book, and has been supportive over the period of its construction. All academics need an editor. For this book Ingrid Laurence edited the initial drafts and offered much advice for the book's improvement. I am most grateful to her – she has made this book a much better read. The book is dedicated to John and Sara Allsopp Lander, who in 2008 went the extra mile for us.

1

Into the World of Roman Pleasure

Pleasure is extinguished just when it is most enjoyed; it has but a small space, and quickly fills it – it grows weary and is soon spent after its first assault.

Seneca, On the Happy Life *7.7*

You embrace pleasure, I enchain her; you enjoy pleasure, I use it; you think it the highest good, I do not think it even a good; you do everything for the sake of pleasure, I nothing.

Seneca, On the Happy Life *10.2–3*

At the Saturnalia . . . Augustus would give gifts of clothing or gold or silver; again coins of every kind, including old ones of the kings and foreign money, another time he would give nothing but hair cloth, sponges, pokers and tongs and other such things with a double meaning.

Suetonius, Life of Augustus *75*

Where do we find pleasure in the Roman Empire? Seneca, a first-century senator, can be our guide here.[1] Surprisingly, for him, pleasure was not to be found in the centre of the city in the forum with its architecture and its temples to the gods, or in the home, but instead was out of sight in the alleyways and within the bars and the brothels of the city. He could also feel pleasure's presence lurking in the dark and steam-filled rooms of the baths. Seneca's nose could sniff out pleasure from the smell of perfume on a man or wine on his breath. He could hear it in the belch of the drunken man.[2] When he went home, Seneca lived in a house that provided notable luxuries. As he says himself, he could be accused of enjoying pleasure in his own home, the manifestations of which can be noted: at dinner, in the furniture of his home, the presence of an aviary, trees planted for their shade rather than their produce, wine that was older than Seneca himself, his wife's earrings that cost the annual revenue of a household, the presence of young well-dressed slaves and meals that were served with care, including meat cut by a professional carver.[3] These were all signs of pleasure or luxury, which could be defended as being subject to the control of the rich man. The truth of the matter was that the Romans might love the ideal of living without pleasure, but few actually did – unless they were beggars living under the bridges over the river Tiber and begging near the temples of the city.[4] However, for the wealthy Romans, pleasure was always ready to ambush them, to possess them, and to destroy any pretence of its opposite virtue.[5]

THE ROMAN GIFT

Rome was the first cosmopolitan metropolis with a population of more than a million people, of whom many had access to the goods produced across the Empire that stretched from the Atlantic Ocean in the west to Iraq in the east, from Britain in the north to the upper reaches of the Nile in the south. Goods flowed into Rome in abundance and their consumption took many forms, but the most revealing is that of the gift. Martial, writing in the second half of the first century CE, wrote a book of epigrams (known to us as *Epigrams* Book 13) that was modestly priced at 4 sesterces,[6] containing 123 mottoes that could be attached to gifts (real or imagined). The gifts are not themselves huge investments: some incense, pepper or some beans.[7] Many of the gifts have a geographical provenance attached to them, providing information on the exclusiveness or renown of a region for its production of certain types of produce found in Rome. There are gifts to be given by both rich and poor pointing to the presence of a consumer culture in which the gift was an important part of the market place.[8] What these gifts show us is an insight into the availability of consumer choice.[9]

The setting for the gifts would appear to have been midwinter,[10] but despite this there was a huge variety of produce available for consumption at the dinner table. The produce of the fields of Italy is fully represented: beans, groats, flour, beets, rapes, cabbages, mushrooms, truffles, to give just a few examples. Other gifts included a range of livestock and game familiar to visitors to Italy today: goats, pigs, ducks, a garland of thrushes, goose liver, rabbits, deer and others. The produce of the sea is also represented by gifts of live mullet kept in salt water, sea bass, turbot, oysters, prawns and sea urchins. Hunting of wild animals produced further gifts: an oryx, a stag, a wild ass, a roe deer, a foal of a wild ass; some of these may have been alive rather than dead – certainly the gift of a gazelle was a pet for a small son. There are imported products: lentils and beans from Egypt, figs from Syria and the Greek island of Chios, Sicilian honeycombs and honey from Athens, Pannonian birds, as well as Libyan pomegranates that were now grown in the suburbs of Rome as well as regional specialities from Italy: Lucanian sausages, asparagus from Ravenna, oil from the town of Venafrum. There are also some exotic products: dormice, swans, flamingoes, the womb of a pregnant pig and the womb of a virgin pig – all delicacies to be given away. What we might call processed foods are also represented. The expensive sauce known as *garum* is listed alongside an amphora of a cheaper variety called *muria*. There are also 19 regional wines listed.

What the list of possible gifts illustrates is an emphasis on consumption and choice of produce. The gifts vary from the basic to the most elaborate and exotic. They take us from Italy across the Mediterranean to producers in Syria and in Egypt, as well as in the northern provinces, represented by Pannonia. Winter as a season associated with a shortage of produce was overcome by the transportation of goods from one province to another, notably roses sent to Rome from Egypt, that had been cultivated so that they would be available for the construction of garlands in winter.[11] The choice of gifts allows for the buyer to make a statement about their character. The moralist might content himself with some beans, but the lover of the exotic might provide the most elaborate, foreign and outlandish gift. A gift could also make a statement about the character of the recipient. A gift of murex shells from which purple dye was extracted could highlight the effeminacy of the recipient,[12] whereas a gift of sorb apples, which were thought to prevent an upset stomach, might not have been for his consumption rather for his young male sex-slave.[13] Similarly, onions were not just a gift of food but a statement about the nature of the recipient's wife, old and in need of onions as an aphrodisiac.[14] The gifts were made not just for their immediate usage as food or drink, but were statements about taste and were chosen with a view to the well-being of the recipient and a wry laugh on the part of the readers of the epigrams. The sensations catered for included those of taste (food and drink), smell (perfumes and roses), and the facilitation of sex.

THE SATURNALIA

The context for understanding these gifts is the festival of the Saturnalia, coinciding with our own modern winter festivals of December. It was the time when all were in theory equal, with children, women, slaves, the poor and senators sitting at the same table to take their pleasure.[15] At first sight, this reveals an equality of all at the festival. However, the action of gift-giving differentiated a person's friends according to their relationship – those perceived as of little value received a small gift, those of great value a beautiful one. The period of gift-giving would seem to continue throughout the Saturnalia, which would have facilitated the recycling of unwanted gifts to others, but what was important was the giving of a gift, as much as the item itself, since the act of giving recognized the bond between two people.[16] However, the value of a gift given required a gift of a similar value in return or the relationship was seen to be unequal.[17] The recipient of gifts might look upon a variety of products of quite different qualities from basic necessities to the most refined luxuries. Martial reviewed the combination of the exotic gifts received by the wealthy Sabellus, which included the basic necessities of flour and beans, alongside pepper, frankincense, Lucanian sausages, Syrian grape syrup, jellied figs in a Libyan jar and a product from Spain.[18] Whereas the poor man made a gift to his patron of a small gift that might later be recycled to another. But this did not matter, the action of gift-giving and receiving recognized the relationship between the persons involved and provided a material expression of it, regardless of whether their wealth was equal or unequal. The visible interaction of persons of different status, in a context of excess and indulgence in pleasure, was for many Romans the very essence of pleasure and luxury which needed to be restricted to the period of the Saturnalia – a mere seven days.[19] However, moralists, such as Seneca, saw the activities of the festival, characterized by a drunken and vomiting mob, extending right through the 365 days of the year.[20]

Today, we are familiar with the excesses of consumption in winter, at Christmas, and the effect of this season of celebration and gift-giving on the economy. The media in October happily predict a 'bad Christmas' for high street retailers, and later in January further discuss the results of it. However, underlying this in our own world is the role of the gift in stimulating or facilitating economic development, something that we share with the Romans.

Wine was transported across the Mediterranean in amphorae.

The presence of a season of gifts with a secure set of trade routes across the Mediterranean Sea was fully felt for the first time in the first century CE. It shows up in the records of pottery and amphorae (containers for the transport of liquids) found in a recent excavation beneath the House of the Vestals in Pompeii: only in the first century CE was Pompeii awash with products from all over the Mediterranean – Greek, Spanish and Italian wines; Spanish *garum* competing with the local variety; and varieties of pottery previously unknown during the first century BCE. On the very eve of the eruption of Vesuvius (August 79 CE) some crates were delivered to a house that contained 37 lamps produced in Northern Italy and 76 pottery bowls of two very similar types made in Southern Gaul (modern France).[21] The find has really defied archaeological explanations: why should such a shipment end up in a single location in Pompeii, and what would the owner do with such a uniformity of products? The material had come a long way and has a certain rarity value: the 76 bowls represent 50 per cent of all similar Southern Gaulish wares (in the pottery forms know as *terra sigillata*) found in Pompeii. These were not destined for sale in a nearby shop (there is no evidence for such a local enterprise connected to this house); instead it seems likely that what we have in this house is a box of gifts to be broken down into smaller numbers and distributed. The consignment's arrival at the end of August or mid-September (79 CE) coincided with the tail-end of the sailing season and certainly all such gifts needed to have been transported to their location of sale or consumption by the gift-giver by the end of September or mid-October. We might imagine the gradual rise in prices of imported gifts once the sailing season had closed and the stock of available gifts from overseas was gradually decreasing as the Saturnalia approached. For the gift-giver, their consumer choice of imports may have become increasingly limited as time moved on with the result that products from closer at hand became of greater interest – the absence of imports could lead to a dependence on Italian products transported by land right up to the Saturnalia itself.

The gift-giving economy of the winter season could bring in new products, and/or ever more exotic ones, but once these products had been tasted or consumed, the demand for them may have increased and been made available by other means apart from gift-giving. The bars of Pompeii are found to contain not just the local wine, famous for its hangovers, but also a whole range of different wine imports alongside the very best of Italy – Falernian, sold at 16 times the price of a local wine. *Garum* from Spain as well as local products were found in numerous bars,[22] as was a pastry in a form similar to a Cornish pasty. It is hard to determine whether these were luxuries prior to the first century CE; the excavations beneath the House of the Vestals has shown such a variety of goods to be absent; yet such a variety is the characteristic of the wine amphorae found at almost any location in the city by the time of its destruction. This might suggest that the act of gift-giving of imported products widened their distribution and resulted in the demand for a greater availability of produce in the bars of the city, but did not lead to the population drinking high-quality wine all of the time. Instead, a range of produce was available that was suitable for consumption at different occasions. This may have caused some previously exotic gifts to become products associated with a monetary value that could be consumed regardless of the season of the year.

To return to Martial's gifts in *Epigrams*: these included Italian and imported goods and presented the gift-giver with options regarding the type of gift to present to the recipient, or with the question what gift best constituted or described their relationship: a traditional one of beans or a few olives from

Picenum in Italy or some figs from Libya or Syria? The choice was an important one – there were those who rejected the imported in favour of what they saw as a traditional Italian rusticity, in which there was no place for the new-fangled or effeminate luxuries of the Orient. The message is clear: not everyone engaged with the world of pleasure or, at least, made a show of not so doing in public. A young man was seen, typically, to want luxuries or novelties: Spanish wool dyed with purple from Tyre, a high quality toga, Indian sardonyxes, Scythian emeralds or simply 100 newly minted coins; whereas we can expect an old man to be gratified by the novelties of his own youth, a generation or more earlier, which represented a tradition of gift-giving to be embraced by the young giving to the old.[23] What we see here is how the gift, as an object, created a material presence for the purely social relationship between two people. The range of gifts found in Martial's last two books of *Epigrams* presents us with the material from which we might read the variation in social relations from the young to the old, the rich to the poor, the modern to the traditional, and so on.

Gift-giving was so marked at the winter festival that a region of Rome was renamed after the clay images that children of Romans gave to the children of slaves within their own families.[24] This region, called the *Sigillaria*, came to produce not just these images but items of ever greater complexity,[25] and it is in this region of Rome that we find the gift market which included among its wares a small book by Martial.[26] Martial produced in book form a series of pithy lines to accompany such manufactured gifts (which we know as *Epigrams* 14) and his work provides us with a guide to what was for sale in the shops of the *Sigillaria* and what might be chosen as a gift – there are 223 items in all. The gifts have some familiarity, but also reveal a different world: a stylus case for a boy or a variety of writing tablets; gaming equipment for the Saturnalia: knucklebones, dice and cashboxes; wine cups and drinking vessels; tables; a variety of lighting equipment; balls for exercise; strigils or scrapers and oil for use at the baths; hunting equipment; a barber's toolkit; a soldier's sword and belt; musical instruments; clothing (anything from slippers to a breastband or a toga); wool for the manufacture of cloths; caged birds (nightingales and talking parrots); a chest of medicines; whips and sticks for beating slaves and children respectively after the festival was over; texts of the classical authors from Homer through Cicero, Sallust, Vergil and on to Catullus, Ovid and Lucan. As in his previous volume, Martial includes food items, but these are fewer: a bread roll in the shape of the

god Priapus with his erect penis, a pig, sausages and cakes for boys. A variety of
items could have been given to improve the appearance of the recipient's body:
a toothpick, an earpick, hairpins, combs, hair dye and lengths of barbarians'
hair for the manufacture of extensions. There were also small statuettes in a
variety of materials from terracotta to gold: a victory, Leander in marble, the
beautiful boy Brutus had loved, a hunchback, a lizard slayer, Hercules and a
hermaphrodite. There were animals for sale: miniature mules, lapdogs from
Gaul, hunting dogs, a monkey, and, listed alongside them, sex-slaves, a young
boy and a young girl, together with others including a stenographer, an idiot,
a dwarf, boys specializing in comic acting, a cook and a confectioner. The
Sigillaria was a haven of the exotic that catered for the Romans sensations; gone
were the rings of yesteryear,[27] but the statues from which the district got its
name remained prominent in the list of gifts.

Not only were there new goods available for the Romans to gain pleasure from
in the first century CE, new habits developed. Pliny the Elder, who died during the
eruption of Vesuvius in 79 CE, reports that some 50 years earlier a new form of
pleasure was introduced: drinking on an empty stomach. It was a practice famous
among the barbarians of Parthia (modern Iraq and Iran) and foreign to the world
of Rome.[28] The result for many Romans was drunkenness and vomiting, but for
some, such as Novellius Torquatus from Milan, fame for his spectacular ability
to hold his drink and never to slur his words. We need to note here that the idea
of a room for people to be sick in, a *vomitorium*, is an invention of the modern
mind. Compared to us, the Romans had a different relationship with the action
of vomiting: it was something that could be beneficial to a person's health and
a variety of products could be taken to help a person vomit – parsnips, radishes
and salt to name but a few from Pliny the Elder's *Natural History*.[29] Others are
identified to prevent sickness: sesame seeds combined with wine or basil on its
own.[30] The drunk, unsteady and about to be sick or recovering from a meaningful
vomit, was a theme of scenes depicting the drinking party at Pompeii. There is
even a fresco of a man actually spewing his guts while his companion holds his
head. The desirability of vomiting depended in part on the time of year: for the
Romans it was a good thing in winter, but not in summer, with negative effects
for the constitution of the body.[31] The Saturnalia in December was therefore a
perfect time for excessive consumption that could well have been accompanied
by the celebrants gagging and retching, which would have been regarded as

healthy – if perhaps unsightly and needing to be undertaken outside the dining room. However, the introduction of drinking on an empty stomach throughout the year no doubt produced some unseasonal vomiting in the summer months, and a need to control the pleasure of intoxication. The Saturnalia, by contrast, was the time in which pleasure reigned and luxury could be indulged in and was a time for most, including senators, to demonstrate their engagement with pleasure to their inferiors: free citizens and slaves.[32] This was the season when the toga-clad Romans shed their togas and partied.[33]

The Saturnalia was the time for gift-giving by men to other men and by women to men; women received gifts on the Kalends, or first day, of March, for the festival called the Matronalia,[34] usually from the men they had given gifts to at the Saturnalia.[35] No further gifts could have been imported to Rome between December and March since the shipping lanes of the Mediterranean were closed for winter. The March festival was very different from that of the drunken carousing at the Saturnalia; it is a difference we see reflected in the works of Martial: his first four books were full of sex and naughtiness suitable for young men, but his fifth book has a different focus and was for the reading by virgin girls and married women.[36] Indeed, the first four books may have made suitable presents to be given to men at the Saturnalia and his fifth book for women in March – like many societies, the division of the male and female genders pervaded many social institutions: even the type of books read by men and women. In the pre-Julian Roman calendar, March had been the first month of the year and was associated with birth both of the year itself and of children – it was on the first day of March that Juno Lucina had a temple dedicated to her in Rome. She was the goddess who brought children into the light of the world and was the deity associated with the process of childbirth. There is a contrast here between the Saturnalia held in the dark days of midwinter and the Matronalia of Juno that marked the beginning of the year and the birth of children. The giving of gifts by men certainly stretched back into the distant past of the second century BCE, where we can find in a Roman comedy a wife waking her husband up before dawn to demand money for a present for his mother-in-law.[37] The Matronalia has a lesser presence in the literature that survives, but it is clear that on this day the city of Rome was full of people delivering presents,[38] and it continued to be a prominent survival that Christians observed in a traditional format alongside the celebration of the Saturnalia.[39]

The festivals of December and March, associated with the giving of gifts to men and women respectively, highlight the abundance which Rome and Italy could draw on to create exquisite items for friends and family, while at the same time humbler or more traditional gifts could be given. The two, luxury and meagreness, go together to define each other – Rome was a society that worked on polar opposites: living–dead; male–female; child–adult; war–home and luxury–miserliness. The giving of a gift presented both the giver and the recipient with an image of each other via the choice of item. The gift symbolized the unspoken or unarticulated assumptions about the person to which the gift was to be given and, as we saw from the sheer variety of gifts, the range of gifts reflected the variety of tastes in Rome. What was important was to participate in gift-giving and the receiving of gifts; it was not so much a duty as a pleasure, as can be seen from Seneca's treatise *On Benefits*. The festivals were not the only time at which gifts might be given, indeed the presentation of social inferiors with 'benefits' is a frequent reminder of how gift-giving reinforced the power of the elite. Interestingly, the giving of gifts between husbands and wives (and vice versa) was severely restricted by law to prevent the overall impoverishment of either party through love and affection. The gift to another was a sign of abundance or a sign of a wealth of resources to be given to others, often of a lower status.

GIFTS OF THE EMPEROR

The ultimate giver of gifts was the emperor. He was the man, or rather super-being, who provided for others. He supplied the plebs in Rome with free corn. He distributed money to them as a present. He supplied them with visual spectacles. The emperor Titus, who opened the Colosseum in 80 CE, would proclaim a feeling of woe that he had not benefited one of his subjects for the period of a whole day with the exclamation over dinner: 'My friends I have wasted a day'.[40] The relationship between the plebs in Rome and their emperor was characterized by gifts from the emperor to his people; it gave rise to the expression that the plebs, by the end of the first century CE, were no longer concerned with politics, only 'bread and circuses'. Their devotion to their emperor was expressed on the first day of each new year: men, rich and poor, went to the forum or the palace to fulfil a personal vow for the emperor's safety. They threw a small coin into the pool, the Lacus Curtius, where tradition had it a battle for Rome's survival had turned; others took gifts up to the palace. The total numbers involved in these small offerings was considerable. The first emperor, Augustus, used the money to buy and dedicate a statue in each of Rome's 365 neighbourhoods, such as that of Apollo in the district of the sandal makers.[41] The just emperor, as the provider for all, could not simply accept a gift and needed to demonstrate his munificence by using the money to provide statues in each neighbourhood of the city. Other emperors regulated the types of gift they might receive, but still the good emperor would not accept even these for himself.[42]

It was the emperor's pleasure to provide for his people in the city of Rome. No other citizen, whether senator or freed slave, could put on games in the city. In 64 CE, with the commander of the Praetorian Guard, Tigellinus, Nero put on one of the parties of the century.[43] It was an expression of his great love for his people. The setting was the Campus Martius, an area of theatres, parkland, and, at its centre, a large artificial lake, the Stagnum of Agrippa, which was fed by water brought from more than 20 miles by aqueduct to Rome. It was here that Nero later built the first large-scale bath and gymnasium complex, or *thermae*. The water from this beautiful pool drained into the Tiber via a 800-metre canal, which was adorned with sculpture. The party was arranged around the lake – taverns and brothels were set up on the shores and at night the groves on the shore line were illuminated and rang out with song, while the centrepiece of the party, a large raft covered in purple cloth and cushions, was rowed around the lake by male prostitutes or towed by other vessels adorned with ivory and gold. Nero dined in style, while others drank in the taverns. Prostitutes strolled naked through the groves and on the shores of the lake, and noble women, virgins and married matrons alike, were found in the brothels. Social conventions were outraged: a slave had sex with his female owner, a father watched his daughter have sex with a gladiator, and the event culminated with Nero, dressed as a bride, marrying a freed slave. The drama of this wedding was played out with a dowry, witnesses, a marriage bed and a torch-lit bridal procession. This was not a one-off event; Nero's reign was punctuated by such parties in which a landscape of pleasure dominated the city of Rome.[44] His people were presented with the gifts of empire: pleasure without any limitations and the overturning of social conventions, except one: the emperor provided pleasure for all and was at the centre of the spectacle. A grateful populace in the first century CE might have seen this as liberation, but the later moralists in the senate of the second century CE were outraged. Nero extended the festive spirit of a winter festival, the Saturnalia, characterized by excess, to the whole year. His reign marked a short-lived, 12-year period when pleasure was extended as a gift to the people over the course of the whole year, rather than being contained within the shackles of the winter festival – a matter of a few days. The emperor had the power to deliver a new world of pleasures to his people. He could choose to give them what only the elite had access to in their homes and distribute his gift within a landscape of glitter and light, with himself as the centre of attention. This was much more than bread and circuses; it was excess on a new scale in which the people could become part of a public culture of pleasure that had previously only been enjoyed by the aristocracy behind closed doors.

2

The Emperor's Pleasures

It is a man's pleasures, yes his pleasures, which tell us most about his true worth, his gravitas, *and his self-control. No one is so dissolute that his work lacks all semblance of seriousness; it is our leisure which betrays us. It was at leisure that the majority of the emperor Trajan's predecessors spent time on gambling, debauchery and extravagance, thus replacing what should have been their relaxation of their serious concerns with a different form of tension – the pursuit of vice.*

Pliny, Panegyric: 82

Augustus could not lose of the charge of lustfulness and they say that even in his later years he was fond of sex with virgins, who were brought to him from all places, even by his own wife.

Suetonius, The Life of Augustus: 71

Later, when emperor, at the very time he was correcting public morality, Tiberius spent a night and two whole days in feasting and drinking with Pomponius Flaccus and Lucius Piso, immediately afterwards making one the governor of Syria and the other prefect of the city.

Suetonius, Life of Tiberius: 42

Caligula could not control his natural cruelty and viciousness . . . he was a most eager witness of the tortures and punishments, revelling at night in gluttony and adultery . . .

Suetonius, Life of Caligula: 11

ROME'S FIRST EMPEROR

The murder of Julius Caesar on the Ides of March in 44 BCE produced a new sort of Roman, one who did not forgive his enemies, but mercilessly avenged

them; one who at the age of just 19 raised an army and resisted all attempts by
well-meaning senators, ambitious generals and others to wrest power from him.
This was a man who broke the rules of human behaviour; as a young man he
had the ambition and direction of one much older.[1] His name was Octavian, the
adopted son of Julius Caesar. He would wage wars against his Roman enemies
ruthlessly until all were exterminated or loyal to him.[2] Seventeen years after the
murder of his father, Octavian changed his name by state decree to Augustus –
meaning 'the increased'. Not only did he have a new name, he had a new role as
the first Roman emperor. For Rome and its citizens this was a new beginning
– a monarchy in all but name,[3] and all the lavish pleasure pursuits that came
with it.

Augustus could do anything. He had more power than anyone else in the
state, with 28 legions under his personally appointed commanders. Unlike any
other senator, he had his own bodyguard – the Praetorian Guard. He bestrode
the world like a colossus, backed by more money than any other senator, and this
he used with panache. He supplied his people with free corn. Half a year's wages
was bestowed on as many as 250,000 citizens at a time. He rewarded soldiers
with more than 400 million *sesterces* and double that in grants of land on the
completion of their military service. His finances equalled and almost exceeded
those of the state. He rebuilt the temples and public buildings of Rome so that
they gleamed with their white marble quarried at Carrara. His gladiatorial
games were an event never seen before: 10,000 men fighting, 3,500 beasts
destroyed, a sea fight of 30 warships manned by 3,000 sailors on a purpose-built
artificial lake. Whereas other senators may have been millionaires, Augustus was
a billionaire. The total bill over his reign was 2,400 million *sesterces* – no one else
could match this level of gift-giving. But that was not all. Augustus was the man
who was seen to pursue a policy of armed conflict over the most distant parts
of the globe, creating diplomatic relations between Rome and India for the first
time.[4]

The Romans, for their part, were grateful for their emperor's success. A
formal thanksgiving to the gods was made regularly. Augustus, in his *Res Gestae*,
enumerated the 55 occasions and the 190 days over which the people made
their gratitude for his existence known to the gods. Every five years, vows for
his health were decreed, and when after five years the vows were fulfilled, games
were held to celebrate the longevity of their emperor. Some 80 silver statues of

him were spontaneously erected by the plebians of Rome; he took them down and re-cast the metal into images of the gods. On his return from campaigns, altars were decreed to Fortuna Redux – literally the return of good fortune. On another occasion the day of his return became known as the Augustalia, and it was a festival to be celebrated each year. There was also an altar set up on his return to Augustan Peace – even his enemies knew that it was Augustus, their emperor, who ensured that their pleasure-filled lives would not dissolve into the carnage of civil war.[5] Most people adored this new type of human being, the emperor who protested he was not a god, yet after his death seamlessly became one.

So how was an emperor, whose social position was between that of a man and a god, to take his pleasure? Roman mythology was replete with the actions of the deities – but the gods were often depicted as drunken, and even rather miserable. Augustus, the original emperor, was to set the tone. His biographer Suetonius, writing later in the second century CE, set out to present a rounded account of his character – not a chronological story of his life from birth to death, but an overview of all the facets of the man. Suetonius included wars and politics, but these were placed alongside the health, the body and even the underwear worn by the emperor.[6] Much was also written about how the emperor pursued his private life and enjoyed the world of pleasure, made infinite by both his position and his wealth.

Surprisingly, Augustus' lifestyle appears austere. He lived in a house on the Palatine Hill in Rome that was modest compared with those of his friends or even that of his daughter.[7] Life in the house was traditional, with the imperial women expected to spin and weave the cloths for those in the household. In spite of this modest upbringing – or perhaps because of it – both his daughter Julia and his granddaughter, also called Julia, were deemed by Augustus to pursue unacceptable pleasures, and were banished by him from Rome.[8] The sayings or mottoes of Julia were recalled years after her death, as exempla of the statements of a fun-loving woman in her thirties; quite a contrast to the austere comments of her father.[9] Julia was confined to an island and denied every luxury, including wine and male visitors. After five years she was moved back to the mainland of Italy but was still banned from Rome and all its pleasures. Despite Augustus' moral thunderings against his daughter, though, the pair were actually alike in all but gender. Augustus was a famous adulterer, with friends and members of his household identifying suitable married women, adult women and virgins for his pleasure; a process that involved their examination naked, in the manner of the slave market.[10] His second wife Livia had been snatched from her husband at a dinner party, so the story goes. Livia even found virgins for him herself; afterwards these would be discarded as just more girls who had lost their virginity to the emperor's passion.[11] But such behaviour was one thing for Augustus and quite another for his daughter – he was a man and she was a woman; his traditional household could accommodate his behaviour but not hers.

Dinner parties were another constant feature of the emperor's household and were populated by a huge variety of guests. The emperor himself was a light eater and drank sparingly, but there were three or six courses for his guests, all lavish but not luxurious.[12] There were good conversation, music, stage shows, professional storytellers and an opportunity to witness Augustus' real passion – gambling.[13] Suetonius quotes a letter from Augustus to his adopted son, the next emperor Tiberius, which reveals the dynamic of the emperor's gaming board:

> 'We spent the whole of the Quinquatria [a five-day festival dedicated to Minerva] very merrily, my dear Tiberius, for we played all day long and kept the gaming board warm. Your brother made a great outcry about his luck, but in the end did not come out far behind in the long run; for after losing heavily, he unexpectedly and little by little got back a good deal. For my part, I lost 20,000 sesterces, but because I was extravagantly generous in my play, as usual. If I had demanded of everyone the stakes which I let go, or had kept all that I gave away, I should have won 50,000. But I like that better, for my generosity will exalt me to immortal glory.'

A meal with Augustus involved gambling and he even provided his guests with money to ensure that they could play for high stakes, giving each of them 250,000 sesterces for this very purpose.[14] Augustus is not simply enjoying the fun of betting, but is also indulging in that very distinctive Roman pleasure of gift-giving. The guests might well remember the night when they won money off the emperor, who magnanimously allowed them to keep the stakes as well as their winnings. When he died, this generous man became a god.

SUCCESSORS TO AUGUSTUS

Tiberius, the second emperor, was a man of complexity. He had flourished under Augustus as a competent general, but withdrew from public life to live a life of learned leisure on the island of Rhodes and only re-entered the political arena following the deaths of Augustus' grandsons and heirs apparent, Gaius and Lucius.[15] In this period, he was famous for a great love of wine and drinking, pursuits which earned him the nickname Biberius Caldius Mero, meaning the drinker of hot unmixed wine – a pun on his full name Tiberius Claudius Nero.[16] Historians have regarded Tiberius as not the first choice of heir to the legacy of Augustus. However, on taking up the reins of government, Tiberius did not leave the city of Rome for two years and then for the next nine was always in Rome, close by in the neighbouring towns or on the coast at Antium.[17] He attended the senate and the courts diligently. But the feasts continued, some are reported by Suetonius.[18] What is more, he established a magistrate or officer of pleasure and appointed a leading expert: Titus Caesonius Priscus, who was a Roman knight. Tiberius also enjoyed the pleasures of the city and dining with the great nobles of Rome, and any woman could be chosen to be brought to his bed. Refusal released the full wrath of the emperor and the destruction of the woman in the courts at the hands of informers.[19]

What changed his reign was the death of his son Drusus in 23 CE. He left Rome for the cities of the Bay of Naples and its islands, a region still known today as Campania. He never returned to Rome. The emperor, now in his sixties, was intent on solitude and eventually made his home on the island of Capri.[20] Here, he ceased to be on view and was subject to all the Roman suspicion of those who lived a secret life. There are stories of orgies and the hiring of sex experts to put on shows to turn on the aged emperor; bedrooms were painted with sex scenes and the woods of the island were filled with boys dressed as the god Pan and girls in the guise of nymphs. This was an island where the emperor's pleasure came first. He was reputed to swim naked with young boys, who swam between his legs and were trained to sexually excite him.[21] His eccentricities included keeping a pet snake and having a passion for cucumbers.[22] Capri was also the place where the emperor viewed executions and punishments of those whom he feared – and there were many.[23]

Tiberius' pleasure island was the world into which young Caligula, at the age of 19, entered and remained with him until the old emperor's death five years later. Here, he learned the excesses for which he was later to become notorious. He enjoyed the tortures and executions, committed adultery, and trained as a dancer and a singer to perform at the wonderful feasts.[24] On his accession to the throne, he was hailed as a dream emperor: young, handsome and resident in Rome.[25] His first actions included rewarding his people by extending the winter festival of Saturnalia, distributing 300 *sesterces* to the plebs in Rome (a third of the annual salary of a Roman legionary) and throwing lavish banquets for the senators, the Roman knights and their wives.[26] Importantly, he revived the practice of Augustus of putting on games and gladiatorial shows, an area neglected by Tiberius.[27] This was a man courting popularity, but also playing the part of a god: his image replaced that of Jupiter and he extended his palace towards the forum, so that he might emerge from the palace via the temple of Castor and Pollux, where he walked as a god and expected to be worshipped by his people.[28] Like Tiberius and Augustus before him, Caligula slept with any woman who was available, or who was told of the emperor's desire, and he often left the dinner table with them to return later to recount the erotic acts to his guests, including the woman's husband.[29] The husband was humiliated, but as the emperor reminded his grandmother, Antonia, he had the right to do anything to anybody and that included dinner guests, members of his family and the people of Rome.[30] Indeed, it would seem that this demonstration of his access to pleasure and humiliation was also a demonstration of his powers. Caligula was an all-powerful deity and set forth to fulfil the role given to him. However, a soldier's dagger revealed the frailty of this conceit.

The idea of the emperor as a god did not end with Caligula's assassination. His successor, his uncle Claudius, was portrayed in statues as Jupiter. Whereas Augustus had taken down statues of himself, now the statues of the emperor represented him not as a man but as a divine being. It was a strange idea for Claudius, given that he had been kept out of public life by the emperor Tiberius and had lived in a private world of scholarship, drunkenness and gambling in his home with gardens in the suburbs of Rome or in his villa on the Bay of Naples.[31] Under Caligula, he had a public role and held the consulship twice, but he was often the object of ridicule at the emperor's table: pelted with olive stones by the guests when he fell asleep and even woken up with blows of a whip or rod.[32] He became emperor at the age of 50. Like Augustus, Claudius was an emperor who gave his people money, buildings and monuments, a new aqueduct and games. He even extended the Roman empire across the ocean to conquer Britain.[33] Claudius continued the practice of the imperial dinner party with 600 guests and was a great lover of food and drink. After eating his fill, or even more, he would sleep with his mouth open (a slave placed a feather down his throat so that he would vomit and relieve his stomach).[34] His passion for women, we are told, led to his seduction by his niece Agrippina, and the law permitting an uncle to marry his niece allowed them to wed, following the execution of his previous wife Messalina, who was notorious for her sexual appetite.[35] Like Augustus, Claudius was a gambler and even published a book on the subject and fitted his carriage with a gaming board.[36] Posterity views Claudius as the servant of his wives and freed slaves, who catered for his every need. However, the emperor presented to us is a pleasure-loving, generous man in the mould of the deified emperor Augustus. Claudius liked to eat and drink rather more than his abstemious predecessor, but basically the pattern of imperial pleasure was set: dinners, drinking, gambling, sex with whomever the emperor fancied and the occasional demonstration of imperial anger to frighten the unwary (whether the emperor took pleasure in executions is addressed in Chapter 10 of this book). Like Augustus, on his death Claudius was deified – admittedly with some criticism. But he was deemed a god nevertheless, and like his statues in the guise of Jupiter, it is clear he took his divine status to heart during his lifetime.

His stepson and successor Nero would, of course, take these pleasures to the limits with parties for the people – but ultimately, he was building on a pattern that had been established by the imperial family from 27 BCE with the rise of Augustus through to his own accession in 54 CE. Many of the chapters of this book examine Nero's actions and whims through to his death in 68 CE, and with it the final demise of the Julio-Claudian dynasty established by Augustus. But was this pattern of pleasure replicated by the next imperial line, the Flavians, who came to power following the civil wars of 69 CE?

A NEW REGIME OF PLEASURE – THE FLAVIANS

The first of the Flavians, Vespasian, was in fact at pains to distance himself from his predecessors in public. His statues portrayed him as he was – a 60-year-old man with a lined face and thinning hair. His son Titus, aged 40, appears as a younger version of the statue of his father – this new dynasty looked different to those who had come before. These emperors were army commanders who had led soldiers to victory in Britain and Judaea and whose ultimate achievement was the sacking of Jerusalem. Their justification for their position as emperor, and subsequent divinity, depended on their rise from obscurity and a series of prophecies and miracles performed in the East.[37] Vespasian was a widower at his accession and chose not to remarry, but enjoyed a relationship with a woman called Caenis, who was deemed a concubine rather than a wife, due to her status as a freed slave.[38] The new emperor was not one to have sex with just anybody, and was devoted to Caenis – but after her death he had numerous concubines. Like his predecessors, he established new monuments across the city, including the Colosseum, and was generous to all. The pleasures that entertained this deified emperor were simple ones. He did not subscribe to the Augustan ideal of gambling and sex with freeborn women, or the drinking and feasting of Tiberius or Claudius. Instead, his life was controlled and dominated by business and the simple pleasures of his concubines, bathing and dinner, where he could demonstrate his rustic humanity and wit. He was a man who got up early before dawn, attended to his letters and other official documents, then received friends, dressed himself, and went to deal with business in the morning. When that was over, he took a drive and went to bed with one of his concubines. Upon waking, he visited the baths, then on to dinner, where his witty sayings and quotations from Greek classics punctuated the meal.[39]

Vespasian's eldest son, Titus, had a very different upbringing. He had been the playmate of the emperor Claudius' son, Britannicus. He had learned horsemanship and weapons training; he made speeches and wrote poetry in both Latin and Greek. Like Nero, he could sing and play the *cithara* (lyre).[40] Unlike his father, he drank and ate through the night, and he had a whole troupe of eunuchs and effeminate males. To top it off, he fell passionately in love with the Jewish queen Berenice, whom he had promised to marry.[41] To some, he looked like a second Nero, but Suetonius is adamant that his banquets showed some restraint, and he managed to pull himself back from the brink of disaster. He sent Berenice away from Rome, and even abandoned his effeminate male friends who would later become famous stage performers.[42] His generosity as emperor was unsurpassed. However, his short reign featured three disasters for the Roman people: the eruption of Vesuvius and destruction of both Pompeii and Herculaneum; the great fire in Rome in 80 CE; and his own premature death. He was succeeded by his younger brother, Domitian. Just 30 years old when he took the throne, he had already gained a reputation for tyranny in the reign of his brother and father. He was an adulterer in the guise of the Julio-Claudian emperors, but also a great giver of games and money to the people of Rome, as well as banquets for the senators and Roman knights. He restored buildings across the capital.[43] However, this was a man who revelled in his role as emperor and took pleasure in the destruction of his enemies.[44] He was a sadist famous for using his stylus to stab flies in the seclusion of the palace. In public, he was greeted by his submissive subjects as their lord or *dominus* – an acclamation forbidden by Augustus.[45] His leisure was different in some ways from that of the Julio-Claudian emperors: taking an early bath and long lunch, eating little and drinking less in the evening, holding banquets that ended early and without the excesses of drinking bouts.[46] Sex was a preoccupation for Domitian. He depilated his courtesans himself and swam with prostitutes; he even seduced his married niece, who was then forced to abort his child – a medical procedure from which she did not recover.[47] These were the actions of a tyrant rather than a god in the making, and Domitian lost his life to an assassin.

THE POLITICS OF PLEASURE

One of the problems about learning about the pleasures of these early emperors is that many of their deeds are recounted by a single source: the author Suetonius, who was writing in the second century CE. It begs the question: were all of these desires and actions real, or were they embellishments of the author, which, in today's society, would result in libel writs and expensive legal action? Does Suetonius really know what Tiberius did in secret on Capri? Or has he imagined a pleasure island for a man of old age, in which a deviant emperor, Tiberius, oversteps the mark by having sex with babies? Suetonius also judges these emperors according to their vices and virtues, and in doing so, evaluates the role of pleasure in their lives – an issue considered to be in the public interest.[48] Pleasure differentiates the tyrant emperor who needs to humiliate his guests at dinner from the good emperor who might have a penchant for sex with virgins, but tempers this with more honourable pursuits.

An arguably more objective view on the emperor's pleasures comes from another writer, Pliny, whose work *The Panegyric* is the written-up version of a speech in praise of the living emperor Trajan, delivered in the senate during Pliny's consulship in 100 CE. The work provides us with a guide to what pleasures are permitted for an emperor. There is little unique about the speech, which uses stock examples of praise and blame, and it desperately seeks to create a legitimacy of sincerity while revealing the impossibility of the task under an autocracy.[49] Pliny represents Trajan as an emperor of restraint, unlike so many of his predecessors.[50] His pleasures were dominated by hunting, the climbing of mountains and visiting sacred groves of the gods, as well as sailing on the sea.[51] His leisure pursuits were traditional and those of the young man enjoying the rigours of the great outdoors, even though he was in fact in his forties (a nod to his status as emperor, a different type of human being able to pursue the recreations of youth even though he himself was not young). Trajan's meals were taken in public and shared with his guests. He was seen to join in the conversation, and became the object of admiration among the gold and silver dishes and ingeniously constructed delicacies.[52] Trajan enjoys his pleasure, but it is a public act that is shared, rather than conducted secretly. In building, he shares his pleasure in redesigning the city with his people rather than a palace: he chooses to rebuild the Circus Maximus, 'a fitting place for a nation that has conquered the world, a sight on its own account to be seen, alongside the spectacles there to be displayed: there to be seen indeed for its beauty, and still more for the way in which emperor and people alike are seated on the same level'.[53] It was a place for his people to see him and to facilitate this he had added a further 5,000 seats. The rightful pleasure of the emperor was to bring entertainments to a greater number of spectators, and for the author of their enjoyment to be seen in the imperial box, a sight that only enhanced the spectacle before their eyes.

One of the chief features of good fortune is that it permits no privacy, no concealment, and in the case of emperors, it flings open the door not only to their homes but to their private bedrooms and deepest retreats; every secret is exposed and revealed to rumour's listening ear. (Pliny, *Panegyric*: 82)

It is clear from this that the emperor himself was one of the people's pleasures: the sight of him at the games, his sayings, his laughter and humour and, of course, his generosity to his subjects. But there was another source of pleasure for the Romans in the early second century: speculating about the secret vices of both their current emperor, and also those of the famous leaders from the past, as extolled, to their great entertainment, by Suetonius.

Pleasure humanizes Suetonius' emperors through a pastiche of sensual desires that culminated, in many cases, in vice and condemnation. His writing on pleasure is not the same as that of Seneca or Cicero, who condemn pleasure fairly indiscriminately;[54] he expects, as does his contemporary audience, that his emperors can enjoy meals, have desires, gamble, and have the odd vice or two but no more. What was essential for Suetonius and his readership was that leisure pursuits did not distract the emperor from his duty to run the empire, look after his subjects and even provide the people with the pleasures that they so desired: whether money, parties, games or simply bread. However, the emperor, a man who could do anything and was in many ways a god, could be destroyed by pleasure and, in the process of his destruction, could wreak havoc and chaos on the lives of his subjects – obliterating their comfortable lives and their own enjoyment of the very luxuries that were the source of their emperor's downfall.

3

The Aesthetics of the City

One may say that the earlier Romans cared little for the beauty of their city, since they were preoccupied with other, more utilitarian measures. But later generations, and especially those of the current age and our own times, have by no means fallen short on this score, but have filled the city with many and splendid endowments of their munificence. For example, Pompey, the late Julius Caesar, Augustus, his friends and sons, his wife and sister have surpassed all others in their zeal for building and willingness to meet its expenses.

Strabo, The Geography: 5.3.8

The Campus Martius is the site for most of these new buildings. It is of impressive size, and allows chariot-racing and equestrian exercises to go on without interfering with the crowds of people exercising themselves with ball games, hoops, and wrestling. The many works of art that surround it, the ground covered throughout the year with grass, the ridges of the hills rising above the river, or sloping down to its edge, all look like a painted backcloth of a stage, and form a spectacle from which it is difficult to tear yourself away. And near these is another Campus, with colonnades round about it in very great numbers and sacred precincts, and three theatres, and an amphitheatre, and very costly temples, in close succession to one another, giving you the impression that they were trying, as it were, to declare the rest of the city a mere accessory.

Strabo, The Geography: 5.3.8

The city of Rome was not just composed of houses and streets, it was awash with temples. Eighty-two of them were restored by the emperor Augustus in 28 BCE alone, employing an ever grander style of architecture which borrowed heavily from the magnificent monuments of the kingdoms of the Eastern Mediterranean conquered by Rome's armies. Strabo, at the beginning of the first century CE, faced with the problem of describing Rome, a city larger than any

The centre of Rome (Gismondi's model).

other in the known world with a population of a million inhabitants, marvelled at the way the Romans had surpassed the Greeks in utilitarian projects in the past (roads, aqueducts and sewers), and now possessed a city that was truly beautiful. This beauty extended across three forums and up onto the Palatine and Capitoline hills, surpassing the charm of the landscapes beyond it. This was all new: the first century CE was to see the full development of Rome as the stunning stage set upon which its emperor walked, declaimed, entertained the people, and was seen. At the same time, the act of building was to create a reminder of the greatness of an individual ruler and a mnemonic from which stories of the past could flow.

The beautification of the city did not actually begin with the emperors, but instead had its origins in the actions of the two most charismatic leaders of Rome's Republican past: Pompey the Great and Julius Caesar. Their forays into the aesthetics of the city shaped the actions of their successors to power, and each subsequent emperor attempted to surpass his predecessor in the redevelopment of Rome – a city which at that time did not live up to its standing as the head of an empire stretching from the Atlantic to the river Euphrates. The aesthetic of development was to become one that embraced an expression of power through the majesty of monuments. Rome, as we shall see, becomes the city featuring the largest buildings filled with the most beautiful statues and set in a verdant landscape on the banks of the river Tiber; in all, a place that could bring fresh pleasures to its people.

A NEW ROME IS BUILT

What first inspired Pompey the Great to set Rome's grand redesign in motion was undoubtedly his famous visit to the Greek city of Mytilene, where he viewed the imposing theatre made of stone and reflected that no such monument existed in Rome – and that one should be built.[1] This dramatic new structure, larger than the theatre in Mytilene, replaced the usual temporary wooden theatres, and became not just a place to view the plays of antiquity; it transformed the Romans' whole experience of going out and offered ordinary people regular access to the arts. The rulers quickly realized that inspiring buildings could house awe-inspiring spectacles – where they could take centre stage. The entrance of Rome's leaders at the theatre soon became an occasion when the multitude could express their approval or disapproval.[2] But the audience was rarely disappointed. Pompey's theatre was completed in 55 BCE and dedicated with not only the staging of plays, but also gymnastic and musical competitions, along with elaborate wild beast hunts in the Circus Maximus, featuring lions, panthers, tigers, rhinoceroses, fighting monkeys, and a new spectacle never before seen in Rome: an elephant fight in which condemned criminals were crushed by the mighty animals.[3]

The building of the theatre marked the pinnacle of Pompey's achievement; he was not just a celebrity, but *the* celebrity to see, even from a distance.[4] Pompey was remembered even in the first century CE for his presence and his beauty, alongside his deeds, and was one of those people from antiquity who was, in the words of Andrew Bell: 'striving to make themselves an attractive and memorable aesthetic'.[5] The new theatre, known forever as Pompey's, was the backdrop to this man's presence in the city, with his house close to it. Within

The Campus Martius (Gismondi's model).

the theatre were displayed images of celebrated marvels from around the world, including women giving birth to hermaphrodites, elephants and a snake.[6] The theatre also housed a statue of a victorious Pompey in the nude, holding a globe to represent him as the commander of all the world and surrounded by images of the 14 nations he had conquered.[7] Pompey, in 55 BCE, was almost the *de facto* ruler of republican Rome, although only a few years later he was eclipsed by Julius Caesar. Yet Pompey's presence in the city of Rome lived on after his death through the existence of his theatre, which continued to be revered as an object of beauty centuries later and the focus of consideration of the career of the man who had paid for its construction.[8]

His successors clearly took heed. Although few of Julius Caesar's projects were completed prior to his murder on the Ides of March 44 BCE, we hear about his plans: to build the largest temple of Mars in the world and a great theatre; to create vast Greek and Latin libraries, and to divert the river Tiber.[9] Rome was to become the place with the biggest and greatest buildings in the whole world, with Julius Caesar utilizing his charisma and new architectural spaces as part

The Forum of Julius Caesar as rebuilt under Trajan.

of an aesthetic of power. This can be clearly seen in the incomplete Forum of Julius Caesar, finally finished by his adopted son, the emperor Augustus. Julius Caesar paid the huge sum of 100 million *sesterces* for the site alone, with the idea of constructing on it a temple dedicated to the goddess Venus, whom he considered to be his own ancestor. When it was finished by Augustus, the temple commanded a colonnaded rectilinear space that was constructed quite unlike the traditional forums used for commercial purposes. Instead, the models for this new architectural form were the public squares of the Persians, in which people gathered to learn the laws or seek justice.[10] It also utilized a luxurious new material, white marble quarried even to this day at Carrara in Italy.[11] This new forum was seen as far more beautiful than the previous forum,[12] and within it were marvels from Caesar's conquests and his life: pearls from Britain adorned the breast plate of the statue of Venus, a statue of Cleopatra and one of Julius Caesar himself. In addition, it was in this space that we find the first attested importance of paintings exhibited as public works of art, with Caesar displaying two masterpieces, each depicting scenes from mythology. By the first century CE, paintings such as these, purchased at considerable cost or simply taken from Greece, were placed into the marble facades of buildings and widely enjoyed, for free, by the public, whereas previously they had only been seen by the rich in their country villas.[13] Gazing at the temple from the piazza of the forum, the viewer was reminded of Caesar's power over his Roman enemies and victory at Pharsalus, his divine ancestry in the figure of Venus, and his presence. Just as Pompey was enshrined in his theatre, so Julius Caesar's forum became a stage on which he might dispense justice to the citizens of Rome.

AUGUSTAN ROME

It was the first emperor, Augustus, and his right-hand man, Marcus Agrippa, who made the greatest changes to the city.[14] Agrippa was to be remembered by Seneca as the person who built the most magnificent works, surpassed by no others.[15] As a result, an area of the Campus Martius, adjacent to Pompey's theatre, became known as the Campus Agrippae and was opened by Augustus in 7 BCE.[16] Within this area stood the largest roofed building in the world, the Diribitorium. Such was the feat of its construction that after the fire of 80 CE it remained unroofed for the rest of antiquity, because of the perceived impossibility of replacing its original construction.[17] Agrippa had also brought into Rome a new aqueduct, the Virgo, that supplied his baths on the Campus Martius with water. The baths were of new type described as Laconian or Spartan, because they were for exercise and the use of oils,[18] as opposed to simply for the process of cleaning the body. Nearby stood his Pantheon, destroyed in the fire of 80 CE and rebuilt by Hadrian in the second century CE (and surviving to this day). The description of the work on Agrippa's building reveals that the Romans were embracing new materials and the craftsmanship of Greece: the column capitals were made from Syracusan bronze and the temple roof was adorned with statues. Meanwhile, supporting the roof were Caryatids like no others found in the ancient world.[19] The building was the tallest on which statues had been placed, a landmark amongst the new monuments of the Campus Martius. The older structures of the area were also restored: the rebuilding of the Circus of Flaminius was undertaken by Agrippa's sister Polla, and the female relatives of Augustus were in charge of other monuments; for example, his sister, Octavia, restored and enlarged an existing portico and it was duly renamed the Porticus

Octavia. The result of all this work was viewed through the critical eyes of the Greek geographer Strabo (*The Geography*: 5.3.8; see the epigraphs to this chapter). It is clear from Strabo's description that the redeveloped area of Rome had become an object of beauty to be admired, to be enjoyed in the Campus through exercise, and to be gazed upon. The new city of monuments rising next to the Tiber was set in landscapes reminiscent of the countryside, with the green spaces intersected by monuments; while towering over them stood twin peaks: the Pantheon of Agrippa as we have seen, and another monument, the Mausoleum of Augustus. This enormous tomb was begun in 28 BCE, again described by our Greek geographer:

> The Mausoleum, a great mound near the river on a lofty foundation of white marble, thickly covered with evergreen trees to the very summit. Now on top is a bronze statue of Augustus Caesar; beneath the mound are the tombs of his kinsmen and intimates; behind the mound is a huge sacred precinct with wonderful promenades; and in the centre of the Campus is the wall, this also in white marble, round Augustus' crematorium; the wall is surrounded by a circular iron fence and the space within the wall is planted with black poplars. (Strabo, *The Geography*: 5.3.8)

The Mausoleum was a dynastic monument within which the ashes of emperors, their kin and associates were to be entombed, and was the destination of the funerals of the imperial family throughout the first century CE. What is interesting about Strabo's account of the buildings of this region of Rome is that some thought had clearly been given to the aesthetics of the colours, namely the contrast between the gleaming white marbles and the green of the grasses, evergreen trees and poplars. The mixing of the crowds for exercise and the Campus Martius as a burial ground also reveals a city undergoing expansion, where the functions of commemoration of the heroes of the day, the emperor and his family, took place within the urban landscape of the pleasures of leisure pursuits: exercise, horseriding and chariot racing.

Augustus' building projects extended beyond this new zone of marble, and included a new forum next to Julius Caesar's in response to the increase in legal business in the city. The colonnades were filled with statues of prominent figures of Rome's history, and became the places of legal appointments – a banker from the Bay of Naples might meet a client at the Statue of Gaius Sentius Saturninus at the third hour of a specified day.[20] However, it was also yet another venue for the display of the power of Rome, with the temple of Mars the Avenger at its centre, a reminder (if one was needed) of Augustus' vengeance delivered onto the murderers of Julius Caesar, and a reminder to others of the power of Rome.[21] It was part of a programme to demonstrate in the architecture of the city the *dignitas* (dignity) of the empire. This was not a light matter; Caesar defended his own personal *dignitas* when he crossed the Rubicon in northern Italy with his army in 49 BCE, uttering the immortal phrase *alea iacta est* (the die is cast), and heading for Rome. The eventual price of the defence of his *dignitas* was one million lives lost in civil war.[22] The buildings of Augustan Rome were themselves seen to have another virtue, *auctoritas* or authority, a quality Augustus could boast that he excelled at.[23] Authority was the feature of his command of the state, rather than the naked wielding of power. His forum, together with Julius Caesar's and the remodelled old forum dominated by the temple of the divine Julius, created a different view of the centre of power. The focus had shifted from the confusion of annual elections to permanency and a presence of the emperor. The cost of his building work in Rome, 100 million *sesterces*, was irrelevant to the new ruler of the world,[24] but what it created was a different aesthetic of urbanism: marble-clad monuments, set in a landscape, with the additional feature of art works on display to be enjoyed by all. The new monuments of Rome justified Augustus' boast that he found Rome a city of clay and turned it into a city of marble.[25]

ROME RISES FROM THE ASHES

However, if you were to look beyond these monuments of the new regime, you would find a very different city of narrow winding streets and apartment blocks, in which more than a million people lived and worked. Life here was not so pleasurable. The scale of the city was unlike any other and was irregular, full of an alien populace who were described as the *plebs sordida* by Rome's aristocracy.[26] The streets were shaded by the tall buildings around them, to the point where sunlight did not penetrate down to ground level. Quite a contrast to the novelty of the Campus Martius with its open spaces for exercise and gleaming white monuments which were later joined by Nero's new baths and gymnasium. But the great fire of Rome in 64 CE, during Nero's reign and lasting some nine days, would sweep away these irregular streets and jumbled tenements. As much as two-thirds of the city was destroyed, and Nero temporarily rehoused the people in the space of the Campus Martius while he perfected his plan to build a new type of city. His vision was a Rome of wider streets, measured rows of buildings, limited in height, and porticoes running along the facades of the apartment blocks.[27] What we see is a new aesthetic of planning that let the sunlight into the streets, while protecting those on the pavements from it. This was the city that Tacitus and the other writers of the second century CE inhabited, but it was only constructed out of the ruins of the fire of 64 CE.

There was also a glittering highlight of Nero's new city, the Golden House. Built on the burned area of the Esquiline Hill, Suetonius provides us with a sense of this new spectacle in the centre of Rome:

[The house] has a vestibule, in which stood a colossal statue of Nero himself, 120 feet high; the area the house covered was so great that it had a mile-long portico with three colonnades; it also had a pool which resembled the sea and was surrounded by buildings which were to give the impression of cities; besides this there were rural areas varied with ploughed fields, vineyards, pastures, and woodlands, and filled with all types of domestic and wild animals. All the structures in the other parts of the palace were overlaid in gold and were highlighted with gems and pearls; there were dining rooms whose ceilings were equipped with rotating ivory panels and with pipes so that flowers could be strewn and unguents sprayed on those below; the foremost dining room was a rotunda, which rotated day and night like the heavens; there were baths through which sea water and medicinal spring water flowed. (*Life of Nero*: 31)

The aesthetics of the palace are not dissimilar to those of Agrippa and Augustus' Campus Martius, and the statue of Nero, double the height of the new apartment blocks, would have been a landmark seen from the hills of the city.[28] This was the place for the emperor to live, but it was also a very public space of reception rooms, dining rooms and baths, populated not just by the emperor and famous sculpture, but also dedicated to the people.[29] Nero the artist was on display to his people, and it seems plausible they would have been invited in to see the wonder of architecture that was enhanced by the use of gems and metals from across the empire, and to view the species of animals in his game reserve.[30] The pleasure palace was not just for the emperor, but for those who visited it with all its wonders of the natural world, a source for Pliny's knowledge of a number of elements in his *Natural History,* written after the palace had been abandoned. The problem we have when dealing with this pleasure-loving emperor is that the writers of antiquity after his fall invoked his actions as examples of despotic luxury. If we look at the archaeological remains, we see architectural innovation,

The Colosseum constructed over Nero's Golden House.

even evidence of an architectural revolution, and a new setting for the display of the emperor within a domestic world, rather than within the public space of a theatre or forum.[31] Here, the emperor could entertain his people in person and display to them the spectacles of empire. The latter included works of art brought from Greece, including one of the most famous from antiquity – the Laocoön group, representing the priest who denounced the acceptance of the Trojan Horse and his sons being attacked by two snakes.[32] The sculpture was suggested by Pliny to have been made in marble as a common project of three artists: Agesander, Polydorus and Athenodorus from Rhodes.[33] Significantly, in the Renaissance it was found within the Golden House and is now displayed in the Vatican Museums – a piece that quite literally altered Michelangelo's approach to the representation of the human form (see plate 4 between pages 120–121).[34]

In contrast to Nero, who after his death in 68 CE was condemned for his extravagant building and creation of a landscape of parkland, his successor Vespasian conspicuously inhabited the gardens of Sallust, rather than the palace.[35] The new emperor opened this domestic space of the gardens to all and in this environment he utilized the landscape of the park and its architectural setting for a display of his *civilitas* in the reception of his subjects: rich or poor.[36] The new Flavian dynasty needed to distance itself from the Neronian 'excesses' and to create a different ideology that placed Vespasian and his two sons, Titus and Domitian, in the public gaze, yet demonstrated their humility as servants of the people.[37] Their grandest political act was to build a very different sort of pleasure palace from the Golden House, this time not principally for the benefit of the imperial family, but for the people. They called this monument the Colosseum. This enormous amphitheatre – the largest in the empire and built right over the lake and gardens of the Golden House at the very centre of the city – was possibly the greatest of all monuments, and today remains a symbol of Rome itself.

The Colosseum was not completed within the lifetime of Vespasian. It was his son Titus who opened the new monument, which quickly became one of the wonders of the ancient world. It was seen to surpass the pyramids of the Egyptians, the walls of Babylon and any architectural achievement of the Greeks; in short, this was the monument to inspire awe and achieve fame.[38] It could hold at least 50,000 spectators, who entered through 80 entrances and made their way through stucco-painted corridors to their seats, where they viewed the greatest show on earth. Titus dedicated this new amphitheatre with the slaughter of 9,000 animals; women and men appeared as hunters; men fought each other in single combat, and in groups as though soldiers; and there were numerous re-enactments from mythology that resulted in the deaths of the participants.[39] It was a show for his people.[40] However, the Colosseum was not an isolated monument. Vespasian and his son Titus were involved in the redevelopment of the whole area that had been the entrance to the Golden House: a new set of baths was constructed, the colossus of Nero had its face recut so that the statue now depicted the sun god, and the temple of the deified Claudius was completed. Recent archaeological research has also demonstrated that the arch later rebuilt and dedicated to Constantine, next to the Colosseum, was originally a Flavian triumphal arch. Further on was the fountain, known as the Meta Sudans – the turning point of the triumphal processions into the Sacred Road that had at its crest the Arch dedicated to Titus' victories over the Jews. The Colosseum sat within a landscape of other Flavian monuments that highlighted their success in warfare and distance from Nero, expressed by an

ideology of duty to their subjects that is revealed in the building inscription:
'The emperor Caesar Titus Vespasian Augustus ordered the new amphitheatre
to be constructed from the spoils of war'.[41]

Where Nero's flamboyant style had been situated in a palace, the Flavians
quite literally presented the contents of the palace and the spectacles of the
empire to the people, via the shows in the Colosseum, the new Baths of Titus
and importantly within the new Temple of Peace adjacent to the Forums of
Julius Caesar and Augustus. The form of this temple precinct included plants,
statues, a map of the world and a map of Rome itself in considerable detail. It
was also a place where all Romans could enjoy the grand works of art collected
by Nero:

> Among the works I have referred to, all the most celebrated have now been dedicated
> in Rome by the emperor Vespasian, in his temple of Peace and other public buildings.
> Nero's rapacity had brought them all to Rome, to be placed in reception rooms in the
> Golden House. (Pliny, *Natural History*: 34.84)

The precinct of the Temple of Peace was ranked by Pliny the Elder, alongside
the Forum of Augustus, as one of the most beautiful in the world.[42] This view is
confirmed by another contemporary, Josephus:

> Vespasian decided to erect a Temple of Peace. This was built quickly, in a style to surpass
> all human imagination. He drew on limitless resources of wealth: he embellished it with
> ancient masterpieces of painting and sculpture, so that in that shrine were assembled
> and displayed all the objects which men had once travelled the world to see, when they
> were kept separately in different countries. Here too he stored his especial pride, the
> golden vessels from the Temple of the Jews. (Josephus, *Jewish War*: 7.158–62)

There was a speed to the Flavian projects; the Temple of Peace was dedicated
in 75 CE and the Colosseum and Baths of Titus in 80 CE, four and nine years
respectively from the start of construction.[43] Pieces of sculpture were collected,
but others were new, and fresh wonders were to behold in the latest materials
used:

> The Egyptians also discovered in Ethiopia what is called basinates, a stone which in
> colour and hardness resembles iron . . . No larger specimen of this stone has ever been
> found than that dedicated by the emperor Vespasian in the temple of Peace, the subject
> of which is the Nile, with sixteen of the river-god's children playing around him. (Pliny,
> *Natural History*: 36.58; see also 36.27, 34.53–84; Darwall-Smith 1996: 59–60)

The Temple of Peace was unlike the Forums of Augustus or Julius Caesar; it was a monument for leisure rather than business and could be described as an open-air museum.[44] It brought pleasure to the zone of the bustling forums full of statuary from the Augustan age. Here, the Romans could exercise their minds in the classification of statuary ancient and modern, and at the same time, view the booty of Vespasian, the bringer of peace to Rome after the civil wars of 69 CE.[45] It was a short walk from here to the old republican forum or Forum Romanum, where Titus built a temple to his deified father.[46]

Vespasian and Titus had also been involved in the rebuilding of the city that had continued to contain evidence of the destruction wrought by the fire of 64 CE, as well as its most important temple of Jupiter on the Capitol, that had burned down during the civil conflict of December 69 CE. Vespasian directed the rebuilding of the temple of Jupiter, and also that of the Capitol, even removing some of the rubble himself and providing incentives for the redevelopment of private property.[47] The Flavians had reconfigured Rome with their presence at its very centre, seen by a world of visitors to the new structures of leisure: the Colosseum and the Temple of Peace, but also inscribed across the existing spaces of the city – on the Capitol with a new temple to Jupiter and in the most ancient forum facing the temple of Julius Caesar.

ROME RISES AGAIN

However, in 80 CE another fire was to destroy much of the city, including many of the monuments of the Campus Martius, all those of Augustus and Agrippa, and the Capitol, with Rome's temple to Jupiter.[48] In the emperor Titus' own words 'I am ruined'.[49] He placed money and the objects and statues from his villas at the disposal of a team of Roman knights for the restoration of the city's public monuments, but died in 81 CE before these projects could be completed. His brother, Domitian, took on the task of restoration of the Campus Martius and other monuments across the city, including the temple of Jupiter. It was a huge task and one that Domitian engaged with fully. On the restored buildings, he placed his own name rather than that of the original builder.[50] The format is, as ever, on a grander scale than any predecessor could anticipate or any rival could begin to afford. Plutarch considers the grand gesture, after the death and condemnation of the memory of Domitian:

The greatest wealth now attributed to any private citizen of Rome would not pay for the cost of gilding alone of the present temple [of Jupiter], which was more than 12,000 talents [288 million *sesterces*]. Its columns are of Pentelic marble, and their thickness was once most happily proportioned to their length; for we saw them in Athens. But when they arrived in Rome, they were recut and scraped, they did not gain as much in polish as they lost in their symmetry and beauty, and they now look slender and thin. However, if anyone who is amazed at the costliness of the Capitol had seen a single colonnade in the palace of Domitian, or a basilica or a bath or the apartments of his concubines ... (*Life of Publicola*, 15)

Plutarch presents us with a Domitian, who like Nero, had a mania for building; however, he ignores the necessity for the emperor to not just rebuild the monuments of the city, but to surpass his predecessors at building. And the city of Rome did seem to have the resources to overcome any setback caused by a major fire. Indeed, fire was a means for the creation of suitable plots for some of the grandest redevelopments of the city, whether the Golden House, the Colosseum, or the Domitianic monuments on the Campus Martius.[51] Each emperor was seeking to create buildings and urban landscapes that were ever more beautiful and, in doing so, regarded cost as largely irrelevant. This sentiment was understood by Julius Caesar 150 years earlier, when he borrowed money to construct temporary buildings for his first games in 65 BCE.[52] However, the end result of the new emphasis on Rome as a city of monuments of beauty was the series of magnificent buildings found in Strabo's description of the city. The buildings were not only imposing in themselves, but were landscaped with plants, created from stones quarried in far-off lands and displayed statues of both antiquity and recent times. The landscape of Rome was to fuel entries in Pliny's *Natural History*, whether examples of rare stones, plants or statues. The city had become a spectacle of empire, and every aspect of it could be enjoyed by the public.

When we look at ancient Rome, we are shocked by its size: one million people crowding the streets and the forums as they eked out a living. Many modern historians chart the dangers of the city from disease and fire.[53] Yet, perhaps, we miss appreciating the amenities of the city of Rome that gave pleasure to all: the gardens, the baths, the circuses for chariot racing, the three theatres on the Campus Martius, the Colosseum and the Temple of Peace. It was a larger city than any other, but had little in common with, say, the provincial town of Pompeii, destroyed in 79 CE by the eruption of Vesuvius. Rome had unsurpassed levels of urban amenities and facilities for the pursuits of leisure activities. The Campus Martius and Nero's Golden House featured landscapes that brought the countryside into the city in the form of vast parklands populated by colonnades, baths, other public monuments and statues and paintings.[54] Pompeii might produce its bath buildings, theatres and amphitheatre, but what it lacked was Rome's landscaping and the interconnection of spaces that joined the forums together and connected them to the Temple of Peace. The result was a centre to the city that was experienced kinetically, with each space opening from another to reveal new marvels of the city to the traveller, or fresh wonders recently constructed by the current emperor to the inhabitants.[55] By the end of the first century CE, Rome outshone all the cities of the world – a far cry from the days of the emperor Augustus who began embellishing a city that did not, at that time, reflect the majesty of its empire. Rome burned in 64 CE and burned again in 80 CE, and was rebuilt and revived after each phase of destruction with grander monuments. In time, it was popularly perceived that the 'good emperors' (Augustus, Vespasian or Titus) had built beautiful edifices, and the 'bad emperors' (Nero and Domitian) had created monstrosities. Even so, the Roman people still reaped the benefits. Martial, relaxing in the beautiful baths on the Campus Martius, once mused: 'What was worse than Nero? What was better than Nero's Baths?' (*Epigrams*: 7.34). There was a legacy for the city even from the worst emperors of Rome's past.

4

A Little Place in the Country

You must be careful, particularly if you are building yourself, not to overstep the limit in expense and magnificence. Indeed, in this area much harm lies even in the example set. For most men eagerly imitate the actions of their leaders in this matter in particular. Take the excellent Lucius Lucullus: who imitated his virtue? But how many imitated the magnificence of his country houses. But a limit ought to be set, and brought back to an intermediate level. The same intermediate standard ought to be applied to all questions of one's needs and life style.

Cicero, On Duties: 1.140

Gellius is forever building. Now he lays down thresholds, now fits keys to doors and buys bolts, remodels and changes now these windows, now those. Gellius does anything you name, just so long as he's building, so that he can say to a friend who asks for money that one word: aedificio – am building.

Martial, Epigrams: 9.46

PLEASURE PALACES

By the end of the first century CE, wealthy Romans had developed a passion for creating rural retreats that redefined the experience of pleasure.[1] Some of these villas were a day's journey from the bustle of the city of Rome – others were further away still on the coast of the Mediterranean. The wealth of attractions that these retreats offered were beautifully captured in the writings of the poet Statius, who visited many of the villas of the rich and famous, and attempted to recreate his sensations of wonder in words.[2] The places he remembers and describes have been created by pleasure herself.[3] And rather than a listing of bedrooms and bathrooms along the lines of a modern-day estate agent's brochure, what Statius gives us is an idea of the sensual experience each villa has

Villa at the Capo di Sorrento on the Bay of Naples.

to offer. In visiting the Villa of Manlius Vopiscus near the modern town of Tivoli (ancient Tibur), he describes the cool of the house compared to the summer heat outside. He reveals that the noise of the river Anio flowing between the two sections of the villa murmurs rather than thunders, and discovers there are views from rooms of both the river and the ancient woodland.[4] Then, of course, there are the riches of the interior decoration, with gilded beams, glittering coloured marbles, images of water nymphs in every bedroom, statues in bronze, ivories, gems and a feast of decoration on the walls, floors and ceilings. Every amenity awaits the traveller, from the smoking bathhouse to feasting by the banks of the river and onto bed and slumber induced by the murmur of the river.

It is clear that Statius, writing towards the end of the first century CE, celebrates material wealth with joy. It is in stark contrast to Cicero's opinion (see chapter epigraphs), expressed a century earlier, calling for restraint. Indeed, many Romans from the Republican era saw palaces of pleasure as deceitful luxuries to be condemned for occupying land that should be dedicated to the more honest pursuit of productive agriculture. But by the end of the first century CE, pleasure had won. Although there would still be critics, the sensual perception of the landscapes of the rural retreats of the rich were no longer to be condemned. The countryside had ceased to be inhabited by boorish rustics, and instead had attracted sophisticated city dwellers, who brought with them the architecture, materials and technology of Rome. In their villas, the owners could demonstrate their superiority through the construction of gilded ceilings, citrus wood, imported marble, columns, mosaics, fountains and collections of antique sculpture.[5]

Perhaps the most famous Roman villa still remembered today is that of Pliny the Younger on the coast close to Ostia, which was described by its owner in a letter to a friend in the last decade of the first century CE.[6] Pliny declares that the attractions of his villa are the house itself, the amenities of its location and its extensive seafront. Being only 17 miles from Rome, it can be reached at the end of a day's business via either the road to Laurentum or the road to Ostia. There are woods and meadows on which flocks are pastured in winter. The house is described with an owner's modesty, as large enough but not too luxurious. Parts of the house are sheltered from even the worst weather, whereas others are designed for use in fine weather only. There are views of the sea, but also views of the meadows and mountains inland. Some rooms are set up to get the morning sun and others the evening rays. Other parts of the house are silent and the wind can only be heard during major storms. There are rooms for the slaves and freed slaves of the household that are good enough for guests. There are dining rooms, a bathhouse and a gymnasium. Bathing and exercise were an integral part of life in these houses, and Pliny duly mentions his heated swimming pool and ball-court that caught the warmth of the setting sun. The sensations of warmth in winter and coolness in summer dominate the description of the villa, as do the sounds – 'a dining room where nothing is known of a high sea but the sound of the breakers' – and the views – 'the dining room looks onto the garden and encircling drive, a view as lovely as that of the sea itself'. A covered *porticus* or colonnade led from the villa towards the sea. It is described as being as large as a public building, with windows facing both the sea and a terrace with scented flowers leading to a suite of rooms within which views of neighbouring villas, the sea and the wooded slopes of the hills could be seen. At the same time, the *porticus* is far enough away from the main house so that there is no human noise present, even at the celebration of the Saturnalia.

The only thing that the villa lacks is running water, says Pliny, but good water is abundant from the villa's wells. Unfortunately, this means that unlike at his villa in Tuscany, there is no sound of flowing fountains.[7] The view of the coast from the house or from a boat is a landscape festooned with other villas, which are so large and great in number that they appear to be like a series of cities. All of these attractions, Pliny hopes, will encourage Gallus, the friend to whom he is writing, to leave Rome and visit his maritime retreat, where the amenities exist to rival a life in the city. What Pliny does not mention in his description is anything about the interior of the villa, its decoration, the presence of marble, of statues or any of the features that Statius as a guest found so conspicuous in the villa of Manlius Vopiscus near Tivoli. Interestingly, in discussing his property in Etruria, Pliny does include the mention of marble but concentrates again on the views, the amenities and the layout of the house. Perhaps he felt that it was rather tacky for an owner to list his possessions; or maybe he was holding back on the details until his guest arrived, when he could wow him with the decor. Then again, maybe he recalled his own uncle's condemnation of all such symbols of material wealth,[8] and worried that some may still share his view.

The proliferation of such coastal retreats is also clear from wall decorations. This genre of maritime landscape painting had been introduced under the emperor Augustus to fill the houses of the elite, and provide a picture of villas abundant in *portici* or colonnades leading right down to the sea, of landscaped gardens, groves, woods, hills, fish ponds, canals and rivers, and a coastline populated by people walking, sailing, travelling on donkeys and in carriages to their villas, fishing and hunting (see plate 1 between pages 120–121). There was also a whole subgenre of witty scenes of men staggering as they try to carry women.[9] These were landscapes of human technology recasting the natural landscape to manufacture an image within which people, rather than mythological characters, existed. Their popularity is attested by our knowledge of some 300 examples of these frescoes from the Bay of Naples.[10] These images highlighted not just the villas on the coast, but also their *porticus* or colonnade(s) which were clearly designed to resemble the public architecture of the cities of Italy. It's a feature that is found in Statius' encounter with the villa of Pollius Felix sited on the coast of the Bay of Naples. Statius' poem approaches the villa by boat from Naples.[11] His attention is first drawn to the domes of the smoking bathhouse, and then shifts onto other features of this villa as vast as a city – a *porticus* or colonnade reorganizing the rocky landscape for the pleasure of the guest and owner of this vast villa. Once inside, the thrashing of the sea below is only heard as a pleasant murmur to accompany the pleasant views across the sea towards other elaborate villas on the coast, or across the neighbouring vineyards inland with new viewpoints established from each room. Nature had been reshaped to create an architecture of pleasure within which decoration was derived from imported products: exotic marbles and antique collections of sculpture. This is the architecture of the city, but transposed from the culture of the urban street into a world of scenic views and leisure pursuits.

Today we can get a glimpse of the grandeur of these pleasure palaces when we visit the surviving remains of the villas at Stabiae on the Bay of Naples. These structures were extensively explored in the eighteenth century, with many of their more magnificent frescoes removed to the royal museum in Naples (today the National Archaeological Museum) or to the Antiquarium in Castellamare di Stabia. One piece found its way to the British Museum in London, with further extensive excavations made in the middle of the twentieth century.[12] However, visitors can still explore the excavated remains that include colonnades, walkways, dining rooms, bath suites and bedrooms, and admire the stupendous views across the bay of Naples. The scale of the craftsmanship involved in the construction of these villas can be appreciated through an understanding of the modern conservation of the sites. In July 1950, Francesco Tammaro, a specialist restorer of mosaics, began his work not on the floors of a dining room but on its vaulted ceiling and was to produce a *magnifico disegno* for the restoration of the ceilings. Tammaro was to extend his skills to the restoration of the fresco of Ganymede in September of the same year. His work was deemed to have been *bellissimo* but *molto complicato*. Eighteen months later, Tammaro was still at work in the same dining room. The skills of the modern restorers and the meticulous way in which they work have produced stunning transformations to the images on the walls found at excavation sites. Their work is laborious and labour-intensive, and their efforts can be easily undone by the ravages of time, and budgets inadequate to address even the most basic of conservation efforts. Meanwhile, what is revealed at Stabiae is only a fraction of what was there in the first century: a landscape populated by villas stretching right along the coast, each with its walkway and *porticus* from which the landscape of the bay could be viewed; while internally the decoration of the rooms and baths created a new form of architecture for the countryside – *pseudourbana*.[13]

LIFE IN THE PLEASURE VILLA: NATURAL AND UNNATURAL PLEASURES

So what did people in antiquity do in these vast palaces with their stupendous views? The paintings of the seascapes found at the Vesuvian sites indicate a whole series of activities: riding donkeys, travelling in vehicles, hunting and fishing. How these were organized at the country villas is explained by Pliny in discussion of the lifestyle of the retired senator Vestricius Spurinna.[14] Older men, unlike their younger counterparts, needed a fixed routine or regimen that might be followed each day; Spurinna excelled in Pliny's eyes as having the perfect pattern for an elderly man. Unlike a younger man in the city, Spurinna stayed in bed and only got up at the second hour (i.e. two hours after daybreak), when he called for his shoes and walked for three miles round a *gestatio* designed as part of the villa for exactly this purpose and measuring a circuit of one mile.[15] This was an exercise of both his body and his mind: if he had friends staying they would discuss serious matters; if he did not a slave read a book aloud to him. Following his walk, he sat down and the conversation or the reading continued. There followed further exercise; accompanied by his wife or a friend such as Pliny, he drove a carriage around a specially constructed hippodrome attached to the villa.[16] Spurinna took the opportunity to regale Pliny with tales of men of the previous generation. After the carriage driving, the old man returned to his *cubiculum* or private chamber or sat again outside to compose poetry in either Latin or Greek.

The next action of the day was the baths. Spurinna removed his clothes mid afternoon and walked in the sunshine if there was no wind, and then threw a ball prior to bathing. Finally, there was dinner taken from dishes of Corinthian bronze, items that he owned and admired before his guests, but without the mania of a bronze collector. The pleasure of eating was broken up by the performance of a comedy and the meal extended into the hours of darkness. What becomes clear from reading about the life of Spurinna at his villa is that the entire architecture, and that of Pliny's own retreat, was set up for the performance of exercises to maintain the body: walking circuits, a hippodrome, a ball court and the baths; while permitting the retirement of the owner to his *cubiculum* to work on a literary enterprise. Entertainment included the performance of plays while dining. The architecture not only enabled a pleasant existence filled with literary thoughts, philosophical conversation and witty anecdotes about the past, but also was set up to maintain the man when faced with the challenges of old age. The architecture of the villa created a routine that was not found on the farm, which was so dear to the old men of the second century BCE. Now at the turn of the first to second centuries CE, the manmade landscape of the villa was what sustained a person in old age and created the possibility of a virtuous, yet structured, leisure. To deviate from Spurinna's regimen was to face the possibility of old age creeping up on the body like a disease – a feature of Roman life that, like the rocks and mountains underlying the villas, needed to be tamed and controlled.

The first century CE saw a rapid change in the consumption of goods and the embellishment of pleasure villas; far faster than the developments reported in the previous century.[17] The earlier period had seen the start of this process, with the very finest house in Rome being eclipsed in terms of beauty by more than 100 new palaces in the city over a period of 35 years.[18] Now, a century later, the pleasure villa was so much a part of the landscape that it became an object of philosophical and rhetorical attack; a symbol of all that was seen to be wrong with the Roman society's emphasis on material consumption.[19] The elder Seneca regarded the pleasure villa as imitating nature to recreate woods, mountains, fields, seas and rivers – but completely divorced from the natural world where these items had existed previously, a world that Seneca regarded as unknown to the owners of such imitations.[20] He saw these villas as unnatural as the childless man. Others saw the luxury villa as the symbol of the destruction of the labouring peasant, the latter's livelihood replaced by residences fit for a king with their vast fishponds.[21] These attacks on the very types of villas that had so impressed Statius and others can be viewed as part of a critique of change that created a perception that Italy had been transformed from the historical fiction of a landscape of peasant self-sufficiency dependent on a benevolent aristocracy, into a land designed for pleasure-obsessed aristocrats (including, heavens above, quite a number of wealthy freed slaves). These aristocrats were dependent on the labour of slaves, the import of exotic goods and living in ever larger and more luxurious palaces.

In spite of all their rhetoric (and in many cases, stoic denial of the author's own wealth), these critiques reveal the extent of the villa culture of the elite, and the new essential elements that signified status – a large house in the city and a luxurious villa on the coast or in the mountains. Critiques used the same language that Statius had employed in praising the villa and identified the same features as the symbols that held meaning. Where Statius might admire the transformation of nature, Seneca saw a confusion of natural categories with foundations laid out into the sea, or cliffs cut away to create artificial inlets – the land became the sea and the sea became the land in his reading of the transformation of nature for the building of an environment of pleasure.[22]

Nowhere was this mixing of categories seen as more inappropriate than within Rome itself – indeed, it was the very condemnation of excessive luxuries here that led to the vast building of pleasure palaces outside the city walls. Much of the criticism was focused on the lavish lifestyle of a single individual from the previous century: Lucullus. For a time a leading politician and even successful commander of armies, Lucullus was a man who chose to retire from the political fray of the end of the Republic and instead live a life of pleasure within his gardens (horti) in Rome. His gardens, a century later, were still regarded as the finest and had not been eclipsed by the escalation of luxury.[23] What Lucullus created, in parkland now occupied by the public gardens known as the Villa Borghese, was the landscape of the villa within the city – an abode to rival his retreat on the Bay of Naples. The character and morality of this man was seen to be represented by his horti in the city: encumbered by luxury. Pliny the Elder, whose knowledge of natural and manmade phenomena was unrivalled, condemned the construction of gardens or horti, which contained both villas and pleasure parks, within the city of Rome.[24] Recent excavations beneath the Villa Medici have revealed extensive use of water within the gardens and the architecture of Lucullus' parkland would have facilitated the entertainment of vast numbers, whether with dinner, or plays, or for the celebration of religious rites and festivals.[25] The true extent of luxury within such gardens has also been demonstrated by a more extensive study of another set of urban gardens, the horti Lamiani.[26] There is excavated evidence from these gardens of marble floors, gems for wall decoration, as well as fragments of wall paintings. Two of the most famous sculptures from antiquity were found in these gardens: The Esquiline Venus, and the Emperor Commodus dressed as Hercules alongside other marble statues that included that of an old shepherd. The *horti* clearly provided the setting for the creation of three-dimensional images of mythical and real landscapes, that we are familiar with today from their survival in two-dimensions as frescoes on the walls of houses and villas close to Pompeii, Herculaneum and Stabiae.[27]

Prices for these gardens in the late republic were enormous: 11.5 million *sesterces* was paid for the 250-hectare *Horti Scapulani*; smaller plots or those in a less central location could be found for just over a million.[28] A decent set of urban *horti* would set a Roman aristocrat back almost as much as the cost of his palace on the Palatine Hill close to the forum: we find Cicero buying a house here for 3.5 million *sesterces*, whereas his great rival Clodius paid 14.8 million for a rather more luxurious property.[29] What the difference in prices paid for both houses and gardens demonstrates is that the funds available to Roman senators for the purchase of property in the city varied considerably. Those who could afford the costliest properties, whether palaces near the forum or pleasure gardens on the periphery, were the subject of jealousy. The philosophy of stoicism provided a means by which a Cicero could continue to feel smug about his house on the Palatine, a lavish property, while recognizing that his neighbours commanded considerably greater funds for the purchase and embellishment of their houses. This factor allowed a middle-rank Roman aristocrat to maintain that his property was lavish but not luxurious, just as he was neither a miser nor a spendthrift. It is a philosophy that provided a means not to envy those wealthier than oneself, and also provided a way to condemn the richer than oneself as revelling in luxury and decadence. Those men who produced the literature that condemns luxury, in particular gardens and villas, were not the wealthiest and hence our picture underplays the construction, use or purchase of the pleasure garden as a means to create an image of personal power based upon the command of resources. Moreover, the landscape of the *hortus* had much in common with the palaces of Hellenistic Kings with their theatre, stadium, gymnasium and a *stoa* (a Roman *porticus* or colonnade) – all elements that were not only found in the *horti* within Rome, but also reproduced in the villas of Spurinna and Pliny outside Rome. The ultimate example is the Villa of Hadrian outside Tivoli, constructed in the early second century CE, and it can still be visited today for those who wish to experience the architecture, landscape and views associated with the pleasure gardens and villas at first hand.[30]

The garden of the House of Octavius Quarto, Pompeii.

What made *horti* and villas places to be condemned as symbols of luxury was not just their decadence, but their association with a certain type of lifestyle that was seen as almost anti-Roman. Lucullus, for example, lived in his *horti* when he was an adult Roman in his prime. What made his lifestyle unacceptable was also a withdrawal from public life into this world of conspicuous luxury.[31] He was in effect rejecting the very idea of engaging with the state or regarding the state and society as having any relevance to his life. Since the Roman state with its laws and justice was seen to be part of the natural order, the rejection of the state was linked to the construction of the artificial landscapes of the grand villas and urban *horti* – a similar link to a rejection of nature was made with any public figure who was unwilling to have children.[32] The lifestyle of the owners of the *horti*, such as Lucullus, may have been not dissimilar from that of Spurrina, but they were to be condemned. These men did not need to keep old age at bay and were regarded as a resource that was needed by the state – their refusal to take part in public life was the main issue, and was to be explained not entirely in terms of lifestyle choice, but also in terms of a form of moral corruption caused by an unnatural engagement with, or an over-indulgence in, pleasure. It was fine to withdraw to a garden on the outskirts of Rome, on a public holiday, to discuss with friends philosophical questions while surrounded by architecture, vegetation and winter sunshine. After all, it was in just this setting that Cicero could imagine the magnates of an earlier age, Scipio Aemilianus and Laelius, and some budding young politicians discussing the nature of the Republic.[33] It was quite another thing to do so every day of the year and refuse, as an adult in the prime of life, to take part in the affairs of state.

This was exactly the problem for Nero when he first built his Golden House in the heart of Rome (see Chapter 3): his life was regarded as dominated by pleasure in his new palace, rather than by the affairs of state.[34] What was seen as a violation of city space in all these cases was the replacement of functioning space of *negotium* or business with a space designed for *otium* or leisure. In the order of things set out by Pliny and other authors, *otium* was fine in its place: outside Rome, and undertaken at the right time – in old age or otherwise at times of national holiday, when all would be at leisure. It was seen as unnatural to bring the landscape of the villa into the city, just as it was seen as unnatural to build a villa out into the sea. Such things were deemed to be a luxury too far, in a similar way that we would criticize symbols of excesses today, such as the dog owner who does not walk his dog himself, but employs a professional dog walker; the inappropriate use of four-by-four vehicles in the narrow streets of the city; or the destruction of 'natural' resources and the creation of pollution that we now know contributes to global warming. The latter was of course unknown to the Romans, but we now know from analysis of historic evidence of pollution found in the Greenland ice cap that it was their society that was the greatest polluter, as well as the greatest consumer of resources, prior to the advent of industrialization in the nineteenth century.[35]

GARDENS FOR THE PEOPLE

Lucullus was not the only magnate from the final years of the Republic to own gardens in Rome. His great rival Pompey had his gardens on the Campus Martius not far from his theatre constructed in 55 BCE – the first to be built from stone in Rome.[36] Plutarch tells us that he opened his gardens to the people, and they went there to collect money in return for their support of Pompey's candidate in the election of 61 BCE. The landscape of Pompey's gardens were similar to that of the *horti* of his rival Lucullus, with an important difference: this was public space for the enjoyment of the Roman plebs and a place for their entertainment, for vast public banquets. This was not private luxury, but public magnificence given to the people of Rome.[37] Where Pompey led, Caesar followed; his gardens across the Tiber were opened to the public, and on his death bequeathed to the Roman plebs as a public space for their enjoyment. Here was the venue for the great public banquets that punctuated Caesar's rise to power, disposing of vast quantities of food sourced from shops all over the city of Rome, the grand scale of which could have caused inflation in the prices of food.[38] At his triumphal banquet in 46 BCE, Caesar, for the first time, served the public four different types of wine that resulted in a new system of classifying wine according to its quality.[39] In September 46 BCE, Caesar served up food to 198,000 guests with his friend Aulus Hirtius donating 6,000 lampreys, with each of the 22,000 tables of nine diners being supplied with an amphora of the finest wine.[40] This was a meal greater than anything seen even in the court of the Kings or Pharaohs of Egypt – it was a feast for all, and afterwards they followed Caesar home via his new forum. A year later, the event was to be repeated in October to celebrate the final defeat of Pompey.[41] It was only natural for Caesar to celebrate his triumph over his rival on a grand scale, while at the same time emasculating any rival banquets put on by other aristocrats by forbidding them on grounds of the need to conserve resources.[42] Pleasure was to be provided by one man: Caesar, and was something that was to be maintained by his heirs – the Roman emperors. As a direct result, gradually the *horti* in Rome became the property of the emperor and his family, or became public spaces.[43] There was little room in the emperor's Rome for men to own properties that might compete with the emperor; to do so was to be his rival, with dire consequences. Instead, the plebs enjoyed the amenities of the gardens of the aristocracy of the previous century, and the aristocrats constructed their villas and pleasure gardens at a discreet distance from the capital. Thus, the landscapes of pleasure spread over a greater area of Italy and were enjoyed, at least at Rome, by a far greater number of people. It's fair to say that life for most Romans was considerably more fun for people under the monarchy established by Julius Caesar than it had been under a senatorial aristocracy.

5

The Roman Body at the Baths

What was worse than Nero, what was better than his baths?

Martial, Epigrams: *7.34*

The baths were a feature of the cities of the Roman Empire that disappeared from European cities by the end of the sixteenth century. These were places that not only provided the means for cleaning the body, but were also places at which men and women could come into contact with the bodies of others. The encounters were often sexual and the architecture of the baths created a quasi-public place of pleasure and encounter.

Michel Foucault, 1984b: 251

You never invite anybody [to dine], Cotta, unless you have bathed with him; the baths give you a guest. I used to wonder why you had never asked me to dinner. Now I know you didn't like me in the nude.

Martial, Epigrams: *1.23*

Hostius Quadra's depravity was not restricted to only one sex, but he was voracious for men and women alike. He had mirrors made specially to reflect distorted images . . . they were set up at angles around the room, so when his arse was penetrated he could see all . . . and he relished the exaggerated size of his own penis as much as if it were real. He used to cruise the baths checking penises, recruiting from the ranks of those who measured up.

Seneca, Natural Questions: *1.16*

There were two places in which Romans shed their clothes: the baths and the bedroom. While the bedroom was private, the baths were a public venue in which all from the lowest to the highest undressed, apart from their bath sandals, and were observed by others.[1] The public baths had spread across Italy from the third century BCE and by the first century CE were an essential feature of nearly every town across the Empire. Identified clearly by Tacitus, baths became a basic element of Roman culture that former barbarians would adopt in that process of becoming Roman.[2] Bathing involved the individual experience of heat, cold and nudity resulting in a series of sensations that were felt for the most part by the skin, but there was another aspect: bathing was a social pleasure experienced with others.[3] Our own connection in the West with these features of social life, so prevalent in the Roman world, was cut at some point in the sixteenth century, as Michel Foucault has observed. However, the sensations of heat, steam and nudity have been reinvented in the modern gay bathhouses of North America – a setting that has provided one modern writer with an insight into the sensory pleasures experienced by the ancient Romans.[4]

A STUDY IN NUDE

Bathhouses with the basic sequence of rooms: a *frigidarium* (cold room); a *tepidarium* (warm room) and a *caldarium* (hot room) have been identified right across the Roman Empire.[5] This structure of heated space can be found in the Stabian Baths at Pompeii in the second century BCE, and also in the Central Baths under construction in 79 CE on the eve of the city's destruction. Bathing in Roman culture utilized a set of hot and cold spaces, so that the naked body could be heated up and cooled down. The baths were the only public places, apart from the brothel, where Roman males were naked and their bodies on display.[6] For the moralists, the baths could take on the immoral tones of the Greek gymnasia, in which young men exercised naked – a practice adopted in Nero's Rome.[7] We find women bathing naked and there is evidence of nude mixed bathing from the first century CE onwards.[8] A female view of male nudity is neatly summed up by a witty incident involving the emperor Augustus' wife, Livia. A group of naked males mistakenly entered her presence, an insult to her chastity and modesty, that she deflected with the remark that 'To a chaste woman this was no different from looking at naked male statues'; a remark that plays up the possibility that, unlike the empress Livia, other women found the male body fascinating.[9] Nudity was such a key feature of bathing that it defined the whole experience for the Romans, and made the bathhouses such a unique feature of city living. The rooms in the baths constituted a series of sensory

The *caldarium* of the central baths in Pompeii.

spaces in which the human body experienced a variation in heat to produce sweat, to breathe in steam, to have one's vision obscured by steam and to be immersed in cold water. This was part of a process of cleaning the body, which included the sensation of having one's skin oiled, massaged and scraped – a pleasure in its own right and an action that defined a person as Roman.

The baths built in the first century CE were rather different from the earlier venues for bathing: they were light rather than dark. The changes in and spread in the usage of window glass permitted the baths to become better lit than they had been at an earlier date, as can be seen by visitors to the Central Baths in Pompeii, when compared to the earlier Stabian Baths. It has to be said though that in the first century CE there existed both the new well-lit baths and the older and much darker baths – giving Romans the choice of whether to bathe in rooms where they could see and be seen by others, or in ill-lit darker rooms where the bodies were obscured.[10] They also had the choice of mixed sex bathing, or segregated, and again we find the distinction in the Stabian and Central Baths in Pompeii. The darker and much earlier baths were segregated, whereas the up-to-date Central Baths anticipated no form of segregation.

The act of bathing was, in many ways, institutionalized, with the baths heated up to a high temperature at midday, cooling to a perfect temperature two hours later and becoming rather tepid as the sun began dip below the horizon.[11] The basic process of becoming clean could take as little as an hour or could be undertaken at a more leisurely pace. Those who worked all day, the hired labourers or those who through obligations of duties were detained by the rich might not get to the baths until they had cooled; whereas the rich or the idle would bathe at the eighth hour of the day and enjoy a bath at a perfect temperature. Hence, the experience of pleasure would have varied according to wealth.

Nudity was not a particular problem for the Roman moralists; what was much more controversial was the fact that the baths gave people pleasure. This led Seneca to characterize the baths as the antithesis of the temple, the forum or the walls of the city with their association with virtue.[12] Within this dichotomy, virtue is seen as elevated, exulted and regal; whereas pleasure was lowly, servile and weak. Virtue was seen as having dusty and calloused hands, and the Romans of the past were praised for needing only to wash their arms and legs on a daily basis.[13] Not surprisingly, pleasure was seen to lurk in the darker recesses of the baths and sweating rooms. The act of becoming clean was deployed as a means of characterizing others: over-perfumed; smeared with unguents; or wearing cosmetics.[14] This places the baths in the moral discourse on the city just a step away from the brothel, the alleyway and the tavern, where pleasure was certain to reside. This is perhaps confirmed by the fashion among young men of drinking prior to bathing.[15]

The changes in the architecture of the baths were viewed as a measure of how Roman society had chosen to embrace pleasure. Unlike the baths of Scipio Africanus, who defeated Hannibal in 202 BCE, the modern baths of the first century CE contained mirrored walls, mosaics in stones from Africa, pools faced in imported marble with water running from silver spouts, large windows, clear water, and flues for hot air in the walls as well as the floor to create an even temperature from floor to ceiling.[16] Yet, the older darker baths associated with the men of the past continued to exist and were a place where a stoic, such as Seneca, could feel the morality of the past seeping into the pores of his body in the present.

For all Romans, bathhouses offered a full range of sensations. Emanating from them was a soundscape of pleasures taken: the grunts and pants of a man exercising, the slaps of the masseurs on bare flesh, the splash of a man jumping into the swimming pool, voices in song reverberating from the vaulted spaces of the baths, the shrill cries of the hair plucker and yelps of his clients, and the calls of the vendors of sausages, cakes and other foods.[17] The modern baths of the first century CE became the location in which to observe the degenerate: transported from 'a' to 'b' in a sedan chair, lifted by others from their bath, and even instructed by slaves at what time to bathe – they had in short become enslaved to pleasure and lost touch with their human existence.[18] Sweating could even be equated with an effeminate desire to maintain a thin physique.[19] These men had turned their backs on nature and lived in luxury, all revealed via their bathing habits. The good man might even bathe in cold water only.[20]

CLOSE ENCOUNTERS

The heroes of Petronius' novel the *Satyrica*, Encolpius and Ascyltos, were invited to Trimalchio's house for dinner, meeting up with the great man for the first time in the baths.[21] The narrative of what has become known as the Cena (Dinner) of Trimalchio is an imaginary creation of a world of a rich freedman that gives us a vivid picture of the activities in the bathhouses and the different practices observed. At the baths, Ascyltos and Encolpius stroll in the central courtyard, joking with others who are playing games, when they observe the spectacle that is the great man: Trimalchio, the *paterfamilias*, dressed in red, still in his house shoes, playing with a green ball with a group of long-haired youths, who were remarked on by our heroes for their beauty. The wealthy man's two eunuchs were another novelty to be observed: one counted the balls dropped, while the other held a silver piss-pot into which Trimalchio publicly urinates and then dries his hands on the long hair of a slave. In the baths, Ascyltos and Encolpius work up a sweat in a hot room and plunge into the cold water pool, and are far from finished the bathing process, when they realize that Trimalchio has rushed his bathing ritual and is perfumed and being rubbed down after a full bath and massage. Trimalchio hurries and measures the time taken over every pursuit – he is seen as the antithesis of the heroes, a rich freedman with no taste. In contrast, Ascyltos and Encolpius have little sense of time, stroll in the *palaestra* watching others, take their time to raise a sweat in the baths, and enjoy their bath as a sensory pleasure slowly, while observing those around them.

The encounter with Trimalchio in the baths shows us several important points about Roman bathing: there was an awareness of what others were doing; there was a self-consciousness of one's own bathing regimen with respect to the actions of others; and young males were admired for their bodies in the bathhouse. The last were objects to be observed and eroticized. These young men were quite different from children: they were seen medically to be soft and in need of hardening, not with warm or hot baths, but immersion into cold water following exercise.[22] The body of a young man was perceived in antiquity to suffer from an internal heat and if it was heated further in a hot room, this would damage the person or even cause the young man to become effeminate. Significantly, these young men did not bathe with their fathers, partly since at the baths it could be that young men might have an erection – something that their father was not meant to see.[23] Perhaps, fathers did not bathe with their sons once they were over the age of 14 for this reason.[24] The free youths or the beautiful young slaves of others were objectified, and assessed by a male gaze, from which the ancients drew pleasure.[25] The Roman law *Lex Scantinia* would have protected these young objects of desire from the actuality of sexual assault or seduction by older males.[26] However, as many observers in the United States have pointed out: numerous sexual practices have been illegal in some states, but that does not mean that such laws were heeded in private. Like most legislation on sexuality, the *Lex Scantinia* was difficult to enforce, and when it was, the issue was not so much the sexual act that took place, but the context of other legal and moral crises, for example under the emperor Domitian at the end of the first century CE.[27]

Petronius provides a guide to how Roman adults may have viewed the bodies of these young men – a younger sexual partner was seen to enjoy being penetrated and at an age when they were sexually insatiable.[28] Indeed, throughout Latin literature there is a view of the bathhouse populated by men, looking at other men and regarding those they wish to penetrate as insatiable. The pleasure of bathing was enhanced by the pleasure of looking at others and also by the feel-good factor that some people were having a lot of sex.[29] There was a system of body language used to avoid encounters of the wrong kind.

BODY LANGUAGE IN THE BATHS

The ancients were very concerned with the discernment of the character of their fellow man. For example, Tacitus in *The Annals of Imperial Rome* observes how the emperor Tiberius' character was gradually revealed as his reign progressed – finally ending in a period of total terror. To begin with, Tiberius was deceptive and people were unable to read either his words or his body language, but by the end of his reign his despicable character was revealed. The problem for contemporaries was to find a means of determining the nature of the character of their fellow man. One aid to this process was the ancient science of physiognomy, based on an ideal that all men contained a male side equivalent to the deportment of the lion and a female side that was represented by the movement of a panther.[30] The greatest ancient physiognomist was Polemo, whose determination of character was seen as an event. He could read complicated patterns in the movement of the eyes, skin colour, hair on the head and body, as well as the signs of deception found in gestures and in deportment. For example, Polemo could examine any part of a person to discern their character: of a man from Cyrene (a town in modern Libya) whose eyes were flecked around the pupil with dots, similar to millet seeds, some red and some black, that flashed he wrote: he was a 'master of evil-doing', his character was diagnosed as unrestrained in his greed, sexual desires, dissolute habits and brazen desires – 'an amalgamation of every vice'.[31] Not all Romans were as skilled as Polemo, but most were amateur physiognomists, attempting to read the signs in the body of a man's character, prior to deciding if that person would be a good son-in-law, business partner, travelling companion, etc.[32] The best place to observe the bodies of others was in the bathhouse – here, all bathers knew that they might be under observation of their fellow man and even an expert physiognomist such as Polemo.

The physiognomistic observations of the body shaped the way people presented themselves to others at the baths. The real man is seen to lack any signs of effeminacy in his posture or movements; he should walk like a lion with calm shoulders and a carefully controlled neck.[33] Many male children received not just instruction on body language to make them appear more male, but also had their body shaped from birth by swaddling, their noses and penises stretched, and their buttocks moulded.[34] The opposite to the masculine male was the man making jumping steps, with lolling head, furrowed brow, knocking knees, a shifting gaze and a high voice.[35] These were the aspects of gait that Roman children were taught to avoid.[36] This was the body language of an *androgynos:* a person between a man and a woman – what we might call today a metrosexual. It was a short step from this type of man to the *cinaedus* – a man who sought to provide sexual pleasure: either to men by being penetrated and/or to women with *cunnilingus*. The *cinaedus* was given away by his body language: he clasped the hands of others, his arms are turned outward, he admires his own body, his eyes are shifting, and he touches his nose.[37]

These are all attributes that could be controlled and were part of an attempt to mould a body to the ideal.[38] But other characteristics not based on behaviour were seen to be equally telling. Hair on a man's body was a sign of masculinity – generated according to the ancients by a man's inner heat that also produced semen.[39] Depilation, a common feature of bathing, was seen by some as necessary and by others as the ultimate sign of a female man who chose to become less male.[40] However, we need to be clear that there was a middle ground. There are examples of smooth men, such as Cicero's oratorical rival Hortensius, who regarded the shaggy male as the equivalent of the barbarian lacking civilization and culture.[41] Plus, not all *cinaedi* were depilated, we can find hairy males only revealed as *cinaedi* by a sneeze.[42] The debate over depilation continued into the empire. Persius (34–62 CE) pictures himself attracting an outraged moralist while sunbathing nude and displaying his depilated buttocks and groin to all.[43] A suntan seems to have been a feature that males desired and sunbathing was a popular pastime.[44] Males in figurative wall paintings appear consistently bronzed, in contrast to females who appear pasty white.

Generally, though, what a man faced in the bathhouse was a minefield of behavioural norms: should he have his armpits plucked but not his legs or vice versa? Should his massage be gentle or brisk, with or without oil, with cloth or hand, before or after the bath? indoors or outdoors? In a breeze or in still air?[45] To a certain extent, under the scrutiny of a physiognomist this was a no win situation; but others would look for refinement as well as conformity. Perhaps the sense of harmony between the physiognomic moral ideal and the enjoyment of the clean and beautiful body can be best judged today in the nude statues that survive from the Roman world.[46]

THE BODIES OF OTHERS

The Roman view of the body of the eunuch allows us to see the signs of male feminity and their association with what might be described as 'forbidden' pleasures. There is a long tradition in antiquity of castrating slaves.[47] The reasons for this are difficult to judge, but it is clear that the price of eunuchs in the market was higher and hence we might conclude that the castrated slave was a more desirable commodity. It was a practice that was outlawed by the emperor Domitian towards the very end of the first century CE – interestingly it is after the passing of this law that eunuchs become more rather than less prominent at Rome.[48] Perhaps it was their lack of masculinity that created a reputation for loyalty and obedience – qualities that may have also been found in castrated animals.[49] But it is also clear in Latin literature that the eunuchs were regarded as sexually insatiable. For example, in Apuleius' novel *The Golden Ass*, a set of eunuch priests travelled the countryside kidnapping people and forcing them to perform unspeakable sexual acts.[50]

Eunuchs were both female in terms of them being not men and also female in the sense that they were *cinaedi*. They had been changed and had taken on a female form. Perhaps the most famous eunuchs of the ancient world were the priests of Cybele, who followed their goddess's lover Attis in his act of self-castration. The loss of masculinity is presented to us by Catullus (poem 63) as a total abdication of all male responsibility as well as male sexuality, in which the body becomes the repository of a set of values.[51] The eunuch priests would serve not a male but a female master – great Cybele, creating a further gender inversion in addition to that caused by the removal of testicles. The motivation for self-castration is suggested to have been not dissimilar to the modern justifications for sex-change surgery.[52] This articulates a desire within some young males to become female, in not only the sense of the *cinaedus* giving pleasure to active males, but in the transformation of their body into a different form. That form was visualized in art, and the value of one piece by the painter Parrhasius was said to have been 6 million *sesterces* – an indication of the painting's popularity (the emperor Tiberius kept it in his bedroom for his own personal enjoyment). This would suggest eunuchs were an object of beauty. The fact they also caused disquiet might be because they created a different ideal of the form of the 'male' body. In any case, the eunuchs were required to bathe at a different time to others at the bathhouses. Even so, we can assume that eunuch slaves attending their masters were present at the baths – even if they were something of a rarity.[53] Certainly, Statius could envisage the scarring resulting from castration being seen – and only in rare cases going unnoticed.[54] Like others at the baths, the eunuch was subject to the gaze of others and scrutinized with the same care as the bodies of other bathers

THE NEW LUXURIES OF THE IMPERIAL *THERMAE*

Martial, writing towards the end of the first century CE, frequently places the setting of his numerous witty epigrams in the context of the baths.[55] The *Thermae* of Agrippa, Nero and Titus all make their appearance, along with other marble clad baths often built of brick, hard stone and concrete in the manner of the Central Baths in Pompeii. These buildings were defined by their natural light and good quality water.[56] These contrast with dark and draught-ridden older baths in Rome.[57] The best baths were the newest: the *Thermae* of Titus were preferable to the *Thermae* of Agrippa built a century earlier. Interestingly, the most sophisticated bathhouse in Rome was not a vast structure, but the small yet well lit and luxurious bathhouse owned by Claudius Etruscus – the ultimate bathing experience in light, well decorated and with excellent water quality that rivalled even that of Baiae.[58]

What Martial himself prefers is not just luxury, but well-lit spaces – where he could see the decor of the building and the clearness of the water in which he was bathing. It is only in such well-lit bathhouses that his comments on the bathing habits of others could work. The naked body was there to be seen and commented upon.[59] Scrutiny of male genitalia was included, with the size of Maro's penis commented upon and circumcised Jews duly identified by the crowds of bathers.[60] At first sight, it seems to be a very male space, in which male conviviality was expressed over the size or shape of a penis and also male sexual encounters. However, it is clear that in the first century CE men and women bathed naked together and edicts were only issued to prevent the practice in the second century CE.[61] Martial's comments on women bathing naked with him are instructive: he regards mixed bathing as normative and for a woman to refuse to bathe with him as a sign that she was embarrassed by the shape or smell of her body.[62] But as with all matters of Roman bathing, there were choices to be made – and a woman could opt for a single sex space.[63] And as we have seen, the new well-lit imperial baths in Rome existed alongside the darker and smaller intimate spaces – these, like other small and dark bathhouses, might be described as those of a *cinaedus*.[64] And even the light and airy baths had their darker nooks and corners. What we find in the well-lit baths is an eroticization of the body rather than sex actually taking place – it is a meeting place of lovers rather than the location of sex.[65] Only when we move from the well-lit spaces into the darker recesses of the baths do we even find declarations of love and propositions of sex.[66]

INTO THE PLEASURE DOME

Nowhere could the Roman world of pleasure come more alive than in Baiae on the Bay of Naples. It was a coastal retreat whose baths were key to its popularity, as they were fed from natural springs of hot sulphurous water. It was a place for the sick to recover and for the healthy to immerse themselves in pleasure.[67] This was not a town but a collection of villas and bath buildings that were constructed not so much along the coast but out into the sea – a subject condemned by the moralists, but a practice that continued well beyond the first century CE.[68] So hedonistic was Baiae's reputation that the very mention of a visit to the retreat in a speech could condemn the character under discussion. Cicero did much more in his assassination of the actions of Clodia, a widow in her 30s:

> The accusers are dinning into our ears the words debauchery, amours, misconduct, trips to Baiae, beach-parties, feasts, revels, concerts, musical parties, pleasure boats. (*Defence of Caelius Rufus*: 35)

The great orator then turned the tables on such accusations by suggesting Clodia had done all of these things in Baiae herself, before suggesting that the woman had seduced a young man who was her neighbour in Rome:

> Does not then that notorious neighbourhood put us on the scent? Does public rumour, does Baiae say nothing? Yes, Baiae does not merely talk but even cries out that there is one woman whose amorous passions are so degraded that, far from seeking the privacy and darkness and the usual screens of vice, she revels in her degraded lusts amid the most open publicity and even in the broadest daylight. (*Defence of Caelius Rufus*: 47)

Despite its reputation, or perhaps because of it, from the middle of the first century BCE the aristocracy in Rome migrated *en masse* to Baiae in April, and remained for several weeks at a time. It was a place thronged with the wealthy and famous.[69] Baiae had gathered to it new forms of entertainment and new forms of pleasure, all referred to by Cicero. But ultimately all was built on the pleasant warm water of the thermal springs. Later, Baiae would be the location for Augustus' criticism of a young man visiting his daughter Julia – she, like Clodia, was another of Rome's famous thirty-something adulteresses.[70] At the very end of the first century CE, Baiae became synonymous with the emperor Domitian, an idle man compared with his industrious and living successor, Trajan.[71] It was a place to which men came and left broken-hearted or women came chaste and left as adulterers.[72] The landscape of pleasure was populated by drunks on the beach, riotous sailing parties, and lakes resounding to choral songs – scenes familiar throughout the Mediterranean in the twenty-first century.[73] The popularity of Baiae as a pleasure magnet can be seen from the geographer Strabo's comment that the villas and baths created an area the size of the large city of Puteoli.[74] More importantly, the measurement of the merits of a villa was set with reference to those of Baiae and the beauty of the shoreline.[75]

What is so objectionable about Baiae to many ancients, is that pleasure could be seen in all its forms – Seneca could list a catalogue of vices after only an overnight stop. Rather than lurking in the darkness of the baths, at Baiae pleasure openly announced itself; just as Clodia openly took her pleasures in Baiae in daylight under the gaze of others, rather than in the darkened privacy of her bedroom.[76] It is perhaps the natural and open luxuries of Baiae that inspired the fundamental changes in the bathhouses that were being built in the cities at the end of the first century CE – they became light places in which the bodies of men and women were seen and their actions were watched.[77] For Romans, pleasure was no longer lurking in the dark, but in full view, moving its limbs, seen in mirrors and reflected in clear pools of water.

6

Roman Erotics

Hic ego cum veni futui, deinde redei domi. [*I came here, fucked and then went home.*]

Corpus Inscriptionum Latinarum: 4.2246

Driver, if you could only feel the fires of love, you would hurry more to enjoy the pleasures of Venus. I love the youth Venustus; please, spur on the mules, let's get on. You've had your drink, let's go, take the reins and crack the whip . . . take me to Pompeii, where my sweet love lives.

Graffito Pompeii, Corpus Inscriptionum Latinarum: 4. 5092

Secundus has buggered boys who wailed.

Graffito Pompeii, Corpus Inscriptionum Latinarum, 4. 2048

If a boy has the fortune to be born beautiful, but does not offer his arse for the enjoyment of others, may he fall in love with a beautiful girl and never manage to bed her.

Graffito Stabiae, AE 1996: 400)

Your penis commands, make love.

Graffito Pompeii, Corpus Inscriptionum Latinarum: 4.1938

The discovery of Herculaneum and Pompeii reshaped the eighteenth century's view of Roman society. Those who had read their Cicero and even dabbled in Martial and Juvenal were not prepared for what they were to see in the eighteenth-century king of Naples' museum – a secret room full of sexually explicit wall paintings and depictions of male genitalia (now in the twenty-first century open to the general public). For much of the twentieth century, the images in the brothels of Pompeii were considered so scandalous that they were off-limits to female tourists and those who were reading an English translation of Martial's *Epigrams* would have found sexually explicit Latin translated not into English but Italian. Books on Roman sexual life were published, but it was not until the 1980s that the subject was subjected to a rigorous investigation.

Today, the sex lives of the Romans remains an area of some debate. Michel Foucault, an intellectual giant, weighed in with his *History of Sexuality*, which constructed Roman pleasure in ways quite different from those found today. His critics include Amy Richelin, whose book *The Garden of Priapus* analysed sex in Latin literature within a feminist framework.[1] The publication of the sexually explicit scenes of group sex discovered in the Suburban Baths in Pompeii added a further stimulus to the study of sex in the first century CE. John Clarke set these paintings in the context of other explicit imagery and related his findings to those discovered in Latin literature.[2]

But perhaps the most accurate way to gauge how the Romans found pleasure through sex is to look at the archaeological evidence from the city of Pompeii, particularly the graffiti – basic statements whose truth is unverifiable: Iucundus is the greatest *fellator* or Secundus is a really good shag.[3] This of course doesn't reveal so much about the practice of sex itself, but it does say a lot about the discourse of sex in graffiti that took place on the walls of the city: claims and counterclaims of prowess and passivity. It is inevitably male in focus and origin, for the most part, but was seen by men, women and children. The extent of patriarchy in Rome is revealed in the Augustan laws with regard to adultery. A wife sleeping with another man had committed a crime under this law, whereas a husband had only committed adultery if he had sex with another man's wife: hence a married man might have sex with his slaves, prostitutes and other unmarried persons with impunity. Perhaps we need to move away from these laws that were formulated for an elite, and concentrate instead on the discourse on sex found in Pompeii that is a step away from the sexuality found in high literature, law and philosophy.[4]

VISUALIZING SEX

The images from the Suburban Baths in Pompeii are framed so that the bodies of those taking part are on show, erect penises are present, and/or the act of penetration of males and females is highlighted. These images are carefully placed above a series of numbered 'lockers' from I through to VIII, each luridly depicting a variety of sexual positions and pleasures: in I a woman straddles a man's erect penis; II a woman is penetrated from behind; III a woman sucks a man's penis; IV a dressed man performs *cunnilingus* on a naked woman; V two women have sex; VI a man penetrates a woman from behind and is in turn penetrated by a man; VII a man penetrates another man from behind, whose penis is sucked by a woman, who in turn is receiving *cunnilingus* from another woman; VIII a poet with grotesquely enlarged testicles reads from a manual on his own.[5] What is more difficult to read from these scenes is their meaning: is this fantasy or reality; is it serious or humorous; did such things happen in practice or only in theory; what are the statuses of the participants: are they slaves, are they prostitutes? All are questions that are almost impossible to answer. What is clear is that the scenes were to be looked at and pleasure was to be gained – whether from laughter or from fascination.[6] Interestingly, the changing room was painted over with a thin coat of paint and scenes I to VIII were obliterated prior to the destruction of Pompeii in 79 CE, perhaps reflecting the short-lived acceptance of these images as suitable decor for the changing room.

There is something very different about the display of sexual pleasure in the Roman world of the first century CE. It can occur where we expect it, as in the famous brothel at Pompeii, but it also appears where we do not expect it. What did the guest think when drinking from a cup that shows in elaborate detail two men copulating? The beautiful silver drinking vessel known as the Warren Cup, now owned by the British Museum (purchased in 1999 for £1.8 million), shows two scenes of adult males penetrating younger males, while another male watches through a half-closed door.[7] The drinking vessel has been dated to the first century CE and placed in the province of Judaea, but similar silver vessels have been found elsewhere, including in Pompeii: a vessel from the House of the Menander silver hoard showed an adult male with a female partner. The guest invited into a house would have seen scenes of sex painted in detail on the walls of the house. In the House of Caecilius Iucundus (a banker today made famous by the Cambridge Latin Course), we find a scene of a couple in bed. That was not located in a bedroom but in the peristyle or garden space of this famous house – the detail is elaborate and includes the reflection of the woman's face off the rear wall. Does this mean that the Romans were less hung up about sex, or blurred the boundaries between what we today call homosexuality and heterosexuality? This type of evidence might fuel ideas that the Romans had sex with anything that moved: male or female. However, what is perhaps significant is that scenes of sexual penetration on the walls of houses feature almost entirely a single male and a single female partner – either with the female straddling the male partner, the male penetrating the female partner from behind or the female partner reclining with a leg raised and the male kneeling to penetrate her.[8] We do not find images in the houses of Pompeii of males penetrating males; to locate these we need to look on silver and pottery vessels or in the changing room of the Suburban Baths. Similarly, to locate images of *fellatio,* it is to lamps and pottery vessels that we need to go to, rather than in the brothel and the houses of Pompeii – the exception to this is of course the changing room in the Suburban Baths. Images of *cunnilingus* are extremely rare, appearing on lamps in the context of a '69', or mutual oral stimulation, on the part of a male and a female participant – the scene of *cunnilingus* in the Suburban Baths is again unique.[9] This survey suggests that there is a texture to the representation of sexual pleasure in antiquity: males penetrating females was the most common form of representation, females performing oral sex on males was not unknown, the '69' position can be found, males penetrating males is less common, *cunnilingus* performed by a man is very rare (by a woman unknown). Over this texture is another: the ability to reveal the naked human figure or body or object of desire in the scene – a view of the (female for the most part) body that is penetrated.[10] It's a feature that concurs with Ovid's instructions to women to choose a sexual position that makes the most of their physical features: face, back, bottom, legs, height, thighs, breasts and hairy genitalia.[11]

WRITING SEX

The Roman view of sex was not the same as our division between heterosexual and homosexual. Instead, the Romans placed an emphasis on the active penetration of others and developed a vocabulary to describe the penetration of human orifices.[12] It is worth dwelling on the verbal description of sex and to assess the general pattern of language that we find in the graffiti of Pompeii.[13] The verb *futuere* described the penetration of a vagina: 'Here I screwed many girls'; the verb *pedicare* described the penetration of an anus: see the chapter epigraphs; and *irrumare* was used to describe the penetration of a mouth: 'L. Habonius mutilates Caesonius Felix and makes him suck it.'[14] A man who penetrated the orifices of others might be described as a *fututor*, a *pedicator* or a *irrumator*. These were all positive characteristics of a man. In contrast, the man who was penetrated was the object of derision, and the Romans developed a language for such persons. They were described as *cinaedus* or *pathicus* – a man who gave pleasure by being buggered: 'Vesbinus you *cinaedus*, Vitalio has buggered you'; *fellator* – a man who gave pleasure by sucking cock: 'Secundus is a cocksucker of rare talent'; or at the most extreme *cunnilinctor* – a man whose mouth was for the Romans in effect penetrated by the woman: 'Iucundus licks the cunt of Rustica.'[15] The medical writer Galen makes it clear that the *cunnilinctor* was seen as a person even more revolting than the *fellator* and *cunnilingus* is associated with old men, the impotent and the castrated eunuch.[16] These terms mostly applied to men, but did have their female equivalents and we find women described as *fututrix* and *fellatrix*.[17]

This language used to describe sex and sexual preferences can be mapped through the graffiti from Pompeii to reconstruct the preferences of society in the first century CE.[18] Of the sexualized verb forms found written across Pompeii *futuere* is by far the most frequent, representing 78 per cent of the total; *pedicare* is less frequent at just 20 per cent of the total; and *irrumare* is a rarity at just two per cent. The graffiti from Pompeii also deploy the words *cinaedus*, *fellator* and *cunnilinctor* as insults to others. *Cinaedus* is the most common insult used (54%), followed by *fellator* (39%) with *cunnilinctor* appearing rarely (1%). However, with regard to *cunnilinctor*, we need to recognize that the descriptor tends to be the verb form *lingere* with the noun *cunnus* – taking this into account the number of *cunnilinctores* increases to equal the number of *fellatores*. Hence the overall pattern points to the penetration of mouths (by men and women) and the penetration of anuses being used as a means of insulting other men in equal proportions. The pattern of verb forms might be more significant than the use of words as insults, and indeed, the penetration of the vagina was the orifice that was most written about at Pompeii. This coincides with the form of sex most frequently seen in wall decoration, not just in the brothel, but also in the exquisitely decorated houses of the city. Thus it can be concluded that for the Romans, vaginal penetration was the most common form of sex represented.

PEDERASTY

The second scene on the Warren Cup shows a man having sex with a boy. The age of the latter is defined by his lack of muscle in contrast to the man – it is thought this boy is not fully grown. He is defined as a youth, rather than as an adult. This takes us into an area of pleasure that today we find distinctly disturbing. There is evidence in literature for adult males in the Roman world having sex with male and female children.[19] The opening quotation from a poem written in a peristyle of a house in Pompeii features the crossing out of the word boy (*puer*) and its replacement with the word youth (*iuvenis*). This was to replace the idea of love of a pre-pubescent boy with the longing for a youth – the name Venustus is a fictional name commonly found in Roman love poetry as an object of desire.[20] The distinction between innocent boys and knowing youths is made by Martial, when he equates the boys with virgins and youths with easy girls.[21] Another of the opening passages stating that Secundus buggered underage boys is made clear by their association with wailing – these may equate with Martial's first category or might refer to very young slaves. There is no getting away from it, Roman men were attracted to young boys up to a certain age – that age may be defined as the point after puberty that the body developed hair on the buttocks and on the face. As Niall McKeown has pointed out, there was no lower age limit. What this perhaps points up is that Roman society was based on slavery with a very large percentage of all slaves produced within the empire.[22] The slave was, in effect, an item of property with which its owner (male or female) could do pretty much whatever he wished. Martial conjures up some of the most vivid imagery: a wife finding a husband penetrating a boy is repeated and can be found in other authors too.[23] So it is clear is that the body of the slave was objectified and eroticized from an early age, in ways that today we would find unacceptable, disturbing and intolerable. Sex was also part of a systematized form of violence that permeated the slave's existence within the Roman household. However, there is also a place for mutual pleasure within sexual relations that cross the free–slave boundary, seen clearly in Petronius' *Satyrica*, in which beautiful favourites are exploited and exploit their position and role as objects of sexualized beauty.

UNDERSTANDING ROMAN PROSTITUTION

Today, the brothel in Pompeii must be the most visited place of the city, a highlight of nearly every tour group snaking its way round the site. Those who enter the dark and narrow confines will find a small hallway with five rooms leading from it (a structure mirrored on the upper floor). Above the lintel of each doorway is a single scene of a man and a woman having sex.[24] The furnishings of the paintings are those of the lavish household, a marked contrast to the stone bed and pillow found inside the rooms of the brothel. What is made clear by the graffiti that advertised the services of prostitutes in Pompeii was that they were cheap: Felix would give a blow-job for the price of a cup of wine – 2 *asses*, whereas Epulia charged more – 5 *asses*; Glyco charged 2 *asses* for *cunnilingus*, but Maritimus charged more, 4 *asses*, and accepted virgins.[25] Attica's services were advertised: vaginal sex outside the Suburban Baths for 16 *asses*.[26] Two men, Felix and Florus, charged respectively 4 and 10 *asses*.[27] Mostly, there are names of the prostitutes and one advert implores the visitor to neighbouring Nuceria to ask for Novellia Primigenia in the street of Venus.[28] Three men took the prostitute Tyche to the corridor leading from the street to the theatre on 21 November 2 BCE and paid her 5 *asses* each; not only did they do this but also precisely recorded the event with full and accurate accounting of the total paid – 15 *asses*.[29] There are about 150 graffiti that refer to individual prostitutes in Pompeii, many with prices and offers of *fellatio* and *cunnilingus* being specified – the very acts that were regarded in Latin literature as resulting in the defilement of the body.[30] Hence, at one level, the purpose of prostitution might be seen as the provision of services that husbands and wives would rather not do themselves.[31] Yet, at another level, we may be seeing in the classification of a woman by name as a cheap prostitute specializing in *fellatio* a denigration of her character. Whichever way we choose to look at the problem, commercial sex was cheap and available. There were a number of brothels in Pompeii, and it seems that prostitution was a characteristic of the Roman city, and that sex with a prostitute was an expectation of visitors.[32] Interestingly there were both male and female prostitutes in Pompeii, with the males servicing male and female clients.[33] Debates have raged over who the customers were in the brothel, and perhaps John Clarke is correct to assume it was the slaves.[34] Thus prostitution was a

The largest brothel in Pompeii was cramped and today is difficult for tour groups to visit.

service industry to ensure that the slaves of the city had a relatively simple and cheap way of having sex. The presence of prostitution removed sex and slaves from the household, and perhaps it also ensured that these slaves did not have sex with freeborn members of the family – a scenario imagined by Martial.[35] On a less pleasurable note, prostitution would have consumed any savings that slaves had made with a view to buying their freedom.

THE ROMAN ORGASM

The need for low-cost prostitution to fulfil the slave's human need for sex can only be understood with reference to how the Romans viewed the orgasm. The orgasm is a facet of the human body that has been found to be particularly difficult to describe or represent.[36] Perhaps this is the reason why modern historians of Roman sex have very little to say on the matter.[37] This is something of a surprise since it is the Romans who were the first people known to conceive of sex between a man and a woman as resulting in a mutual orgasm.[38] Women, as well as men, were defined as achieving pleasure through sex, or as one male writer observed 'no other moans were heard than those of pleasure and gratitude'.[39] What seems important to the male writers is that their actions induced the pleasure of their female partner and these heightened their own sense of joy.[40] Ovid identifies women over the age of 30 as the ones who take most pleasure from sex – significantly, it is women of this age group who are portrayed as the famous adulterers of the Roman world. Sex is seen as a sensation to be learned by younger girls, and what we find in Ovid's instructions to young females is a playful parody of the sex manuals 'written' by women (but perhaps read by men as well as women) in antiquity, but like many things from two millennia ago the actual details elude us.[41] Unfortunately, we know little about women's pleasure from sex, because we lack a female voice in the surviving literature from antiquity. But, perhaps it is worth recalling the witty saying of Augustus' daughter Julia when he contrasted her skimpy dress with the one she had worn on the previous day: 'Today I am dressed for my husband, whereas yesterday I dressed to see my father.' All knew, apart from her esteemed father, that she was a notorious adulteress.

For Ovid, men did not require instruction, but needed only to hold back their orgasm to ensure their woman's pleasure. Men sought the recognition of their ability to give pleasure to women, an accolade found in Pompeii: 'Fortunatus, you sweet soul, you mega-fucker. Written by one who knows', or we find in the brothel that 'Phoebus fucks well' illustrated by a face and a penis.[42] The veracity and authorship of such statements may be in question, but the ideal of bringing pleasure through sex is there.

Sex and orgasm were seen by ancient medical writers as essential for most men and women to maintain them in good health.[43] Female puberty was a medical condition, which was only cured by sex.[44] It was thought that the body became over-full with fluid that needed to be released – visualized by Horace as the presence of an erect penis and a choice of either literally feeling as though his body was bursting or fucking a passing slave boy or slave girl.[45] A point reinforced in a graffito from Pompeii: 'When my worries oppress my body, I use my left hand to release my pent-up fluids', and may have led one slave owner to remark, 'Take advantage of the cook, whenever you like'.[46] A bar in region VI of Pompeii (6.16.33) is decorated with dressed masturbating male figures and a large ejaculating phallus. This, to us, seems a bizarre set of imagery – but perhaps we should view the water flowing from the penises of statues in the house of the Vettii as similar: a continuous ejaculation.[47] There are also numerous images of Ethiopians with over-large penises ejaculating.[48] What is clear is that all human beings, both free and slave, needed to have sex and were expected to have sex, or to become sick.

ROMAN HOMOSEXUALITY?

The Romans' sexual practices are difficult to categorize. We can identify males penetrating orifices of males and females without the category of bisexuality arising – the important fact is that they are active in this sexual equation, and the penetrated is passive: a woman, a slave or a younger male. The male in contrast who was penetrated was regarded as a *cinaedus* – something akin to a dancing boy. The *cinaedus* was a polluted category – a person who had given pleasure passively.[49] Latin literature and graffiti are full of criticisms and derision of the *cinaedi*, in a way not dissimilar to how we would today describe as homophobia.

In their teenage years, some of the most famous Romans were penetrated by older men (for example Julius Caesar), yet this did not seem to make them a *cinaedus* as such. Perhaps, what we see is a gradual sexual maturation in young men that transforms them from being penetrated by other men, to penetrating beautiful long-haired slave boys and finally turns them into heterosexual married men, with the long hair of their slaves cut and the slaves dispatched to love slave girls instead of their young masters.[50] The ambiguity of this sexual rite of passage is made clear with examples of married men having sex with slave boys, and there are many examples of the penetrated youths of literature being active sexual partners.[51] But what is equally clear is a strong condemnation of adult Romans who were penetrated and gave pleasure to others by being passive. The force of the rhetoric of shame directed against the *cinaedi* creates the category of difference and also gives a vivid picture of the nature of 'normal' adult sexuality, via a rather distasteful form of homophobia. What is more difficult to prove is that underlying the prejudice is a culture that we would call homosexual. The signifiers of the *cinaedus*, as we have seen in the previous chapter, were closely aligned to those of the castrated male, and were most easily seen in cross-dressing or in long-haired slaves.[52]

The difficulty of the *cinaedus* lies in the Roman idea that this was a feminine man, whose purpose was to provide pleasure – an inversion of an ideal of a man who took his pleasure by penetrating the orifices of others male and/or female. There is something different about deriving pleasure from being penetrated. It points to a limitation to the Roman norms of desire. Nero as a famous deviant both penetrates males and enjoys being penetrated.[53] Such persons might be understood as experts on pleasure and hence had in Roman terms embraced vice, or permitted vice to cross the age boundary that existed between the youth enjoying himself, moving into the age at which a Roman was expected to have been married. The *cinaedus* effectively had not grown up and continued to embrace all forms of sexual pleasure. This was the view of the dominant culture that sought to repress, ridicule and make them invisible.[54] The main element in the repression of the *cinaedi* was the notion that they did not penetrate their sexual partners as well as being penetrated themselves – a concept that modern commentators have accepted as fact.[55] However, there would appear to have been a group of men whose sexual preference for penetrating men and being penetrated by men created what we today might call a homosexual culture, whose members were subjected to the ridicule of the dominant culture of masculinity.[56] The *cinaedus* could be characterized as a transvestite, who was buggered by sailors prior to returning to his wife – where lacking an erection, he brings pleasure to his wife through *cunnilingus*.[57] It is a short step from these actions of the *cinaedus* to those of the self-castrated priests of Cybele discussed in the previous chapter. It is difficult to read these and similar passages – either we have a continuum of stereotypes running from hidden *cinaedus* to transvestite *cinaedus* onto self-castrated eunuch – or we might be seeing a variety of homosexual practices within a subculture/s.[58] Perhaps these two readings are not mutually incompatible: a dominant culture of repression can only thrive if a transgressive subculture is seen as a threat. The symbols of the subculture resided in the use of makeup, depilation, perfume, hairstyle and brightly coloured clothing. Moralists raged against the *pathici* who displayed these symbols prominently. Policing by moral repression might be particularly effective in cities with smaller populations – as is witnessed in the numerous graffiti from Pompeii that accused others of deviant sexual practices (discussed earlier). However, in Rome, a metropolis of more than one million people in the first century CE, the effectiveness of such policing ceased to work and we can locate a subculture of *cinaedi* similar to that found in the growing cities of early-modern Europe – for example London in the eighteenth century.[59] The evidence from Pompeii, in visual images and in graffiti, would suggest that the subculture was less visible outside of Rome in the less anonymous smaller cities. And what is true for homosexual men would have been true for women – there was less surveillance of the private lives of others in the metropolis, a factor that facilitated a greater range of erotic pleasures. At the end of this chapter, readers will have noticed there has been no mention of Roman orgies. Why? The answer to that question is simple: there is no real evidence for them. They are yet another case of the fevered imagination of the modern world, which attempts to sexualize all other cultures past and present.

7

Dining

Pleasure in eating is probably the hardest to combat. For other pleasures we encounter less often, and we can refrain from some of them for months and whole years, but of necessity we are tempted every day and usually twice a day, since it is not possible for man to live otherwise.

Musonius Rufus, 18a

I remember once hearing gossip about a notorious dish into which everything over which foodies love to dally had been heaped together by a popina (bar) that was rushing into insolvency; there were two kinds of mussels, and oysters trimmed, set off at intervals by sea-urchins; the dish was flanked by mullets cut up and served without bones.

Seneca, Letters: 95

Remembering past delights in food and drink is an ignoble kind of pleasure and one that is, besides, as unsubstantial as yesterday's perfume or the lingering smell of cooking.

Plutarch, Moralia: 686C

Eating was an activity practised by the vast majority in antiquity simply to gain the calorific intake to survive.[1] But there were others, mainly the rich, who sought to create new tastes and new refinements to experience new sensations provided by the vast range of produce available, thanks to the expanding Roman empire.[2] Humans often detach the act of dining from the nutritional value that leads to their biological survival, and the Romans were no exception. At the heart of their dining experience lay the social institution of patronage, by which the less rich were invited to dine with their much more wealthy benefactors; yet at the same time the wealthy Roman traveller expected dinner invitations on his arrival at his destination.[3] Underpinning the dinner party was a fiction that all the guests were convivial and equal.[4] The reality was rather different: the Roman dinner as a social institution cannot be underestimated, both for its provision of pleasure and its role in reinforcing hierarchies that existed beyond the dining room. It was a format that was not restricted to the houses of the elite, but was replicated in inns, guild houses and in mass banquets thrown for the public.

According to Roman etiquette, the dinner party took place after bathing so guests were clean and perfumed. You traditionally reclined with eight other diners, arranged on three couches placed by the three sides of a table, with three people sharing a couch; you conversed, you drank, you ate. For the host, the wit in entertaining one's guests was as important as the clever culinary sophistication of the cook. A whole range of sensory pleasures were provided: smell, taste, sound and sight – all shared by the diners. In short, the Roman dinner party was key to what we might describe as *romanitas*, in the same way that we might suggest that bathing created a sense of Roman identity – these are characteristics that were attractive to recently conquered provincials and were to distinguish them from barbarians.[5]

But if the physical setting of nine persons reclining, eating and drinking alcohol might provide opportunities for conviviality between guests of a similar status – free citizens – the dining room was actually a venue in which the social distinctions were made clear, as can be seen in Juvenal's biting *Satires* or in Pliny's observation that different food was served to diners of different statuses.[6]

The distinctions started with age. Only adults reclined together, children sat separately or reclined in a separate *triclinium* (dining room).[7] Hence children were segregated from the intimate pleasures of the adult table, but were seen to have been in the act of learning the etiquette. Dining was an adult occasion in an adult space with adult conversation and adult pleasures to be indulged in. The presence of obscene songs and lovers in the dining room made Quintilian wary of letting children be present at a Roman dinner.[8]

Intriguingly, the dining room by the first century CE was a venue where women reclined with men and distinctions of gender that had previously caused men to recline and women to sit in chairs had been overturned.[9] What differentiates men from women in the dining room is dress, gesture and positioning of sexual partners together, with males reclining with their front facing the woman's back.[10] There were, of course, male-only and female-only dinners in antiquity and we should not suggest that all dinner parties had mixed-sex guests. But where dinners featured both men and women, there was an ideal that both sexes would enjoy the same food, the same conversation and, if husband and wife, later a bed.[11] What Matthew Roller sees in the portrayal of men and women reclining at dinner is the eroticization of the occasion that should lead onto sex – it is notable that the positioning of male behind female at dinner mirrors the most common sexual position found in wall painting at Pompeii.[12] However, there were sometimes disruptions: emperors could take other men's wives away for sex in a *cubiculum* before both parties returned to the dinner.[13] Adultery was linked to the dining room, and drunkenness was seen as the origin of these sexual encounters.[14] The sequence perhaps can be seen as instructive of a Roman view that at dinner, at least, women were not submissive, but were capable of taking action and at least within this space became equal to men – sharing the same pleasures. Naturally, the moralists saw such freedom and enjoyment as destroying the natural order of marriage and a man's control of his wife.

The dinner party was also the occasion at which conventions were flouted resulting in the destruction of reputations. What a man ate was a subject that could be related to his character and moral ambitions and how he behaved at the dinner table.[15] Clement of Alexandria instructed the young on what might be described as table manners – eat slowly, do not belch, do not be a messy eater, do not talk while eating, do not turn your head or roll your eyes while drinking, do not sneeze at the same time as drinking, etc.[16] The dining room, with all its temptations of pleasure that could lead to over-consumption of food or wine, was the *locus* where many a young man was seen to head for personal destruction and a life of vice rather than virtue.[17] A gluttony for food was often linked in damning public speeches with a gluttony for sex, and a man who seemed too fond of wine and food was in danger of being branded effeminate, or a *cinaedus*. It was not just the consumption of food and wine that offended. Nero constructed his new dining rooms within the Golden House to feature pipes to douse his guests with the petals of flowers and perfumes.[18] With the pleasures of dinner went the danger of public humiliation at a later date.

Outdoor dining room in a Pompeian garden.

PLACES TO DINE

The dining room or *triclinium* has been recovered in numerous houses in
Pompeii and Herculaneum. Three couches were arranged in a U shape around
a table. These could be temporary or permanent structures. The ones from
Pompeii are built from masonry and presumably covered with cushions and
woven fabrics. The diners reclined on their left arm and utilized their right
to drink or eat with. As a result, around the table, in close proximity, were
the diners' heads – enabling them to hear each other, look closely at their
reactions and even to study them from the point view of their physiognomy
(see Chapter 5). The diners were seated according to the status assigned to
them by the host: with the most important seat reserved for himself at the
centre of attention. He was deliberately placed here, in what was known as the
consul's place, so that he could preside over the dinner like a charioteer over
his horses. Next to him on one side was his wife or his child, while on his other
side reclined the guest of honour.[19] The seating marked the host out as the

most important person, a position reinforced by the visual association with his honoured guest next to him and with his wife to his connections through marriage. Yet, within the schema, the consul's seat was accessible to messengers and other servants – allowing the host to conduct business while dining.[20] The actual position of others was something of an experiment, within which social hierarchy needed to be balanced with the equality and conviviality of conversation at the dinner table.[21]

The dining couches in their masonry format can be found both within the house and in the garden, allowing a greater flexibility of movement and views. It would seem logical that the outdoor area was the more relaxed setting amid plants and foliage, with the formal dinners taken indoors, yet there's not much evidence for a such a view.[22] Instead, there was a long Roman tradition of eating indoors in winter and outdoors in summer.[23] The comfort of the diners was paramount – they should be warm but not oppressed by the heat. Indoor dining rooms were ideally designed to capture the afternoon sun, if used in winter, and to be shaded from the afternoon sun, if used in summer.[24] For those taking their dinner in the last hours of the day, the outdoor dining room provided a cool contrast to the act of bathing that occurred an hour or two earlier. The frequent addition of water fountains cascading close to the diners provided an additional stimulus of the senses to create an almost bucolic ideal of a meal taken not so much in a garden, but in a landscape away from the bustle of the city that all had experienced in the first part of the day.[25] The garden aped the landscape of the pleasure villas of the rich, with their vistas over a rushing river or the sea. The removal of the dining room from the interior to the exterior of the house is similar to the relocation of a person from the city with its *negotium* (business) to a villa landscape associated with *otium* (free time). Eating outdoors is a different experience from indoors and the setting makes reference to other signifiers of what was pleasant – the sound of water, the link to nature and growing things, the movement of the air, and a coolness that could not have been achieved within the indoor dining room. Yet even the indoor dining rooms afforded a view of the landscape – for example that found in the House of the Labyrinth (Pompeii) gave the diners vistas across the peristyle garden.[26] These, of course, were nothing when compared to Pliny's carefully staged set of five dining rooms at his villa at Laurentum – each of which was constructed to provide views for his guests across the sea, the woods or the mountains.[27]

Sperlonga view from the dining room at dusk.

THE ROMAN DINNER PARTY

There are paintings of dinner parties in Pompeii, notably in the House of the Chaste Lovers. For one modern commentator these are 'implausible', due their sheer scale of luxury, and the lack of covering of the male body leads her to conclude that the scene is soon to 'degenerate into a bona fide orgy'.[28] But the connection between dining and sex made by this reviewer reflects more on how we in the twenty-first century view these images of Romans eating.[29] This view has been shaped by film and the representation of degenerate Romans stuffing their faces, being sick and then stripping off for an orgy. None of this was of course the case: the Roman orgy is a modern fixation and the Romans had sex in private. Yet, the paintings of dinner parties are important: they delineate a point at which conviviality had been achieved.[30] The diners have drunk, as can be seen from the scenes of participants being sick aided by slaves to do so (there was no such thing as a *vomitorium*). The diners, whether of the same sex or not, seem to lose their clothes. The setting can be indoors in some paintings, and outdoors in others under an awning close to the trees. In all cases, the focus is not so much on dining but on drinking. Even on the shrine to a household's gods, we can find a drinking scene: six men recline, while another raises two large vessels at the very centre of the scene.[31] A modern interpretation might see this as a drinking toast, but maybe it is a religious action that preceded a pouring of a libation? There is little food in sight, perhaps reflecting the practice of the first century CE of drinking without eating. Like scenes found in dining rooms across Pompeii, these images are eroticized in a manner that creates the dining room as a space associated with the senses – taste, intoxication and sexual arousal.[32] But like the dinner party, the senses are only temporarily aroused and pleasure is contained and controlled via social hierarchies and expectations of fellow diners.

For the Romans, the dinner party was a stage on which individuals played out roles. The emperors were the masters of the dining stage, and the ultimate examples of the powerful hosts: Augustus excluded freed slaves from his table; Caligula seduced wives of reclining husbands at his; Domitian invited masses of diners to his new palace, and at other times terrorized his guests in intimate surroundings that were a prelude to their deaths; Trajan let his diners converse.[33] All cases reinforced the individual emperor's status, with Trajan perhaps proving the most powerful because he could let his guests converse – perhaps knowing that none would step out of line.[34] But for lesser Romans, too, the host was still the powerful man in the dining equation, he was acknowledged and sometimes took centre stage. The dining room permitted the host to develop and project his own views and his character to his guests.

That's not to say that the host could not get it wrong, as proved by Petronius' satire on the actions and attributes of the fictional wealthy freedman Trimalchio.[35] The freed slave has become a citizen, and has learned the rules, but has failed to understand the subtleties of the conventions of dining in Roman culture. Here is a dinner that is enjoyable in terms of the food and drink, but lacks the sense of conviviality that was seen as desirable. It is an intriguing insight into what Roman guests may have looked for in a good dinner party.

When the guests at Trimalchio's dinner take their seats in the dining room, they have their hands washed in melted snow by singing Alexandrian slave boys – all the slaves sing when undertaking any task. The guests are served delicacies – olives from panniers of a bronze Corinthian donkey: green in one basket and black in the other; around the donkey were silver platters from which dormice and sausages were served. It is at this point their host enters and another dish arrives – pastries shaped like eggs that contain the delicacy of a tiny bird. Trimalchio discourses on the food, which is then whisked away by singing slaves to be replaced by ancient Falernian wine. The next dish is in the form of the 12 signs of the zodiac with each sign represented by an elaborate delicacy – Libra features a set of scales on which a cheese tart was balanced by a pancake with which bread was served. The next dish served by male dancers is made up of sows' udders, birds and a hare adorned with Pegasus' wings – four statues of satyrs at the corner of the dish pour sauce over the food.

Up to this point, the guests have eaten food to the accompaniment of Trimalchio's discourse on life and its brevity, but now, with hunger and thirst sated, the guests start their own conversations – only to be interrupted by their host's strange pronouncements on the nature of the universe.[36] A whole boar is brought into the dining room, that when cut open revealed quails – one for each guest. While the guests consume this delicacy, a slave boy dressed as the god Dionysus goes round serving grapes. Trimalchio leaves the room to visit the toilet and the guests take over ordering wine themselves and telling stories until their host returns to discuss the end of his bout of constipation. He proceeds to interrogate his guest Agamemnon and to denigrate his guest's discourse on rich and poor. A pig is brought in that appears uncooked, but from the cut-open stomach comes roasted sausages and giblets – yet another example of a dish appearing as one thing and then revealing itself as quite another. Trimalchio is now seen to be drunk and suggests his guests dance with his wife – an impulse that is interrupted by the reading of the accounts of his estate at Cumae, which is followed by the appearance of acrobats. There are also actors to perform for their host and then the guests are showered with perfume from the roof. There follow cakes and fruit, while Trimalchio recalls his life story from slavery to freedom and riches. There is a Greek dish to follow: a hen and goose eggs for each guest – that Petronius' hero finds revolting, but he is urged to eat it by his host.

The dinner is running its course and all are drunk. It is at this point that we are made aware of the conversation of the wives of some of the diners; they are drunk and conversing about their role as *materfamilias* (matriarch of the household) and their husbands' slave-boy lovers. Another dessert course is served, followed by thrushes stuffed with raisins, and quinces looking like sea urchins. There is a sense that at any moment, the wives will start to dance -- they are already clapping, but Trimalchio continues with a dirge-like discourse on life and death that features the provisions of his will and monumental tomb. The guests relocate to the private bath-suite in the house (converted from a bakery, a subject of another monologue by Trimalchio), and pass to another dining room as a rooster announces the start of a new day – the bird is inevitably dispatched, cooked and made into pastries. Trimalchio, now plastered, lies down and tells everyone to pretend he has died, at which point Petronius' heroes flee the house at top speed. The pleasure of the food and drink had been great, but their host's conversation and antics had made the occasion unbearable. For the Romans, it was a dinner party flawed by the presence of a freed slave as the host; the pleasures of food and drink were easily destroyed by poor conversation. Clearly, getting the dinner party right could turn freed slaves or barbarians into Romans – getting it wrong would merely reinforce the distinction between persons of quite different status.

EATING AND OVER-EATING

There is a sense of performance at Trimalchio's dinner found in the parade of food and the opening of wrapped dishes only to reveal that they are in reality different from their external appearance. Dishes process past diners and are then revealed.[37] For Macrobius, this feature eclipsed the value of food as a nutritional item.[38] Taste was just one sense stimulated in the dining room: perfumes enticed the sense of smell, the procession of items before a person that included beautiful slaves, furnishings, tableware, as well as the food were a feast for eyes; and singing, music and conversation engaged the aural senses.[39] Emily Gowers sets out the structure of an elaborate dinner in the following way: the *gustatio* – a tasting of roots, vegetables, fish and eggs; followed by the meat course of the *cena*, and ending with fruits and nuts – perhaps followed by a *secundae mensae* [second table] of luxurious pastries, particularly at the Saturnalia.[40] This could be elaborated with additional courses of meats or, in the interests of novelty, reversed.[41] However, the alimentary map of Rome contained both those who might languish in luxury and others who ate fastidiously a feast of beans – Rome was large enough to contain a disapproving Seneca watching the gluttony of others and the extravagant diner, object of the former's gaze and derision.

Gluttony, it has to be said, was an unattractive attribute. It led to the stomach taking over the body and causing the citizen to cease to be of any utility to the state. Cato the Elder deprived a Roman knight of his status as an equestrian on the grounds that his body was too corpulent and hence consumed by luxury.[42] Gluttony was seen to have its origins at a precise point in Rome's history – 187 BCE.[43] However, the escalation of gluttony and the consumption of food was a continuing concern in the first century CE – with Tacitus charting the increase in culinary consumption from 31 BCE through to 68 CE.[44] Two courses had increased to as many as seven or more.[45] Dishes were not simple, but involved a whole range of different ingredients placed together in an ever more sophisticated gastronomic extravaganza – as we can see in the opening passage from Seneca: two sorts of mussels, oysters, sea urchins and filleted mullet.[46] The food might come from every part of the empire to be consumed as gastronomic delights and digested. Flavours from India, Egypt, Crete and Cyrenaica could be used to create what today might be described as fusion cooking.[47] Pliny the Elder was careful to note which famous Roman first served up what exotic animal at a dinner: Hortensius was the first to present his guests with peacocks; Maecenas debuted wild asses.[48] Novelty had its value and to supply their tables, Hortensius and Lucullus kept herds of wild boars just for this purpose alone.[49] The Roman table needed to be loaded with new and ever more elaborate dishes to fuel the ever more sophisticated tastes of the foodies of the first century CE.

Such a foodie was epitomized by Aulus Vitellius. Born in 15 CE, he had spent his boyhood and early teens on Capri with Tiberius, but he came to prominence under Nero governing Africa and then was appointed governor of Lower Germany by Galba in 69 CE.[50] He was, in Galba's words, a man who thought of nothing but eating and thus not to be feared (ironically, this was the man who would later march on Rome with his legions following Galba's murder and become emperor, albeit briefly). His days were punctuated by three or four feasts – the first replaced the Roman light breakfast, the second replaced lunch, the third was held at dinner and finally there was a drinking bout. To celebrate his arrival in Rome, Vitellius' brother presented him with a vast dish called the Shield of Minerva, a fishy mess composed of livers of pike, brains of pheasants and peacocks, the tongues of flamingoes, and the milt of lampreys brought from all over the Mediterranean by the crews of the Roman fleet.[51] The result of Vitellius' continual indulgence was seen on his body: although a tall man, his face was flushed from drinking, and he had a huge belly. When he was dragged through Rome after his downfall, the size of his belly was mocked by the plebs.[52] The pleasure derived from the dinner table had destroyed Vitellius's body by the age of 57 and made him an object to be ridiculed.

Perhaps what is most striking about the consumption of produce was the waste it produced. There are five famous mosaics of a messy floor strewn with the waste of dinner.[53] Ultimately, this organic material was swept up and fed to pigs, dogs and other animals resident in the cities or close to the villas of the rich.[54] The problems of rubbish in the Roman city did not come in the form of organic waste, but that of materials from collapsed buildings.[55] It should be noted that human waste, whether in the form of faeces, urine or vomit, was disposed of for the most part in cesspits – provided that the city was sufficiently high above the local water table for such pits to function.[56] The toilets of the Roman house were often located in the garden at a distance from the dining room – often close to where food was prepared in the kitchen. We can envisage a guest moving through the house to locate the toilet, maybe using the opportunity to view the preparation of the next gastronomic delight. However, it is not impossible that slaves were at hand to brandish a convenient vessel to accommodate their master and his guests' need to pee or vomit – as revealed in the paintings of dinner parties, in which a guest is sick.[57] Vomiting was not uncommon in the ancient world as a means of purging the body, but that medical practice was adapted to allow the body to extend its capacity for food at dinner.[58] Even the abstemious Cicero was so tempted by a heavily seasoned dish of mushrooms and vegetables at a dinner given by Lentulus that he overindulged and suffered from diarrhoea for two weeks.[59] Whether this was overindulgence or simply a case of food poisoning cannot be determined – but what is clear is that the results of eating/over-eating could incapacitate Romans for some time afterwards, while their bodies recovered from the rigours of the dinner party they had so enjoyed.

DINING CLUBS AND PUBLIC DINNERS

The Romans had numerous guilds (*collegia*); some were based around work (e.g. builders), others around religion (e.g. worshippers of Isis), and others were less specific, based around a sense of communal interest.[60] These organizations were viewed with a certain suspicion by Roman authorities, since communal action was seen in some cases to lead to civic unrest and violence.[61] There were rules permitting a guild: to meet to perform rituals, to collect subscriptions for the burial fund, to collect entry fees, to make provision for funerals of members, and most importantly to regulate the guild's annual dinner – including a stipulation that members should not change seats or move around during the dinner in order to preserve the hierarchy of the guests.[62] These were organizations for not only freeborn Romans, but also freed slaves and even those slaves owned by another person. The structure of the guild was hierarchical with magistrates, often better-off freed slaves, presiding over the guilds activities.[63] The guilds, in many cases, had their own buildings that featured dining rooms. These are found across the archaeological site of Ostia Antica – there were certainly more than 40 in number.[64] Perhaps, the most significant activity of these guilds was dining – one agricultural writer regarded this activity as directly affecting prices in the markets in Rome.[65] Looking at the guild houses of Ostia, we find in the carpenters guild house four dining rooms, in which 36 members might recline looking out over a courtyard.[66] The structure of the individual dining rooms is the same as that found in the dining rooms of the houses of Pompeii – but with extra rooms to cater for the higher number of guests. Such buildings were provided in the wills of benefactors, such as Salvia Marcellina for the Guild of Aesculapius and Hygeia (god and goddess of health).[67] She donated a building and 60,000 *sesterces* to provide 60 guild members with food and drink, as well as a distribution of money from interest on the capital sum. The foundation of the guild was celebrated, as was the emperor's birthday and New Year, and there were occasions to celebrate the dead members of the guild. In total, there were seven occasions on which the guild met, and a significant proportion of these occasions involved the consumption of food and drink.[68] Like the scenes of excess found in the wall paintings of Pompeii, the dinners of the guilds were also regarded as occasions on which drinking led to excessive behaviour.[69] What we see in the guilds is a rigid hierarchy within which all knew their place, but at any moment these formal structures (similar to a modern Rotary Club) might descend into chaos under the influence of drink – it was not for no reason that the guilds were strictly regulated.

The dining clubs were relatively small affairs when compared to the mass open-air dinners provided by the elite. These were major events of public expenditure and, in Rome, the amount spent on them had to be limited by a decree of Augustus.[70] It was an area that, in Rome, was to become almost the personal interest of the emperor as benefactor of the plebs. However, outside Rome there was plenty of opportunity for the aristocracy to spend on public banquets. Publius Lucilius Gamala provided a dinner for 1,953 colonists seated in 217 open-air dining rooms in the forum at Ostia.[71] Presumably in poor weather the porticoes of the forum and the basilica might accommodate these large feasts. The public feast was becoming an increasingly common feature of benefactions handed out by the elite to residents in their local cities, eclipsing their earlier expenditure on public buildings by the end of the second century CE.[72] Again, what we see in inscriptions is a strict hierarchy in force; the magistrates, the town councillors, the freedmen priests of Augustus were distinguished from the rest of the citizens of the town and frequently were treated to better food or a much more elaborate form of feasting.[73] Thus, this enjoyable activity strikingly reinforced the social hierarchy of the city – a pattern found in all Roman dining, where guests may enter with the spirit of equality – but all knew their place.

8

Food and Wine

We have come to such a point of delicacy in eating and gourmanderie that as some people have written books on music and medicine, so some have even written books on cooking which aim to increase the pleasure of the palate, but ruin the health of the body. It is at all events a common observation that those who are luxurious and intemperate in food have much less vigorous health. Some, in fact, are like women in pregnancy who have unnatural cravings; these men like women in pregnancy, refuse common foods and have their digestion utterly ruined. Thus, as worn-out iron needs tempering, their appetites continually demand being sharpened either by neat wine or a sharp sauce or some sour relish.

Musonius Rufus, 18a

Look at Nomentanus and Apicius, digesting, as they say, the goods of land and sea, and reviewing the creations of every nation. See them, too, upon heaped roses, gloating over rich cookery, while their ears are delighted by the sound of music, their eyes the spectacles, their palates by flavours; soft and soothing foodstuffs. Their whole body is excited with soft and gentle caresses and, if they didn't stop inhaling from time to time, . . . would be killed by the different aromas. You would say they were in ecstasy, yet it will do them no good, for they take no pleasure in what is good.

Seneca, On the Happy Life: *11.4*

The eating habits of the Romans are poorly understood. Popular misconceptions include the idea that the ancients survived on stuffed dormice and lark's tongues – or enjoyed a cuisine in some way resembling the culinary repertoire of modern Italy. Obviously, many of the ingredients available today were also eaten by the Romans, including a range of mammals, birds and fish. However, there were notable absences: tomatoes, potatoes, pasta, pizza and even pimentos – absences that would render today's Italian cuisine rather dull! It raises the question: what did the Romans eat, and was their food as interesting as the opening quotations might suggest? There is not one simple answer. Cultures throughout history have absorbed new products to produce fresh tastes. In the modern west, we adults feed our children a quite different range of food from what we ate ourselves in the 1960s or 1970s. Food preparation changes and adapts to produce new tastes; it is not static and responds to the availability of flavours and aromas. This is particularly true for the Romans of the first century, who saw a huge expansion of the repertoire of products available – whether that be wine, food, spices or perfumes.[1]

At the heart of our understanding of Roman food lies the cookery book of Apicius. The identity of the author has caused problems. There was an Apicius living at the beginning of the first century BCE who was a renowned lover of pleasure and his name seems to have been adopted by cooks in later ages.[2] There was an Apicius living in the first century CE who created new and ever more refined dishes.[3] Another Apicius lived at the time of the emperor Trajan, and he found a means of sending oysters to his imperial master on campaign in Mesopotamia. Whoever the author of the cookbook was, he was certainly concerned with the preservation of a large variety of ingredients so that they might be available out of season.[4] And the book, whatever its date, has been the inspiration for modern cooks to attempt to recreate the dishes of the Romans.[5] The recreations draw on the 450 recipes, removing the stranger items or unclear techniques used, to produce a very different set of tastes involving a complicated blending of spices and tastes.[6] These are, it has to be said, modern interpretations of Apicius' recipes for the modern palate – it is clear from reading them that it is easy to overdo the quantities of spices involved and what are produced today are a particular cook's experimentations.[7] But as a result, we have a better understanding of the recipes the Romans enjoyed.

Even the poorest districts of Rome were full of a variety of products to delight the urban palate.[8] Food and its consumption even provides many of the names of parts of the city of Rome. The aptly named Forum Boarium housed the meat market, and the Forum Holitorium the vegetable market.[9] The *macellum* or market was another place that sold a whole range of goods.[10] In addition, throughout the city, the streets were thronged with sellers of wine by the glass and snacks such as chickpeas by the plate, for as little as an *ass* (the smallest Roman denomination).[11] Food was cheap, suggesting not so much that it was abundant, but there was a huge number of food sellers who were forced to cut their prices to compete with each other.[12] The Velabrum, a region at the very

Fresco of bread distribution in Pompeii.

heart of the city, could deliver a great range of goods including smoked cheese, while the Vicus Tuscus or Etruscan Street was a place filled with shops selling fish, fruit, poultry, perfumes and luxury items such as silk.[13] The importance of food to the capital of the empire should not be underestimated. And it was not just about taste – as we saw in the previous chapter, the Roman dinner was a visual feast in which the host, the food and the drink all enchanted the guests. Yet, there is a further human sense involved in the derivation of pleasure from food – that of smell.[14]

THE FRAGRANT TABLE

A number of changes occurred to the tastes and smells associated with food over the course of the first century CE. Propertius provides the key to how we should view pleasure derived from food and drink – it is a combination of food, wine, aroma and sex.[15] The aromas of food were accompanied by others such as the perfumes of roses or the smell of a wreath of celery.[16] The scent of myrtle could accentuate the experience of drinking wine.[17] Whole tables at the most wanton banquets would be loaded with rose petals.[18] The guests themselves would be scented with perfumes that could turn the heads of their fellow diners – drawing attention to the person who was most sensuously fragrant.[19] Perfumes included imported scents from Egypt, Judaea and the Italian centres of scent production based in Campania.[20] They were the ultimate luxury, a transitory sensation that was experienced by others – but applied potentially to all parts of the body including the soles of the feet.[21] No doubt scents applied at the baths prior to dinner were still fresh on arrival at the dinner party: all would have smelt of roses.

Over the scent of flowers and anointed bodies was the smell of the food itself. Interestingly, there is a direct linkage between flavours tasted and aromas smelt in the ancient world.[22] Roman food, as seen in Apicius' recipes, was based on the enhancement of the natural flavour of an individual foodstuff by the addition of a compound sauce made from a number of strongly flavoured (and fragrant) ingredients.[23] For example, venison could have been accompanied by a sauce that combined pepper, lovage, caraway, oregano, celery seed, *laser* root, fennel seed and fish sauce. Apicius lists more than 140 different spices, whereas we today across the globe cook with roughly half that number.[24] Considerable trouble was taken to obtain these products from India via Rome's ports on the Red Sea and the Persian Gulf over the course of the first century CE.[25] What we find by the latter half of the century is that spices had ceased to be a rare luxury and had become a standard expectation of the Roman diner, with prices slashed to a third of what they had been in earlier decades.[26] The trade was so significant that emperors and senators recognized an inbalance in trade with India, resulting in a 55 million *sesterces* deficit, and if the silk route to China was included that sum rose to 100 million *sesterces*.[27] What this implies in terms of Roman pleasure is that by the end of the century they were eating food that was highly spiced and highly aromatic; whereas the food at the beginning of the century had been much blander.

Much else had changed over the course of the century. New fish had been introduced into the Mediterranean – Optatus, a fleet commander, had populated the sea between the Tiber and Campania with the parrot wrasse, native to the Caspian sea, even taking care for the first five years to put back all that were caught. Fifty or so years later Pliny could report that these were now frequently caught and were the number one choice for gourmets in Rome.[28] The shifts in taste were apparent and the meals were becoming ever more ambitiously exquisite (as we saw in the discussion of the meal of Trimalchio in the previous chapter). Hence, the cook needed to keep up and maintain a similar sense of taste as his master.[29] As meals had become ever more sophisticated, by the end of the century the cook had gained an army of assistants and specialists – something that we today are familiar with from watching celebrity chefs at work on TV.[30] The price of chefs had increased by 300 per cent and a cook was one of the most expensive slaves of the household, whose artifice in the kitchen could also cost their owner far more through their use of expensive ingredients to titillate the palate of the master.[31]

THE ROMAN PALATE

Today, to add to the traditional flavours of sweet, sour, bitter and salt we have recognised a fifth, umami, derived from a combination of mushrooms and monosodium glutamate. It is described by Sally Grainger as: 'an all round the mouth meaty taste' with cheesy bits.[32] This was a taste the Romans derived from liquamen – the fish sauce related to the more famous relish garum. It was made in antiquity by dissolving small fish and parts of large fish with salt and leaving them to ferment.[33] Underlying many of these was garum or liquamen, a salsamenta manufactured by the fermentation of fish that produced something not dissimilar to the fish sauces used in Thai cooking today or, some suggest, something akin to Worcester sauce.[34] As an ingredient, it is not dissimilar to fish sauces produced in Thailand and other parts of South-East Asia, but with considerably less salt, and as a consequence used Thai fish sauce for cooking Roman food needs to be diluted with grape juice.[35] Alternatively, Mark Grant suggests the following recipe to create the taste of Roman fish sauce: dissolve 400 grams of sea salt in 700 millilitres of water over a low heat and then add 100 grams of salted anchovies with some oregano and a tablespoon of *sapa* (concentrated grape juice).[36] What the modern cooks of Roman food have discovered is that the ancients already had access to the fifth flavour, *umami*, a taste not really associated until recently with the culinary tastes of Europe and the Mediterranean.

Apicius' cookbook is divided into ten sections or books, variously embracing meat dishes, vegetable dishes, compound dishes, pulses, fowl, luxury dishes, quadrupeds, seafood and fish. To gain an idea of the flavours used in the recipes, we can simply look to the originals in Apicius, book by book. The focus of Book One was on preserving and restoring ingredients. Apicius (1.8) advised his readers that fried fish, if plunged in hot vinegar, can be preserved and that cloudy wine can be made clear with a paste made from beans and the white of three eggs (1.6). He also provided tips for restoring fish sauce and honey; for preserving meat in honey or mustard rather than salt; and for storing oysters, olives, grapes, apples, pomegranates, quince, figs, blackberries, turnips and truffles.

Book Two opened with the subject of minced ingredients that might be suitable for the making of forced meats (faggots) and sausages. The book opens with a seafood version (2.1.1) combining prawns, lobster, squid, cuttlefish with a seasoning of pepper, lovage, cumin and *laser* root (a gum available today only from Afghanistan) and suggests other fish-based versions prior to moving onto forcemeat made from offal and brains of land-based animals. Peacock faggots were regarded as the very best, followed by those from pheasants, then rabbits, chickens and young pigs (2.2.6). Often accompanied with a thick or cold sauce, a version of the dish developed by Sally Grainger involves at its heart chicken combined with cumin, pepper and parsley meatballs poached in fish sauce with peppercorns.[37] She suggests serving the faggots with a thick sauce derived from pudding rice, half a leek, dillweed, celery, grape syrup and fish sauce.[38] What is striking about these recipes is that there is a sense of familiarity with the more recent European culinary traditions of faggots, meatballs, fishcakes and sausages – perhaps there is a Roman legacy to an Englishman's bangers, if not the mash. Vegetable dishes are the subject of the third book, and readers will find a wide variety: asparagus, beetroot, cabbage, carrots, gourds, leeks, lettuces, radishes, swedes and turnips. Boiling these vegetables is familiar today; what is less customary is serving up, for example, leeks dressed with oil, fish sauce or wine. Turnips and swedes were mashed and reheated with lashings of cumin, a little rue, some Parthian *laser,* honey, vinegar, fish sauce and syrup. The combination of sweet with sour extended even to serving sweet melon over which was poured a sauce made from mint, honey, fish sauce, pepper and vinegar – an unusual combination that Sally Grainger has found to be a very successful starter for the modern palate.[39]

The cooking principle behind Book Four seems to be the combination of different ingredients: *cattabia* or salad, *pattinae* (dishes) of fish, vegetables, fruit and eggs, meat and fish stews, some soups and other hors d'oeuvre. One salad involved layering bread, chicken, sweetbreads, cheese, pine nuts, cucumber and dried onions, over which was poured a dressing of celery seed, pennyroyal, mint, ginger, coriander, raisins, honey, vinegar, oil and wine.[40] To achieve perfection with this dish, it had to be placed for one hour in the snow to chill it prior to serving. Some of the egg dishes resemble in some ways a modern frittata with the important difference that the vegetables, nettles and spinach were first cooked in fish sauce.[41] These are not alien tastes even for the modern palate, a fact that is confirmed with reference to the stews, one of which combines pork with apricots to produce a sweet and sour taste with a hint of fish sauce – the latter really is in nearly every recipe.[42] It's clear that even in a barley soup or a stuffed gourd, the Romans employed a large number of ingredients to create spicy and aromatic dishes. Book Five, which deals with pulses, confirms this pattern and the Roman reputation for luxurious eating is only confirmed by the number of ingredients, notably imported spices.

Matters are equally diverse in Book Six, which deals with birds for the table. It opens with boiled ostrich, moves onto duck, partridge, pigeon, dove, flamingo, goose and ends with a longer section on chicken. As for sauces, a combination of pepper, lovage, celery seeds, sesame seeds, parsley, mint, onion, date, honey, wine, fish sauce, vinegar, oil and syrup might go particularly well with parrot or flamingo.[43] It needs to be stressed that there was nothing particularly luxurious about eating flamingo, but the tongues were considered a delicacy and were strongly advocated by the first-century Apicius.[44] What is interesting is that Pliny suggests that the flamingo had ceased to be a rare bird, even found in Gaul, Spain and in the Alps – perhaps like the parrot wrasse it was introduced to be served at the Roman table. It is significant that Apicius includes no less than

15 recipes for chicken, served in a variety of ways including in dill sauce, sour sauce, *laser* sauce, its own sauce, and with milk, with boiled gourds or roasted. There are a far greater number of recipes for this domesticated animal than for flamingoes or ostriches, pointing to the probability that the chicken was seen on far more Roman tables than the exotic birds also found in this book.

It is in Book Seven that recipes start entering the world of luxury. It opens with a recipe for sterile wombs, moves onto udders, fattened livers, and we find recipes for a stomach, kidneys, testicles, roasted meats, hams, sweets, flowering bulbs, mushrooms, snails and truffles. Luxury here is defined as a rare part of an animal, the consumption of fuel in roasting it, or the exquisite taste of mushrooms and truffles. The latter, it needs to be noted, were boiled whole, then grilled and simmered in fish sauce, wine, sweet wine, pepper and honey.[45] Strangely, the list of exotic and extravagant recipes ends with eggs and how to boil or fry them. There is a strong emphasis in this book on recipes for sauces to go with meats, something that continues in the following book with recipes for quadrupeds. The hunted come first: wild boar, deer, wild goats, wild sheep and are followed by beef and veal, lamb, piglets, hare and finally ended with the dormouse – the smallest mammal eaten. Meat could be boiled, roasted or the animal could be stuffed from the boar down to the dormouse.

The final books of recipes of Apicius are subtitled 'The sea' and 'The fisherman'. The penultimate book produces dishes featuring lobster, crayfish, electric ray, squid, mussels, sea urchins, oysters, other forms of shellfish, baby tuna and mullet. Lobsters were split and grilled with a pepper and coriander sauce, or were boiled and accompanied with sauces that might involve pepper, lovage, parsley, cumin, honey, vinegar and fish sauce, a combination that appears in several recipes for sauce to go over seafood – mint might replace the parsley.[46] The final recipe in this book is of interest for the history of pleasure, since it is named after Baiae (the centre of Roman excess). Chopped oysters, mussels and sea urchins were cooked in a pan, into which was added chopped roasted pine nuts, rue, celery, pepper, coriander, fish sauce, dates and oil to produce *Embractum Baianum* – or the relish of Baiae.

Reading the recipes of Apicius causes us to question our ideas about Roman food. It was not the act of eating a large number of small mammals (e.g. dormice) that made the food Roman, but the combining of spices and, of course, fish sauce. In these recipes were created a series of sensations that might be recognized as all of the five flavours associated with the human sense of taste. There is a subtlety to the recipes that continues to appeal to modern chefs, who seek to create their own versions of these dishes.[47] More importantly, the recipes for sauces, although seeming to contain similar ingredients, produce quite different results – 12 different sauces for lamb for example.[48] The recipes do not seem that exotic and have much in common with some dishes found in the southern and eastern Mediterranean or elsewhere in Europe.

IN VINO VERITAS

Food was eaten at dinner with wine – the primary intoxicant in the Roman world, causing nearly all other forms of alcohol and drugs to be marginalized or ignored altogether. Drinking wine was the fundamental indicator of a person's engagement with Roman culture and what might be called 'civilization',[49] factors that may have enabled the export of this commodity to regions well beyond Rome's empire, as well as to those well below the status of the elite.[50] Wine prices found in Pompeii reveal that a cup of wine varied according to its quality, from one *ass* for ordinary wine, two *asses* for something better and four *asses* for the best – a Falernian.[51] Children were for the most part shielded from alcohol, due to their absence from the Roman dinner party.[52] It was as young men that the joys of drinking and drunkenness were first learned outside the home with their peer group in their late teens and early twenties. If this was the case, how and where did women learn to drink? There is a long Roman tradition, true or invented, that women did not drink wine in Rome's distant past and that the virtuous continued to maintain a distance from the substance – the generic principle being that drunkenness leads inevitably to sex.[53] One occasion for drinking was the secret female-only festival of the Bona Dea (Good Goddess), at which the wine bowl was misnamed the honey-pot and the substance described as milk – perhaps, as Nicholas Purcell has suggested, as a means to suggest accidental female inebriation rather than the deliberate binge drinking that seems to be anticipated in the lives of young males.[54] Maybe this is the key to understanding the context in which young women discovered alcohol – under the instruction of males, perhaps husbands or other young men, who misled them with a false taxonomy of the liquid in front of them.[55] This is, perhaps, shown in the frescoes that represent drunken, clothed women and scantily clad (more sober) men found in Pompeii.[56] However drinking was learned, the consumption of wine was a pleasure for both adult men and women – the latter indicated by the unusual decree by Augustus that his daughter, exiled for adultery, should have no access to wine.[57] The pleasure derived from wine consumption – and drunkenness – enabled both men and women to break free of some of the harsher social 'rules' imposed upon them.[58] At the same time, how a person drinks and the type of wine s/he chooses projects a sense of personal self-image.[59] Furthermore, the intoxicating quality of wine was tempered by mixing it with water, in contrast to the barbarians who drank it neat.[60]

Just as we saw the Romans introducing new edible produce to the provinces of Gaul and Spain, notably the flamingo, so they also exported the vineyard. It resulted in an influx of imported wines increasing over the course of the first century CE from the Western Mediterranean to complement those of Italy and others imported from the Greek East.[61] Under Domitian at the end of the century, the problem was partly addressed with a restriction on the planting of new vines in the provinces to feed a booming market for cheap wine.[62] What we see generally is a massive overall increase in wine production that in turn supplies a larger market for wine, with the city of Rome consuming as much as 250 million litres transported in ten million amphorae per annum.[63] The bulk is impressive, but along with the expansion in capacity was a move by some Italian growers to producing high quality wines, and their wines held their own.[64] Campanian vines were introduced into Umbria with a view to producing quality wines in that region, a process that is well attested with reference to the use of vines from Greece as well.[65] Interestingly, some varieties of vines were well suited to this process, causing more Pompeian grapes to be grown at Chiusi than at the town from which the grape gained its name, while others including the most prized grape Falernian did not do well outside their home territory.[66] There is a sense of change as new wines came into fashion – for example those from Nomentum.[67] The sophistication of the production of Roman wine has perhaps been underestimated, but a careful reading of Book Fourteen of Pliny's *Natural History* or Book Three of Columella's *On Agriculture* reveals just how much expertise there was to hand and understanding of the returns from vineyards. This knowledge caused some small vineyards to become very valuable and such a desirable asset that even Seneca (who could denounce luxury and pleasure) paid through the nose for one.[68]

The contrast between the mass-marketed wines and what can be described as *grands crus* was in taste, rather than in alcohol content. What we see develop by the end of the first century CE is a definition of quality and a lexicography to discuss those features associated with particular wines. There was a great diversity in types of wine, which varied according to the region from which they were produced and according to the strength of alcohol content.[69] Age was a quality and 200-year-old wines were available: due to their age these were not drunk mixed with water, but were added to more recent wines to improve their flavour. Keeping wine was a sound investment up to its twentieth year, but any longer and one ran a risk; it was only over 200 years that you might see a healthy profit at a rate of 6 per cent per annum.[70] Pliny the Elder, in the second half of the first century CE, could list a hierarchy of wines with 14 *grands crus classés* and 28 *crus non classés*.[71] A few are worth listing to reveal the dynamics of wine connoisseurship. The first class of wines was led by the emperor Augustus' favourite Setinum from the region of the Pontine marshes around Forum Appii on the Via Appia. Also in this first class was Caecuban that grew to the north of the Bay of Naples. Falernian had fallen into the second class of wine due to a greater emphasis on quantity over quality – it was after all available in the bars of Pompeii at only four times the cost of the cheapest cup of wine.[72] However, Falernian from certain vineyards was a highly prized commodity. Just as today there is wonderful Chianti and simply awful Chianti, in antiquity there was good and bad Falernian. The Faustus estate produced some of the best, alongside their excellent Caucinian and Faustian wines. Moving down a level were that of the Alban Hills outside Rome and the wine of the Sorrento peninsula and its neighbouring hills overlooking the bay of Naples. Within this third class of wines, Pliny observes that wines came into and went out of fashion. These wines are all of the very highest quality; the next class was more mass-produced and was served at public banquets – Mamertina from Sicily and Potitiana that was often labelled up as Mamertina. Deception was part of the vintners' art – wine from southern Gaul came with the addition of herbs and noxious powders to alter its colour and flavour. New wines were a feature of the business: Campania had produced in the middle of the century a Trebellician wine just four miles from Naples. Although Spain produced quantity rather than quality, some wines from Tarragona or the Balearic islands caught the attention of the emperor Augustus' wine buyer, who commented: 'The flavour of this wine is new to me, and it is not of a high class, but all the same I prophesy that the emperor will drink no other'.[73]

Today, we have little real idea of what ancient wine tasted like. A Campanian Vintner, Piero Mastroberardino, has been growing grapes within excavated vineyards in Pompeii. Two and a half acres of the 167 excavated acres were devoted to vines from 1996 with the first harvest in 2001. The vines are not ancient varieties but modern local varieties. However, the production is ancient in that vine trellises are placed at a spacing of every four metres and the grapes are grown at a greater density than in a modern vineyard. In 2003, 1,721 bottles were distributed, the first six to Italy's president Silvio Berlusconi and the rest auctioned via the internet. The 13.5 per cent alcohol content is fittingly the strength of a modern wine, said by its producers simply to have 'an ancient aura', if not the taste from antiquity.

DRUNKENNESS AND GOOD TASTE

The centrality of alcohol to Roman civilization cannot be overestimated – drinking wine quite literally defined a person as a member of Roman society. The type or variety of wine might define a person's social status. Pliny could precisely equate the status of a guest with the quality of the wine he would serve them from family to friends to freed slaves.[74] As in most cultures, drinking was a social act with a set of rules and was, to some extent, enclosed within the space of the dining room or the tavern.[75] There was a clear awareness of the effects of alcohol defined in some ways as a continuum from *ebrius* through *ebriosus* to *extra ebrietatem*.[76] How you drank and the extent of your drinking was a reflection of your character, and the notion of alcoholism has been shown by the late John D'Arms to have been absent from Roman thinking. Of course, this does not mean that what we define as alcoholics and alcoholism did not exist – the Romans simply did not construct drinking with our terminology.[77] The immoral or mentally feeble man might drink a lot, but there were examples of successful politicians who drank excessively, even passing out during meetings of the senate.[78] Wine and its consumption was seen as a force for good, but naturally, as with anything to do with Roman pleasure or lifestyles, there

Crossing stones facilitated easy access to the bar across the street in Pompeii.

were still ways to get it wrong and to act improperly. Pliny in the *Natural History* (14.137–48) rounds on the drinking practices that do not equate with his expectations of the enjoyment of nature's gift of wine. Pliny was clear: drinking of wine should take place within the confines of the dining room as an accompaniment to food. But fashion had changed in the early part of the century and drinking on an empty stomach had caught on, and drinkers were seen in the wrong places – at the baths, in public, when your body was already heated up, and when naked rather than clothed.

Novellius Torquatus Tricongius was the greatest drinker of the first century. He had exceptional capacity and would never slur his speech or vomit, and would arrive early for his duties as praetor and as consul. Drinking wine defined the Romans and wine provided them with their primary alcoholic resource that would drop their defences, loosen their tongues, and develop a greater sense of pleasure through drunkenness. The next day, head aching, hands trembling, eyes sore and cheeks sagging, the pleasure of the previous evening was forgotten – what had they said? What had they done? Had they committed a crime? Was it treason or adultery? Perhaps that was the point: the inhibitions of the elite were set aside and they embraced the dangers of alcohol of speaking their minds, of doing things they would not otherwise have done. Perhaps, as Pliny suggests, they had spoken the truth, *in vino veritas*, and would pay the price with their lives when sober.

9

A Great Song and Dance

Actions that are strongly discordant with civilized behaviour, such as singing in the forum, or any other instance of extreme waywardness, are readily apparent and do not call for much admonition or advice.

Cicero, On Duties: *1.145*

It was no longer enough for them to shout and clap as they reclined [at dinner], but, in the end, most of them leapt up and began to dance, making movements unfit for a free man but appropriate for that beat and that kind of melody.

Plutarch, Moralia: *705E–F*

Suppose that someone is making a wise man his heir, and asks him, when he leaves him 100 million sesterces in the will, to dance openly by daylight in the forum before he receives the inheritance; suppose that he has promised that he will – for otherwise the man would not name him as his heir. Should he do what he has promised or not?

Cicero, On Duties: *3.93*

For almost no one dances while sober – unless perhaps he is insane – neither while alone nor in a moderate and honourable banquet. The dance is the final accompaniment to an early banquet, a pleasant locale, and location of many other luxurious activities.

Cicero, For Murena: *13*

In 17 CE, the Roman senator Lucius Norbanus got up and took up his trumpet to greet the day and his morning callers.[1] For us, it seems a somewhat surprising thing for a Roman senator to do. We've been fed a steady diet of senators by the BBC and Sky TV that portrays them as a pompous version of the English aristocracy (with English accents to match). Hence discovering that one of their number played the trumpet or sang or danced rather challenges the whole preconception. There is, in fact, a whole catalogue of the Roman aristocracy performing music, taking part in plays and dancing in the first century CE.[2] And there was a long tradition of all sectors of Roman society enjoying a rich oral culture well before this.

Children were exposed to song from a very early age, when babies were sung to sleep.[3] Rhythm was used in the development of a knowledge of language and basic numeracy '*unum et unum duo, duo et duo quattuor*' and so on, and when a teacher read a text to a class, the pupils chanted it back to him.[4] The rhythm of chants, verses and songs was the substance of education for young men and young women alike, equipping them with knowledge not just of letters, numbers and even literacy, but also a sense of tradition and an ability to memorize song that would continue into adulthood.[5] Music, song and dance permeated all levels of society, from the barmaid gyrating while playing a pipe, flute or castanets, through to members of the aristocracy such as Sempronia in the 60s BCE. She was not only well read in the literature of Greece and of Rome, and able to play the lyre, but was also trained up to dance with greater skill than was considered appropriate.[6]

Like most things that brought pleasure to the Romans, song and dance was often roundly condemned by the moral minority keen to link it with a collapse of conservative values. Citizens such as Sempronia were criticized if they trained hard to dance well.[7] The connection between being a good dancer and immorality would seem to date back as far as the late second century BCE; whereas previous to this time children, male and female, had learnt to dance competitively.[8] Cicero, in the last decades of the Roman Republic, could look on the young men attracted to following his enemy Catiline and characterize them as dancers and singers, who could also be quite handy with daggers and poisons.[9] Cicero saw the appearance of song and dance as symptoms of change for the worse and moral decline of the Roman race, but he also recognized a long tradition of singing at aristocratic banquets.[10] The rise of a critique of the art form can be traced back to the second century BCE when Scipio Aemilianus complained that dance schools were catering for freeborn girls and boys.[11] The most effeminate men, the *cinaedi*, were quite literally dancing boys with whom no respectable man – and certainly no freeborn children – should associate, let alone be drawn into their dances.[12] What we might be seeing here is the influence of Hellenism and the social construction of the musician and/or dancer as a professional, whose ability to entertain extended to sex. The fact that young men continued to dance and to sing, and take lessons to increase their skills, demonstrates the persistence of the Roman's tradition and love for the art form.

In any case, by the first century CE, there had been something of a cultural revolution in the nature of song and dance: first, theatres had been or were being built in most towns of Italy; secondly, under Augustus a new form of pantomime had been introduced that was becoming wildly popular; and thirdly there is evidence that music had become far more sophisticated, with a far greater range of notes. These changes shifted the place of song and dance from being marginalized in the late Republic of Cicero's day to becoming central to the construction of Roman pleasure by the end of the first century CE. Over the course of this century, not only senators would appear on stage, but also their emperor would perform as though he were a professional.

A CENTURY OF MUSIC

There are very few direct attestations of ancient musical notation. The ones that do exist in papyri found in Egypt show an evolution of music from a simple use of two or three notes to accompany a song, through to instrumental pieces featuring 11 or 12 notes, and up to 13 notes have been found in a recently discovered papyrus.[13] This new find provides us with the most extensive piece of music from antiquity. It features the first actual attestation of conjunct and disjunct tetrachords, and it has now been rendered on a modern oboe.[14] This was music to be performed by an expert on a *cithara* (lyre). However, a traditional seven-string *cithara* would not have produced 13 notes, hence it has been suggested that this was a piece to be performed on an 11- or 12-string *cithara*.[15] Alternatively, the complicated instrumental piece from Egypt could have been performed on an *aulos* (flute) with 15 finger-holes – such as one found in Pompeii.[16] What is clear though from this unique find is that Roman music was sophisticated, and when we hear of the emperor Nero learning to play the *cithara* to a professional standard, we should not underestimate the difficulty or the sophistication of the task.[17] What we also find in the late first and early second century CE is the words of famous Roman senators being adapted to be sung to musical accompaniment on the *cithara* by Greek musicians.[18] It is unclear whether this innovation was led by demand from Roman senators or whether it was the creation of the musicians with the intention of providing a new musical product to be consumed by their egotistical Roman patrons. Despite the long tradition of music in Rome going right back to the fifth century BCE, there is a distinct difference in the experience by the first century CE.[19] Stone theatres had been built not just in Rome, but right across the towns of Italy. The impetus came, it would seem, from the construction of Pompey's theatre in Rome, followed by the theatres of Marcellus and Balbus under Augustus.[20] These were not just places at which to see action upon a stage, but, as many visitors today will discover, these are harmonic spaces in which sound waves travel from the performer to the audience. For Vitruvius, the theatre was the place where citizens with their wives and children were seated with the intention of experiencing pleasure.[21] Key to this experience was the construction of the seating so that not only the lines of sight from the audience to the stage were seamless, but also the flow of sound from the stage to the audience was similarly uninterrupted.[22] In setting out the section on the theatre in his work *On Architecture*, Vitruvius drew on Greek theories of harmony that linked the very construction of the Roman theatre to the performance of music.[23] The proliferation of theatres across Italy over the course of the first century CE points to the importance of music and song. At the same time, there were two important developments in music itself; first, as we've seen, there was a greater sophistication and greater range of notes available on more complex instruments; and secondly the adaptation of the Latin language by Greek musicians to produce a new tradition of Roman song that drew on the musical theory of Greece.

LORDS OF THE DANCE

The new theatres of the late first century BCE and the first century CE were also places to watch dance. Under the first emperor, Augustus, pantomime had appeared on the stage and it was said later to have been introduced by Pylades – the most innovative stage performer of the period.[24] This did not mark the introduction of dance as such, but a development of the art into a new form of performance that was to become the most popular attraction in the theatres

The large theatre at Pompeii.

of Italy. It drew on themes familiar to us from Greek mythology that were the substance of Greek tragedy, together with elements of Greek comedy and Satyr plays with their choreographed sections of dance. What Pylades also did was compose a handbook on dancing and develop a distinctive Italian style based on a type of dance found in Alexandria.[25] His own performances were renowned for their expression of passion and variety within each single character depicted.[26] Whereas another dancer of the time, Bathyllus, specialized in comic dance. These were new forms of entertainment drawing on a Greek culture of dance, but transforming these elements for consumption by a public in Rome and Italy. The solo dancer was accompanied by musicians and a chorus, which may have been a development made possible only by the clever new acoustic designs of the Roman theatres. By the middle of the first century CE, pantomime was an art form that had taken hold and even Seneca could admit to being utterly addicted to watching it, a new pleasure devised in Rome that was popularized and disseminated across Italian culture.[27]

So passionate did the Romans become about pantomime that tension often erupted during performances, and the art called into question moral decency. In

the first year of Tiberius's reign (15 CE), violence among the audience resulted
in casualties not just to the theatregoers but also the deaths of four members of
the Praetorian Guard sent to quell the riot.[28] The senate discussed the incident
and proposed that miscreant pantomime dancers could be subjected to the whip,
but the proposal was vetoed. There were measures to ensure that the rioters at
this performance were punished with exile. Plus, other measures attempted to
curb the interaction of the pantomime dancers and the aristocracy – preventing
senators from visiting their houses and forbidding Roman knights from contact
with them in public. The influence of dancers was seen to extend beyond the
theatre to the home, where they were said to have sex with the women of the
house.[29] The pantomime actor Mnester was one of the lovers of the emperor
Claudius' wife Messalina.[30] The violence in the theatres continued until 23 CE
when the pantomime actors were banned from Italy and so began a 14-year period
in which, in spite of numerous petitions, the shows were shut down – only to be
restored by Caligula in 37 CE.[31] The ban did not seem to diminish the Romans'
enthusiasm for their new art form that could provoke such strong emotions.

So why did the state and the emperor see the pantomime dancers as threatening
the state and debauching women? It was partly down to the structure of the
new art form – pantomime involved a competition between solo performers.
This produced a divisive effect on the audience, not seen in earlier dramatic
forms at Rome.[32] Yet there was more, as is revealed by Lucian in his work *The
Dance* (*Saltatio*: 81): the dancer needed not only to be technically perfect, but
also to reflect the human qualities and aspirations of his audience. This, Lucian
maintains, made the dancer a mirror for the characteristics of each spectator. As
a result, the audience often could not contain itself and burst into applause as
it saw a reflection of its own being or soul. This was the pleasure derived from
viewing a great performance.[33] What made the performers so powerful was their
ability to communicate with the audience, to reflect their desires, and to incite
them to express ideas through collective behaviour and violence. The powerful
relationship between dancer and audience did not cease with the performance.
Dance invaded the homes of the Romans with husbands and wives vying with
each other to recreate the moves that were seen on stage.[34] The first century CE
was a new age of dance, a powerful pleasure banned for more than a decade,
but entrenched as perhaps the ultimate spectacle that could then be emulated at
home under instruction.

Fresco panel showing theatre masks from the House of Julius Polybius, Pompeii.

LIFE'S A STAGE

In 59 CE, at the festival to celebrate the shaving of the emperor Nero's beard, Aelia Catella danced in a pantomime.[35] She was 80 years old, and had in all probability in her youth seen the great innovators of pantomime under the emperor Augustus and been inspired to learn the steps that she so ably performed in her old age to applause and wonder. Others of this age group, who had grown up in the Augustan heyday of dance, took part but recognizing their loss of agility willingly joined the choruses. The young joined in too, and the historian Cassius Dio creates an image of all of Rome attending dance schools as well as singing and music lessons. The intention was to perform in public and to be recognized as the best, or at least second to the master of these arts – the emperor Nero.[36] Public performance was something new and seems to lie at the very heart of the Roman state under Nero. Most young aristocrats gained some knowledge of music, dance and singing as part of their general education. However, on the accession of Nero, the new emperor sent for the master of the lyre, Terpnus, who became his teacher. He not only learnt how to play the lyre, but also sought to strengthen his voice – he had lead weights placed on his chest and regularly purged himself.[37] It is significant that at about the same time there was a fad for minor surgery, including penis piercing, that was supposed to be good for both the health and the voice.[38] The logic behind this was that the genitals were considered to have been the loom-weights of the voice, but what is important is that the Romans considered succeeding at public performance so vital they were prepared to undergo this extreme measure.

Nero did not have the best singing voice, but nevertheless he could charm the audience.[39] He had a core of 5,000 supporters – the Augustiani, who would acclaim their emperor as 'our Apollo', while he dished out songs or tragic roles (only taking up pantomime at the very end of his reign) with a mythological content: 'The Blinding of Oedipus', 'Orestes the Matricide', 'The Frenzy of Hercules', 'Attis' and 'The Bacchantes'.[40] Inevitably, the emperor won all competitions, including all of those in Greece, and no rival was safe from the emperor's jealousy.[41] The imperial ruler, on the stage, in competition with members of the aristocracy, young and old, both male and female, seems somewhat surprising. Yet, it seems to have worked – Nero inverted the principles of *virtus* and *dignitas* and engaged with theatre audiences directly.[42] In his performance the audience could identify themselves – Nero was not a Tiberius or a Claudius, but the embodiment of the aspirations of the spectators. The emperor on stage was not a one-off, and we find Nero and the aristocracy performing right across his reign.[43] Even the greatest critic of pleasure, Seneca (at least in the early days), publicly encouraged him to excel on stage, leading the audience with their gestures of acclamation.[44] It can be seen as a form of communication, in which Nero might justify the murder of his mother with his own solo performance of 'Orestes the Matricide'.[45] Nero had a vision of how he should be seen: the professional *cithara* player, the tragic actor, the pantomime and the musician. All arts he pursued with a relentless passion and professionalism with the sole intention of excelling and conquering all competitors.[46] It worked, the audience adored him, and after his death he would be remembered for his role as a stage performer.

THE HOME CABARET

The entertainments that appeared in public were also performed in private, a perfectly respectable distraction to diners attending a senator's function.[47] What becomes clear is that enthusiasm for public performances crosses over into the private sphere. Ummidia Quadratilla, born in 26 CE, lived most of her long life during the first century CE, dying at the age of 79.[48] When she was in her 30s and 40s, she would have seen the great performances of the age of Nero and even at the end of her life, her passion for pantomime remained unabated in the face of the new morality of the second century CE.[49] She supported her own company of pantomime players, who performed at home and on stage in the theatre. They lived in her house and were there to entertain her, but she was renowned in the city for her provision of the players at the theatre, where other members of the audience followed her gestures and paid tribute to her in song (interestingly, though, her grandson was kept apart from these *cinaedi*).[50]

The entire episode of the fictional dinner held at the house of Trimalchio is accompanied by music, song and outbreaks of dancing. Singing accompanies the guests washing their hands and causes Petronius' hero to ask himself: 'I wanted to know if the entire household sang, so I ordered a drink' (*Satyrica*: 31). A slave responded in song and every request of the guests continued to be answered by slaves with song. For the diners new to Trimalchio's house, the experience was like watching a pantomime rather than formal dining. The starters were whisked away and replaced with a new course by a chorus of singing slaves, prior to Trimalchio's rendition of a poem (*Satyrica*: 34). The course was not yet ready to be eaten – bread was distributed by an Egyptian slave boy belting out a tune from a pantomime (*Satyrica*: 35). The next dish was revealed by music and four male dancers, who whisked off the lid of a large dish (*Satyrica*: 36). On to the next course, and a slave enacted the various roles of the god Dionysus, while singing Trimalchio's poetry to deliver the dish (*Satyrica*: 41). The meal, now halfway through, was accompanied again by music as dishes were cleared and a dramatic trick was engaged in to present the diners with a drama, in which an apparently uncooked pig was revealed to contain further delicacies and concludes with applause (*Satyrica*: 47). At this point, Trimalchio and his wife, Fortunata, are on the brink of dance, encouraged by chanting slaves, only to be prevented by an announcement and the entertainment moves on with a performance by acrobats (*Satyrica*: 52–3). Trimalchio is also seen to quickly compose a verse to deliver to his guests and the conversation shifts to literary pursuits (*Satyrica*: 55–6). This is followed by drama to deliver a dish composed of a whole calf (*Satyrica*: 59). Dessert is finally served by a slave imitating a nightingale and accompanied by another slave chanting a medley from the *Aeneid* interspersed with lines from an Atellan farce, culminating in further performances (*Satyrica*: 68). By now, the wives are ready to dance but are denied the opportunity by the entire household of slaves entering the dining room, with the cook performing as a tragedian (*Satyrica*: 70–1). Obviously, this is a satirical dinner, yet it supports a clear structure that is found in other texts – between courses, the guests were entertained with drama, music and song. A dinner was not complete unless there was entertainment put on by professionals to delight the ears of the host and his guests. In the case of the dinner with Trimalchio, there is an aural as well as a visual feast to accompany the taste of the food itself.

SOUNDS OF THE CITY

The popularity of song would have affected the soundscape of the cities of antiquity. This is a difficult feature to reconstruct, because the evidence lies in texts and architecture, rather than oral culture. But it is clear that the cities were places full of noise emanating from the streets.[51] The rich were isolated from sounds of city streets in their villas and gardens that provided a buffer to the racket; many could also chose to desert the noisy city.[52] The din was only increased by the vast construction projects of the emperors, whose industry could drown out the clamour of Rome.[53] Sounds did not cease with nightfall and for the inhabitants, especially the migrants, sleep was something that they were denied thanks to the noises of neighbours and the streets.[54] Sleeplessness was a common malady at Rome, claimed in satire to cause a man's death, and treated with herbal remedies and soothing songs.[55] Seneca (*Letters*: 56) took lodgings above a bathhouse, a situation that allows him to ponder the noises emanating from a city. From the baths, he could hear the strenuous grants and gasps of men exercising in the *palaestra*, the crack of the masseur's hand on the flesh of a bather, the shouts of the score in a ball game, a man singing in the bathing rooms, the splash of a man jumping into the swimming pool.[56] Then there were the voices of those who needed to advertise their services: the hair-plucker, only quiet when working (and his customer screaming); an assorted array of food-sellers – each it would seem with their own very distinctive cries that were associated with their products.[57] The huge range of produce and services sold in the street should not be underestimated – everything was available, from sulphur matches through to iced water.[58] Terms were devised to describe the sellers – *ambulator, circitor, circumforaneus* – that designated their itinerant nature and in the final case located them as circulating around the forum. Others would call at the houses of the rich, especially if they had luxury goods for sale.[59] Some were storytellers, buskers and performers.[60] Shops spilled over the pavements and it's likely the proprietor or his servants to undertook their business as much in the street as within the shop itself, every bit as vocal as their itinerant competitors.[61] The streets of Rome in particular were crowded, not just with people moving across the city, but also with people buying and selling goods – the street, as well as the markets, were the means by which the best part of a million people were supplied. It was only the wealthy who were called on personally by traders or who purchased at auctions.[62] What is clear is the streets resonated with shouts, chants and even songs of the sellers, itinerant players and beggars.[63] Throughout Rome, the culture of the streets as linked to the performances in the theatre, uniting the plebs with the aristocracy in a passionate embrace of a culture of song and dance.[64]

10

Violence

His eyes blaze and sparkle, his whole face is crimson with blood that surges from the lowest depths of the heart, his lips quiver, his teeth are clenched, his hair bristles and stands on end, his breathing is forced and harsh, his joints crack from writhing, he groans and bellows, bursts out into speech with scarcely intelligible words, strikes his hands together continually, and stamps the ground with his feet; his whole body is excited and performs great angry threats; it is an ugly and horrible picture of distorted and swollen frenzy – you cannot tell if this vice is more execrable or more hideous.

Seneca, On Anger: *1.1*

When we think of the Romans, there are many popular images that come to mind – but none so vivid than their sadistic pursuit of violent pleasures. Films such as *Gladiator*, *Caligula* and *Spartacus* or any more recent TV docudrama explore the subject of violence and pain inflicted on other human beings for the enjoyment or pleasure of the Roman rulers of the world. In these films and programmes violence is the feature that separates us from them and is the phenomenon that fascinates directors and producers. For the viewers, it is a certainty that some degree of violence is on its way when a programme about the Roman world (however factual) is due to be broadcast on TV, and it both attracts and repels us. The ancient written accounts of events that fuel these new narratives of Rome are many, such as the emperor Claudius sitting through the mass lunchtime executions of criminals or the emperor Commodus personally dispatching an ostrich. However, violence in Rome needs further examination to seek out its place and to understand how, or even why, the Romans enjoyed viewing the public destruction of their enemies and whether this pleasure in violence was a universal phenomenon or subject to criticism.

PAIN AND PUNISHMENT

There is a story told about one of the close advisers to the emperor Augustus, Vedius Pollio, who was a son of a freed slave. The tale became a famous example of cruelty for those living in the first century CE, but at the same time encapsulates the Roman relationship with violence.[1] The emperor Augustus had come to dine at Vedius' house, and a slave had dropped a crystal goblet that smashed on impact. His owner ordered this young slave to be thrown into his pool of lampreys, where he would be torn to pieces in front of his master and his guests. This choice of death for the slave was seen by Pliny, at the end of the first century, to have been chosen for its spectacle: Vedius and his guests could witness at close hand the offending slave, quite literally, being consumed.[2] However, Augustus intervened to prevent this cruelty, and today the incident remains open to interpretation. Does the proposed punishment represent the Roman pleasure of violence, or did most people, like Augustus in the story, disapprove of treating a slave in this way? We know that Seneca believed men such as Vedius to be hated throughout the city, as well as being detested by their slaves.[3] However, there are other interpretations of the incident: does it show that those of slave descent were more cruel than those of free ancestry? Does the incident indicate the exceptional nature of the pleasure-seeking, yet sadistic, Vedius? Perhaps what is criticized is the anger involved in the punishment of a slave, or is the means of his destruction also seen as inhumane? Regardless, there is considerable evidence that there was an undeniable interest – even excitement – generated by the idea of a slave's death by lampreys by contemporary and future writers.[4]

The disciplining of slaves who were seen to disrupt the entertainment of guests was normal, but the punishment tended to be with a whip rather than resulting in death.[5] Numerous trivial reasons for whipping slaves can be found across Latin literature, and perhaps no reason needed to be given – the existence of slaves was synonymous with whippings by the master or his wife and children.[6] Each day may have ended with the sound of the whip resounding in the houses of the city, but this punishment was at the lower end of the scale.[7] There also existed professionals who were employed to torture slaves – and part of their technique of punishment was to display their instruments before they began their task.[8] These included whips with metal sewn onto the lashes, vertical racks for disjointing the body, or using both hot pitch and fire.[9] For us today, who in part define our notions of civilization with reference to ancient Rome, this degree of violence and the acceptance of a system devised for the infliction of pain on another human is shocking. However, for the Romans this was familiar and unexceptional. We find in Latin literature a familiarity with the implements of torture and an understanding about their use in the humiliation of slaves, who were often punished in the entrance halls of houses with the doors open to the street.[10] The point of the punishment was not just the infliction of pain – which could be stepped from a simple whip to the rack, or branding and burning of the body – but also the total humiliation of the victim.[11]

As we saw with the infamous case of Vedius Pollio, death was the ultimate humiliating punishment; and few punishments came better tailored for that task than crucifixion, a uniquely Roman phenomenon.[12] A master could have almost any slave crucified, and the punishment was so common that the city of Puteoli contracted out this service that resulted in the execution and torture of male and female slaves.[13] We should not see this city as exceptional, even if the survival of this inscription is unusual. Within the cities of Italy, there would be contractors who would crucify a slave for a small fee.[14] The contractor provided the executioner, the person to carry the cross, floggers and whips, if specified by their client, as well as all the equipment including the cross, nails and pitch. Crucifixion provides us with a good example of how the Roman relationship with violence was different to ours and to that of the modern police states of the world: for this ancient civilization, torture and maiming were on display in the homes of the slave owners and in the public places of the city. Violence towards slaves was so commonly seen that it is perhaps not surprising that children grew up to become like their parents – wielders of the whip or employers of professional torturers.

Not everyone accepted this system of violence. Seneca (Letters: 47) advocated, at least in philosophical terms, that the slave was a human being and should be treated with greater respect as a fellow member of the human race. In advocating this position, however, Seneca provides us with a very full account of just how widespread this abuse of slaves was by others in the city: they were treated like beasts of burden, silently serving their master at dinner, some were dressed up like women and others sexually abused by their master. He concludes with the saying 'as many enemies as you have slaves' – a saying that was fuelled by the murder of the Prefect of the City of Rome, Pedanius Secundus, in

61 CE. No culprit was discovered, so the law was enacted that the slaves within the household should be exterminated.[15] The speeches presented by Tacitus within his history of the event reveal a Roman ideal of security derived from the tenseness or insecurity of their slaves, who typically walked on eggshells, expected punishment, and protected the master from other slaves within the household. In the case of the city prefect, his house contained 400 slaves, and the retribution launched on them was relentless, regardless of age, sex or innocence. The protests of the crowds in the streets were ignored by the senate, and the emperor lined the streets surrounding Pedanius' house with soldiers as the slaves were led to the place where they were all burned alive.[16] Tacitus makes it clear that the law required that there should be no pity for the slaves and the law was enforced.[17]

It may be argued, however, that the key to the whole system of violence was not pleasure, but fear. Roman children could be affectionate towards infants born to their parents' slaves, but the connection was not one that was maintained in adulthood; indeed, slaves were objectified as a different category of humans.[18] Were the Romans so attuned to the experience of violence towards slaves that they feared that they themselves could be humiliated and brutalized should fortune turn the tables and the tormented – so familiar with the techniques of creating pain – become the torturers? Seneca, like other authors, expresses a fear of violence and humiliation that was one of the features that defined a person as a slave.[19] Perhaps what we see in these fears is a glimpse into the anxieties developed in childhood from witnessing and hearing the violent attacks and humiliation of slaves within the household.[20] There were also those citizens who had directly experienced slavery – freed slaves like Vedius Pollio – who could not only gain considerable wealth, but also positions in the state as advisers to the emperor. Claudius had a reputation not only for the merciless destruction of the aristocracy, but also for being controlled by his freed slaves. These ex-slaves influenced his decisions, became rich and denied Rome's aristocracy access to their emperor. They also gained a reputation as the most ruthless owners of slaves.

For the Romans, terrified by the possibility that they themselves might be subjected to the very instruments of torture which they utilized to crush their own slaves, the presence of freedmen holding positions of power in the court may have heightened their fear. Seneca (*Letters*: 14.6) might guide us here. He highlights how fear could drive a man to withdraw from public life: 'picture to yourself . . . the prison, the cross, the rack, the hook and the stake which they drive straight through a man until it protrudes from his throat.' Indeed, the historians of the first century well knew how to represent scenes of violence and understood the possibility of their fortunes changing, so that their world of pleasure could be transformed into one in which they were tortured and humiliated. The Roman belief that the goddess Fortuna might raise you up only to then cast you down was reinforced by their own experience, and it was a factor written into the accounts of their recent past, which continued to shape their lives in the present. One of the temples of Fortuna was known as the Temple of Sejanus, following the goddess's whim to raise a Roman knight, Sejanus, up to become not just the prefect of the Praetorian Guard, but in effect the partner in the aged emperor Tiberius' labours – and then to dash him down.[21] At the height of his power, he was able to crush the emperor's son Drusus, who had struck him in the face in anger.[22] Sejanus' humiliation of his imperial opponent began with an affair with his wife, Livilla, and may have even ended with causing Drusus' death either by poison or natural causes – the matter was subject to speculation.[23] Sejanus was seen in antiquity to be the person responsible for the destruction of other members of the imperial family – leaving the way for Caligula to inherit the throne.[24] The details were made public to aghast senators, who sat spellbound as they were read the account of the death of the grandson of the emperor in a dungeon within the palace enduring blows of a whip.[25] Sejanus fell from power and was duly crushed: dragged away with head bared for all to see to prison, then executed and his body thrown onto the Gemonian steps, where the people abused his corpse, finally throwing the mangled body into the river Tiber. Later, his children would suffer the same fate and the days of their deaths were recalled in the calendars of the towns of Italy as a reminder of the dangers of life under the emperors and the fickleness of the goddess Fortuna.[26] It was not just Sejanus and the imperial family who suffered, the entire aristocracy was affected by the struggle in the court and retribution was wrought on his supporters and those who had acquiesced for years after his fall.[27]

While some violence in the Roman world can be seen to be motivated by fear, it does not follow that the ancients meted out indiscriminate punishments to all. In fact, many Romans were quite restrained in the disciplining of their own children – certainly compared with the way they treated slaves.[28] Although they used a whip to punish the child, it was used in a manner that did not humiliate

The riot of 59 CE commemorated in a fresco from Pompeii.

them. Moreover, many genuinely believed that the whip was a necessary item for the discipline of the child or young adult, because, like animals, the young mind had not developed its sense of reasoning.[29] The difference in the forms of discipline for a slave and for a wife or child is made clear with reference to the most esteemed figure from Rome's past – Cato the Elder. He beat his slaves mercilessly, but did not beat his wife or children.[30] The good father might have also used the whip on his son occasionally, but it was a vicious father who used it all the time.[31] Whether the punishment of children was restrained or not, it was certainly brutal against slaves, and it's clear that male Roman teenagers grew up with a passion for violence that would surprise even today's proudest holders of ASBOs. These young Roman citizens had a tendency or potential to attack others. As we have seen elsewhere in this book, the emperor Nero came to represent all such forms of excess and was seen by writers in the next generation as the moral majority's hate figure. At night, the young emperor, 17 on accession, led groups of young men through the city and attacked men and women.[32] He stripped, beat, wounded and murdered, he robbed and burgled, he sexually assaulted both married women and young males. But Nero is by no means an isolated example of the violence exerted during the night by gangs of young men. The young emperor was pursuing night-time activities almost expected of the younger aristocracy within the quarters of the city associated with the taverns and brothels of the poor. Our ancient writers paint a picture of youthful violence fuelled by drink within an environment of the dark city of the night, into which the respectable matrons, young men and older senators strayed at their peril.

As such, there is no way to explain Nero's violent behaviour with reference to social exclusion; he was emperor, but as a young emperor he needed to prove that he had power over others and chose to express this in the way that other young aristocrats did: proving their manhood through acts of meaningless destruction.[33] Such young men clearly took pleasure in delivering violence, and enjoyed the power that it exerted over the subdued victim. They also served to reinforce the fears of Roman society – that they, too, could be injured and humiliated at any point.

WATCHING VIOLENCE

Moreover, it can be seen that these young aristocrats never really lost their passion for violence as they grew up. The first century CE was the time when the greatest number of amphitheatres were built, and these buildings have become the very symbol of Roman identity. They were a place where individuals could express their shared values of punishment and enjoyment of the spectacles of delivering such punishment.[34] At the amphitheatre, the state inflicted pain and humiliation on criminals, ultimately resulting in the death of the condemned.[35] In 80 CE, when the Colosseum or Flavian Amphitheatre was dedicated, Martial wrote a book of poems that described some of the scenes placed before the eyes of the 50,000 spectators.[36] A few examples from his work are enough to reveal the dynamics of violence in the Colosseum. The arena revealed heroes and villains before the attentive audience. Carpophorus, the hunter of beasts, killed 20 bulls and also a bear from the northern extremes of the empire and a lion from its southern borders. He was hailed as a modern-day Hercules.[37] The villains, on the other hand, were publicly punished and part of the enjoyment for the spectators was their humiliation and torment. Laureolus was not only crucified but also exposed to an enraged Caledonian bear. Martial presents us with an image of the man's destruction – a mangled pile of gore that no longer resembled a human body but was still alive – a punishment the man was seen to have deserved.[38] The punishments also brought to life the violence of mythology: a female criminal was decked out as the Cretan queen Pasiphae and mated with a bull.[39] Martial comments, 'believe: we have seen it' (*On Spectacles*: 5). Another criminal played Daedalus; when he lost his wings, he fell to be mangled and maimed by a boar.[40] The understanding of these scenes of violence depended on a knowledge of mythology, which had been a realm for the imagination of violent acts by gods and men alike. Now, the emperor provided the re-enactment of mythology with the outcome that the criminal was to die and be seen to suffer punishment for his crimes.

The emperor also provided the spectacle of exotic animals goaded into a violent display: the enraged rhinoceros, tormented by its human handlers, attacking a bear and a variety of other animals before ultimately impaling itself on some carefully located stakes, thus securing its own doom.[41] The emperor presided over and controlled the violence of this beast and others.[42] These animals were still novelties and they were seen to demonstrate the instinct of anger to all the spectators in the crowd.[43] The exotic wildlife eventually upstaged the bulls of Italy, and became an integral part of the show. Elephants had been displayed at the games for more than 100 years but were still viewed as a fearful sight.[44] Pliny the Elder's discussion of animals in Book 8 of his *Natural History* is full of mentions of the first appearance of this or that animal at the games in Rome, and all endured a violent end. There was sometimes a serious message in the destruction of animals – many were seen to personify Rome's enemies past and present: elephants, for example, represented the defeat of Carthage, a strong and worthy enemy, and the bears anticipated the Flavian victories in Scotland.[45] But it's undeniable that the violent deaths of the animals were scenes to be enjoyed by the spectators. Children may have learnt the pleasure at home in keeping cocks, or in the cockfighting arenas, such as that recently found at Pompeii.[46] The cockerels' feet were fitted with sharpened spurs for the maiming of their opponents and the drawing of blood. Today, we often see violence against pets as the first stage towards a pattern of family violence in adulthood.[47] However, the Romans' relationship with animals was different to our own. They kept pets and displayed a sentimentality towards animals, but at the same time enjoyed the spectacle of their death and destruction. This has led Mary Beagon to suggest that a concept of cruelty or kindness to animals did not develop in Rome.[48] Perhaps, it is unnecessary to examine children's cruelty to animals, since they were already so aware of their parents' violence and cruelty towards the slaves of their households.

Exotic animals may have been key to the games, but it was the fights between the gladiators that were the ultimate spectacle. Like modern-day boxers, these ancient heroes showed a level of courage that was uncommon and developed body strength and size that was impressive. Their ability to fight was also impeded by a peculiar set of arms and armour. For example, the *retiarius* was armed with a net, a trident and a short sword, and fought the *secutor* sporting a large rectangular shield, a short sword and a helmet with small eye-holes. The *secutor* had limited vision from his helmet and restricted mobility compared to the *retiarius* with his net. Yet, the *retiarius'* trident was not a particularly effective weapon and easily parried away – it was the net that was the real danger and if ensnared, the *secutor*'s ability to attack his opponent was further hindered. Another pairing of gladiators was the fight between the Thracian, armed with a small square shield and sword, high greaves and no body armour, and a similarly armed *murmillo* with his distinctive visor helmet with an angular crest: an evenly matched contest. The result was an interesting and bloody spectacle of skill – and an undeniably popular one. The opening of the Colosseum in 80 CE featured 3,000 men fighting in a single day.[49] From these mass contests emerged the heroes of the arena, and their existence depended on a love of the spectacle of warfare – a feature celebrated in the triumphs of the emperors over Rome's distant enemies in Egypt, Germany, Britain, parts of North Africa, Judaea and the Parthians.

The triumph over a defeated enemy was a moment for rejoicing and was the rite that ended the celebration of the enemy's defeat. The repression of the Jewish Revolt had culminated in the sack of Jerusalem in 70 CE, and was to supply the Romans with huge numbers of victims for the arena. Vespasian's son Titus celebrated his brother Domitian's birthday in October 70 CE with splendour that included the destruction of 2,500 Jewish captives by wild beasts, as gladiators fighting each other, or by being burned alive, and more were to die in celebration of his father's birthday in November.[50] These were just a prelude to the celebration of Vespasian's and Titus' victory over the Jews – renowned as the greatest of the 320 triumphs Rome had ever seen.[51] Vespasian and Titus dressed in the garb of the god Jupiter – they led the senators of Rome, followed by their soldiers, in a procession that included booty and richly dressed captives. What was most striking for the Jewish historian, Josephus, were the stages that represented moments from the Jewish War: a prosperous country destroyed, the enemy slaughtered, the enemy in flight, the capture of cities – including siege engines destroying walls, an area deluged in blood, Jews in gestures of supplication, temples on fire, houses pulled down, rivers flowing not with water but with flames.[52] These were scenes set up to represent the might of Rome, but there was also Simon ben Giora, an architect of the revolt: he was dragged by a halter through the streets of Rome and scourged all the way along the route, then led away to be executed in the Mamertine prison. His destruction was proudly announced to applause and was followed by sacrifices and his fate provides a contrast to the triumphing duo Vespasian and Titus, the bringers of good fortune and a new dynasty for Rome.[53] There were public banquets for the people, who not only celebrated the destruction of the Jews and the capture of Jerusalem, but also celebrated the ending of all wars, including the civil strife that had produced four emperors in a single year, 69 CE. The extermination of the Jewish captives was to continue and may have been a feature of the opening of the Colosseum in 80 CE; their presence in Rome may have provided the labour for the Colosseum's rapid construction – the place where many Romans viewed with glee the destruction and humiliation of their enemies.

However, there is much to suggest that the Romans were not only fascinated by fighting men in the arena, but also viewed these figures as the new heroes of the age. The images of gladiators can be found in numerous media in Pompeii: as reliefs on tombs, scratched graffiti, lamps, statuettes, in household shrines and as frescoes in houses.[54] We also find reference to sophisticated, lifelike paintings of gladiators from specific shows appearing on public buildings.[55] They were attractive figures to both men and women; graffiti from Pompeii refer to their sexual prowess as netters of girls.[56] Even Seneca could admire the gladiator's skill.[57] Underlying this fascination with the man who faced death and overcame his enemy was the destruction of his adversary – a scene that was enacted in front of 50,000 spectators expecting a good show from both fighters. This was the scene that all wanted to view and no pity was expressed for the victims.[58] The show was there to be enjoyed.

VIOLENCE AND PLEASURE

So what do we read from the violence that pervaded Roman society from the household to the arena and into the streets at night? Underlying all the forms of violence found in Rome was a need to humiliate the enemy (slave, criminal or adversary) and at the same time a fear that one's enemy might himself do the same to you. These concepts seem at first alien to us in the twenty-first century, but perhaps they are actually rather familiar.[59] The attacks on the United States that became known simply as 9/11 were an attempt to humiliate an adversary.[60] The United States responded with an attempt to dismantle or humiliate Al-Qaeda: bombing its bases, and imprisoning persons believed to be enemies in Guantánamo Bay in Cuba. The images of the humiliation of the enemy were seen by all and exemplified by a man in orange attached to a handcart wheeled by two US soldiers. The image of punishment, rather than that of justice in a court of law, has much in common with antiquity's focus.[61] We have also seen the humiliation of the enemy: the abuse of Iraqi prisoners in Abu Graib prison, a captured Saddam Hussein undergoing a medical examination, and finally his execution filmed – an image of greater symbolic capital than those of his appearances in the courtroom. All are examples of the human desire to destroy and humiliate an enemy. At the same time, these actions are fuelled by a fear of an almost invisible enemy (compare Roman notions of the invisible slave). The Iraq war was justified by a fear of 'weapons of mass destruction' and the possibility of their use by terrorists operating in the West. The bomb attacks in Madrid and London may have proved the potency of this fear, as does the daily carnage in Iraq and Afghanistan – even if no weapons of mass destruction have been located, the fear continues to be enhanced and reinforced within the media. The motivations of all parties in this global conflict would have been familiar to those living in Rome: to grind down the proud – Rome's famous motive to justify world conquest, which on the domestic front was expressed by the humiliation of slaves (the enemy within) and viewed in the carnage at the opening of the Colosseum.

But is there pleasure in the violence? The evidence surviving from Rome and in the media today suggests that yes, there is a satisfaction gained from total humiliation inflicted upon one's enemy.[62] There is pleasure in the knowledge of retribution taken for a crime committed, which could also pre-empt an expected

attack in the future. It seems to be part of the human psyche and was the
substance of Seneca's long treatise *On Anger*: the ugly trait he deemed to be the
cause of bloodshed, poisonings, wars, the downfall of cities and the destruction
of whole nations (1.2.1–2) – in other words the very story of Rome's historical
past. Rome's republic had disappeared following the murder of Julius Caesar,
accompanied by an orgy of violence in which terror and the destruction of the
enemies of Octavian, Anthony and Lepidus was a mission. It was a scenario that
haunted the imaginations of historians for the next two centuries and was made
real in the brief period of civil war during 69 CE.[63] The fear of civil war made the
idea of autocracy acceptable; but autocracy itself was seen as another cause of
violence.[64] Seneca sets out the problem: kings see injuries to themselves where
none exist, and need to inflict injuries on others and seize on opportunities to
do harm on the basis of non-existent injuries to themselves.[65] It is a function
of autocracy summed up by the neat saying of Domitian: no one believes there
are plots against the emperor until the emperor is dead.[66] The emperor, like the
slave owner, could only subsist through a feeling of security derived from his
own ability to inflict harm on his subjects, because they were always plotting
against him; a point perhaps reinforced by the servility of the senate, which
caused the emperor Tiberius to leave the chamber and quote the Greek motto:
'O men fit to be slaves', meaning they were duplicitous and deserving of any act
of violence meted out to them. [67]

    In fact, many believe that the phenomenon of imperial rule did exactly
reproduce the situation of an owner and his slaves. Tacitus' history of the period
begins with accusations in the senate of treason and the mutual destruction of
the aristocrats, overseen by an emperor Tiberius, who refuses to intervene in the
process and lets the laws be enforced.[68] History becomes a listing of enforced
suicides and murders, all documented in the manner of the media today, displaying the carnage before our eyes. We have already seen that teenage Roman men
were particularly capable of inflicting physical violence on others, and it should
come as no surprise that the emperors who most exerted their power through
terror were those who were young: Caligula, Nero and Domitian. Seneca was a
witness to the anger of Caligula.[69] That emperor personally tortured senators
with the whip, the rack and fire as though they were slaves. These tortures were
everyday occurences; what so outraged Seneca is that the punishments meted
out to senators were those designed for the masses and should not have been

applied to the aristocracy, and, of course, that the emperor took an active part in their destruction and pain.[70] But even the emperor himself was not immune to the Roman culture of humiliating and destroying enemies. Nero, on learning that he had been condemned as a criminal by the senate, took his life rather than be dragged naked through the streets of Rome, then beaten to death with rods, and his body hurled from the Tarpeian Rock.[71] However, the emperor Vitellius met his fate in 69 CE:

> They bound his arms behind his back, put a noose around his neck, and dragged him with torn clothes and half-naked to the Forum. All along the Sacred Way he was greeted with mockery and abuse, his head held back by his hair, as is common with criminals, and the point of a sword placed under his chin, so that he could not look down but must let his face be seen. Some pelted him with dung and ordure, others called him an incendiary and glutton, and some of the mob even taunted him with his bodily defects . . . At last on the Gemonian Stairs he was tortured for a long time and then killed and dragged off with a hook to the Tiber. (Suetonius, *Life of Vitellius*: 18)

The passage is chilling but makes clear that the Romans did derive pleasure from such a spectacle. Punishment needed to be seen that day, and Vitellius was not the only victim; his son and brother were also sibjected to this extreme form of killing. 'Strike so that he may feel that he is dying', a motto of Caligula, was shared by those who watched the killing of criminals and the punishment of slaves.[72] This was a form of pleasure that we find hard to understand today, and one that all would condemn – yet we are aware from examples across the world that the Romans were not unique and that humans enjoy and are fascinated by the infliction of pain, suffering and humiliation on others.

11

Collectors and Collections

Please remember that Rembrandt will always be Dutch and while the picture is in America, it is acting as a cultural ambassador of your country, its history and its heritage.

J. Paul Getty, 1976: 273

The shift in my thinking was natural. It is a phenomenon familiar to many private collectors. After acquiring a large number of examples of fine art, one develops conscience pangs about keeping them to oneself.

J. Paul Getty, 1976: 279

THE PLEASURE OF COLLECTING

When we think of the world's great collectors, John Paul Getty's name immediately springs to mind. He set the standard for modern wealthy benefactors of the arts, devoting much of his fortune to the vast collection of works now housed for public enjoyment in the Getty Villa and Getty Research Centre. We tend to view Getty as an innovator in the collecting world – yet there are remarkable similarities between this twentieth-century American and the rich Romans of the first century CE, whose art works were displayed to demonstrate their munificence, and whose collections were subject to many of the same sudden fluctuations in taste and market forces as Getty's.

John Paul Getty's collection, for example, came about not only because of his wealth, but also thanks to the flood of objects coming onto the art market during the great depression following the stock market crash of 1929.[1] For Romans in the first century CE, the crisis of civil war (44–31 BCE and 69 CE) would have created a similar situation to that of 1929 and the tensions that affected the art market in the lead up to the Second World War.[2] So, like

The Getty Villa at Malibu.

Getty, the Romans learned to value objects beyond that of a simple aesthetic appreciation – they collected them because they could. Another similarity to the Getty story is his bequest of his entire collection to his museum in Malibu – a move that immediately had a negative effect on the art market, making items for sale rarer and causing prices to rise. In antiquity, it was the super-rich Roman emperors who became the world's first super-patrons. Their ability to gather pieces to display to their subjects created examples of the first public museums, and their domination of the art world through their wealth and position slanted the market and caused prices to become inflated.[3]

But collecting was not just the preserve of the emperors of the first century CE and their predecessors, the rulers of Hellenistic kingdoms: Alexander the Great or Attalus of Pergamum. Rome was the first society in history to have its own art market, with the prices paid for items remembered and set down for posterity.[4] There was pleasure in ownership of beautiful and expensive objectives and, as John Paul Getty observed, the desire to own such pieces could become a form of addiction similar to that suffered by an alcoholic or a drug user.[5] Rome was a place that was filled with statues and other collectables on display or for sale.[6] It was not simply the oldest items that were collectable, the new were too, and it was an economic demand that was fully supplied by Rome's numerous markets and trade connections, which stretched from the city, across the Mediterranean and into Asia.[7]

As today, when an item of clothing once worn by Princess Diana commands an enormous price, the Romans associated objects with their former owners and paid accordingly. One of the century's hottest collectables were myrrhine cups and bowls, and a single item could cost anything from 300,000 to 1 million *sesterces*. What made them even more valuable were teeth marks of a former owner, for example a famous ex-consul. But even a broken vessel was worthy of display and the condemned often took pleasure in destroying them to prevent their confiscation and ownership by others.

COLLECTING OBJECTS

At the beginning of first century CE, large private collections of statues were also the norm among the rich. In fact, they became so widespread that there was a swelling of opinion that all sculpture should be organized for public display, rather than being held for private individuals to enjoy at their leisure.[8] Much of the art in private hands had been looted from Sicily, Greece and Asia Minor during the late third and second centuries BCE, and Pliny the Elder, writing in the first century CE, saw a connection between the physical presence of these luxurious items and a continuing Roman moral crisis.[9] The private collection became subject to condemnation as an example of a person's engagement with luxurious living – but if displayed to the public, the very same art works were turned into a symbol of that person's generosity or *liberalitas*.[10]

Thus the first century CE saw the enrichment of Roman culture through the ability of all citizens to view such fine pieces. Like modern-day art-lovers, it's clear that the Romans derived not only enjoyment from the aesthetics of the statues and other curiosities, but also took pleasure in learning about the items' age, the artist who had made them and the history of previous ownership (particularly if attributed to a great figure such as Hannibal or an Alexander the

Great).[11] The Romans also took great pleasure in the simple fact of collecting.[12] Some items like statues, as well, produced a sense of moral history. Pliny the Elder can trace the origins of statuary as a phenomenon back to 510 BCE and the founding of the state, but observes these were 'good' Roman statues that were dressed in a toga. It was only later that the draped nude statuary was introduced from Greece, to which the Romans added a breastplate.[13]

Collections and exhibitions were not just limited to sculptures, of course. Indeed, a smorgasbord of curiosities unimaginable in modern times was proudly put on display. The emperor Augustus had a personal collection of the remains of sea monsters, bones of the Giants and antique weapons from the age of the Greek and Trojan heroes.[14] The Giants were said to have been banished from the earth by Hercules and were believed to live beneath volcanoes – hence on the eruption of Vesuvius in 79 CE, many initially thought the Giants had returned to the Earth.[15] When a major earthquake in the reign of Tiberius not only destroyed cities in modern Turkey, but also affected cities in Sicily and the very southern tip of Italy, it was claimed that the bodies of Giants had been found.[16] A tooth was duly despatched to Rome to be presented to Tiberius and the delegates asked him if he wished to view the whole body. Tiberius, not wanting to disturb the dead, asked a geometry expert to estimate the size of the body and the face of the Giant; an image was created and rushed to the emperor, who decreed it was enough to see this, and returned the tooth to the resting place of the 'Giant'.[17] The story was subject to disbelief, even in antiquity – but for many the display of Giants' bones became even more popular. It added to the Romans' belief that nature in the past had reared far larger creatures – including humans.[18]

Another curiosity put on display in the reign of Claudius included a half-man-half-horse or hippocentaur, which was said to have been discovered by a king of Arabia and was sent to the emperor. The creature died on the journey, but was pickled and put on display in Rome. Eventually, it was consigned to the emperor's storerooms and was viewed by both Pliny the Elder and Phlegon of Tralles, who both regarded it as the genuine article.[19] Other items taking pride of place in Rome over the course of the first century CE included a Phoenix from Egypt, later thought by some writers in antiquity to have been a fake.[20] In the previous century a satyr had been sighted in Brundisium and in the later Empire a satyr preserved in salt was presented to the emperor Constantine, and the body of a Triton with gills below his ears could be viewed in Rome.[21] These items reveal the intersection between an imagined world populated by fabulous monsters, the creatures of mythological times, and the representation of these phenomena by artists in sculpture. All sat alongside each other in collections on public display in Rome for the wonder and incredulity of the citizens.

THE PUBLIC DISPLAY OF COLLECTIONS

Collecting was to reach its zenith in the first century CE. The first purpose-built spaces for the display of art works were completed at the start of the century.[22] In 10 CE, the future emperor Tiberius dedicated his newly rebuilt temple of Concordia in the Roman Forum, begun nearly 20 years earlier with a view to the adequate display of antique sculptures from Greece.[23] Sculpture that was some 300 or even 400 years old was consequently brought to the very centre of Rome and exhibited in a new space that featured a broader arrangement of the central room or *cella* to allow for the inclusion of windows in the façade to bring natural light into the room.[24] To add to the beauty of the exhibition space, the light reflected off the polished coloured marbles of the interior walls, and the sculptural format of the design of the new temple extended to its façade, with the steps flanked by statues of Mercury and Hercules.[25] Meanwhile, on the roof, further figures of deities were positioned to promote the temple as a venue for the display of a particular type of imagery.[26]

Within the temple were works in bronze, mostly of deities, signed by the artist: Latona, Apollo and Diana executed by Euphranor; Jupiter, Minerva and Ceres by Sthennis; Mars and Mercury by Piston; an Apollo by Baton; and Aeslepius and Salus by Neratius.[27] There were also paintings by named Greek artists and some oddities: elephants carved from obsidian and a gem from the ring of Polycrates.[28]

But Tiberius' collection was not the first to be displayed by any means, and it is linked to a pattern of public figures using booty from a military conquest for the purchase of art works to exhibit as a monument to their own glory. The earliest example of such a monument was that of Asinius Pollio in 39 BCE, in the Atrium of Liberty, constructed in a complex that included Rome's first public library, perhaps the completion of a project proposed earlier by Julius Caesar.[29] The collection may have included the colossal sculpture of Dirce being bound to a bull, known today as the Farnese Bull and on display in the Naples Archaeological Museum. Another collection was put on display by Augustus' sister, Octavia, within the new Portico that took her name. The collection was simply known as the works of Octavia and Pliny the Elder picks this one out for mention alongside other exhibits established by members of the imperial family.[30]

PRIVATE COLLECTIONS

Such collections fuelled the Romans' thirst for further artistic treats, and led to the demand for the public display of all such art treasures.[31] This was never to be fulfilled, and it's clear that private collections carried on apace. Vast, private displays of sculpture have been found at a number of villas in Italy, and these provide us with a strong image of the Romans, their pleasures and tastes. For example, the sculpture collection excavated at the Villa of Oplontis situated between Pompeii and Herculaneum was created around the theme of sport, and was clearly designed to enhance the enjoyment of watching young men compete. The statues were arranged around a swimming pool or *natatio* 60 metres in length and 17 metres wide and positioned in a line with a backdrop of plane trees, oleander, lemon trees and laurels.[32] The view this created from the villa was of the pool, bounded by a space that may have been a running track, a line of statues, trees and vegetation. Meanwhile, the statues were not chosen at random but fitted their sporting setting: two herms of Hercules, two identical statues of the goddess Nike, an Ephebe or athlete, a statue of the goddess Artemis, a statuette of Aphrodite undoing her sandal in preparation to bathe, and a statue of Dionysus. The central piece of the *natatio* was a large, slightly less than life-size, sculpture of a satyr attempting to sexually assault or rape a hermaphrodite.[33] Such violent and eroticized sculptural groups were favoured themes for the water features of villas in Campania: the famous 'Pan with the Goat' found in the Villa of the Papyri and now in the Naples Museum would seem to derive from Greek examples of the second century BCE that were frequently copied.[34] The possibility of swimming under this cleverly designed sculpture allowed for new angles to appreciate the artistry and its reflection in the water of the pool.[35] The style of the pieces reflect that of a Greek gymnasium, where naked statuary was commonplace.[36] This style was then transposed to the private spaces of the Roman villa.[37]

A greater variety of tastes is demonstrated by the collection of 80 sculptures in marble and bronze discovered in the Villa of the Papyri at Herculaneum, which had been installed in the property over a period of about 100 years.[38] The range of styles perhaps reflects the different individuals who lived there, and the changes in fashion over the period during which the collection was made.[39] A *natatio* similar to that found at Oplontis, measuring 67 metres by 7 metres, was found here, a size that might suggest another gymnasium. Yet the subject matter on display in the sports area is quite different from Oplontis. This indicates that the selection of sculpture for particular spaces was far from formulaic and was subject to the intervention of the collector, the availability of sculptural types for purchase, and perhaps also fashion.

The very individual pleasures of the owners of the villas are also clearly reflected in the sculpture collections and their settings. This is beautifully demonstrated at the imperial villa at Sperlonga, where in 1957 finds of colossal sculpture groups representing scenes from Odysseus' wanderings were discovered: most notably the Cyclops Polyphemus being blinded by Odysseus, and the sea monster Scylla attacking the crew of the ship (see plate 4 between pages x–x). The latter caused much excitement, since it was signed in Greek by the sculptors who produced the most famous piece of sculpture in antiquity – the Laocoön group. What makes the find more valuable is its situation in a cave on the seashore, in which the emperor Tiberius dined on a journey to Campania in 26 CE.[40] The villa can still be visited and in the early evening at the rear of the Grotto visitors can experience the setting sun reflecting off the water within the cave (see image on page 92). It is an atmospheric setting, which would only have been accentuated by the statuary that is now displayed in the neighbouring museum. These works of art were installed in the early first century and were likely to have been present on Tiberius' famous visit. Further examples of caves and statues of Odysseus and Polyphemus or of Scylla have been found at other imperial villas, and it has been suggested that these later imitations of the original ensemble enjoyed by Tiberius at Sperlonga went on to define an imperial space for dinner, drinking and conversation.[41] So it's clear that the collection of appropriate sculpture was key to the Romans' experience of pleasure, whether they were enjoying physical exercise, the sensation of swimming in a setting surrounded by art works, or the mental gymnastics of the dinner table.[42]

But even the dinner table itself and other furniture were collectable items.[43] Many bronze and marble tables were produced in the first century by craftsmen drawing on a repertoire linked to the culture of Greece, and actual examples survive from Herculaneum.[44] There were two types of table, the *mensa* from which food was eaten and an *abacus* or sideboard on which was displayed the fine silverware of the household.[45] Like so many collectable items, the *abacus* was viewed as a luxury introduced in the second century BCE, but the practice of using it is well attested in the first century CE. It was on the *abacus* that the owner of a house could display his taste. The importance of doing so is clearly seen in the tomb of Gaius Vestorius Priscus built by his mother, Mulvia Prisca, to the north of the Porta Vesuvio at her own expense.[46] The frescoes within the tomb enclosure were designed to portray the young man's life: his sense of duty is represented by a toga-clad Gaius addressing his fellow citizens; there are scenes of gladiatorial combats, images of Gaius in his *tablinum* or public office space in his house, and a drinking party – alongside which is an exquisite fresco of an *abacus* laden with a collection of silver drinking vessels. Similar vessels to these were found hidden in a box beneath the baths in the House of the Menander at Pompeii.[47] The very fact that these vessels were hidden in 79 CE defines them as valuable and collectable – in total it weighed in at almost 24 kilograms, and their value as silver plate was confirmed by writers of the time.[48] Another major collection of silver vessels known from Campania was found in a villa at Boscoreale, but sadly these were sold and distributed in museum and private collections across the world.[49] More recently a similar find was discovered in one of the the dining rooms of the 'inn' at Moregine and examples have been documented across the site of Pompeii.[50] In the hoard from the House of the Menander, there is a mixture of silver vessels for drinking and silver plates off which food could have been eaten. The beautifully decorated silver vessels display scenes from the mythology: Hercules' labours, the marriage of Venus and Mars, rural idylls, chariot racing and depictions of animals. The vessels match in style as a set, but all the drinking vessels are differentiated by the scenes portrayed on them – one guest might drink from a cup featuring Hercules, while another would be supping from a cup depicting scenes from the life of Dionysius. The range of imagery was immense, from those depicting the dynasty founded by Augustus on the pieces found at Boscoreale to the scenes of male–male sex on the Warren Cup.[51] The date of manufacture of these pieces is now thought to run from the first century BCE through to the middle of the first century CE.[52] The vessels were accumulated over time or were purchased as a ready-made collection.

THE ROMAN FASCINATION WITH HUMAN DIFFERENCES

But for the Romans, collectables were not confined to inanimate objects. Humans too who had unusual characteristics were also sold to collectors for the pleasure of their owners. The story of the auctioneer, who at the sale of a costly chandelier of Corinthian bronze threw in with it a slave called Clessipus, makes the point. The collector of ancient bronze was also in the market for a slave, whom Pliny the Elder describes as hunchbacked and ugly.[53] The slave was then displayed by his new mistress naked at a dinner party so all the guests might enjoy viewing his body that was so different. (Clessipus, however, had the last laugh: on the death of his mistress, he inherited her fortune.) The ownership of slaves with an abnormality was something of a fashion in the first century CE. Julia, the granddaughter of Augustus, freed her slave who was recorded as the shortest woman alive.[54] The wife of the moralist Seneca owned an expensive and misshapen dwarf by the name of Harpaste.[55] There exists in Latin literature a full range of human oddities that might rival *Ripley's Believe it or Not!*, Barnum's group of physically different humans who toured Britain in the nineteenth century, or the sideshows that have had a recent revival in the United States.[56] These human oddities commanded a higher price than other slaves at Rome with a specific market being devoted to their sale.[57] What is clear is that the Romans paid high prices for these slaves, and thus we have to conclude that they enjoyed a fascination for quirks of nature.[58] When you think that today, 1 in 33 births results in a congenital disorder, humans born with such conditions in ancient times could not have been particularly rare. What made these people so valuable was the very fact of their survival beyond birth and infancy.[59] Even so, a Roman with money could buy a person who was very short, or who was culturally defined as simply being very ugly, and put them on display in much the same way as they did their bronze statues.[60]

In his role as the super-collector, the Roman emperor in particular was always in the market for the purchase of the playthings of nature, and the courts of the bad emperors were filled with petulant dwarfs, precocious boys with very small heads, and in the case of Nero a whole variety of 'monsters'.[61] Such people were in the unusual position of being recognizably different, yet had access to the most powerful man in the state.[62] They had in the past been viewed as prodigies of the gods' displeasure, but were aligned to the divine – the representation of the two-faced god Janus, for example, bears a remarkable similarity to that of adult conjoined twins.[63] What we see by the first century CE is a shift in their significance from signs of the displeasure of the gods to valuable assets to be collected and displayed.[64] Like other collections, the emperor displayed the human curiosities in his possession to his people. At the games, Augustus put on display a member of the elite, Lycius, who was 2 and weighed just 17 pounds, yet was famous for his very loud voice.[65] There is also considerable evidence for dwarf athletes and dwarf dancers from antiquity, as can be seen from the numerous small terracotta figures that have been found of dwarfs dancing, playing music or being involved in combat sports from boxing to gladiatorial fights.[66] Not only was the body of the tallest man put on display in the public Gardens of Sallust, but also those of two Roman knights who grew to the stature of 3 Roman feet (slightly smaller than our modern foot).[67] In fact, any strange birth resulted in the infant being sent to the emperor. Phlegon of Tralles (*Book of Marvels*: 20, 23) records in the reign of Nero: a four-headed, eight-armed and eight-legged boy being brought to the palace for his inspection in 61 CE; another arrived in 65 CE with a head in the shape of that of the god Anubis. Later ancient writers, of course, were to put a different slant on these oddities. For them, such collectables were simply symbols of the real human monsters – the emperors themselves.

12

Pleasure Transforms Roman Culture

It was an altered world and of the old unspoilt Roman character not a trace lingered. Equality was an outmoded concept, and all eyes looked to the orders of the emperor.

Tacitus, Annals of Imperial Rome: 1.4

While the glories and disasters of the Roman Republic have been chronicled by famous writers, and intellects of distinction have chronicled the Augustan age, until the rising tide of sycophancy deterred them, the histories of Tiberius and Caligula, of Claudius and Nero, were falsified through cowardice while they flourished, and, when they fell, composed under the influence of still rankling hatreds.

Tacitus, Annals of Imperial Rome: 1.1

The Senate was overjoyed . . . The delight of the knights fell little short of the Senate's. Respectable citizens who were attached to the great families, clients or freedmen who had seen their patrons condemned and exiled, now revived their hopes. The plebs sordida, who had grown familiar with the pleasures of the theatre and the circus, the most degraded slaves, and men who had squandered their property and lived on Nero's discreditable bounty, all were miserable and greedy for news.

Tacitus, Histories: 1.4

The result was that those who had recently rejected the Roman tongue now conceived a desire for eloquence. Thus, even our style of dress came into favour and the toga was everywhere to be seen. Gradually, too, the Britons were led astray with the allurements of evil ways: colonnades and warm baths and elegant banquets.

Tacitus, Agricola: 21

In the study of Roman history, much is made of the creation of the monarchy that we know today as the Roman Empire. The process was under way by

50 BCE, but was not completed until 27 BCE with further consolidation during the long reign of Rome's first emperor, Augustus. This was a major change, not just in constitutional history, but in the very nature of Roman society.[1] It can be substantiated with reference to law, politics, literature, architecture, sculpture and even mythology.[2] What gets lost in the history of Rome over the course of the first century CE is a sense of the place of pleasure.[3] Pleasure is a fleeting sensation, seen by Seneca to pass quickly into the oblivion of memory. It is something that is difficult to recall or to represent in language, regardless of whether the pleasure be one that engages with sight, taste, touch, smell or even pain.[4] In Republican Rome, perhaps the ultimate symbol of hedonism was the pirates who ravaged the Mediterranean: elaborately dressed, *cithara*-playing, heavy-drinking and with a ruthless love of luxury.[5] By the first century CE, with the pirates eradicated by the emperors, the imperial ruler himself had become the symbol of unrestrained pleasure. Emperors and pirates have much in common within the Roman mindset – neither have any real restraints placed upon them; indeed, the pirates' exercise of power would have been familiar to many living under Nero. The only means to articulate resistance to the emperor was by suicide – a self-presented death that avoided the humiliation of a trial for treason and retained a person's material wealth for their children's enjoyment.[6] Captives of pirates and citizens of the emperor's Rome were both subject to the pleasure of the person who held power over them. Like later folk heroes, a Nero could distribute largesse to the poor, while ignoring or even robbing the rich.[7] Even Trajan, an emperor seen as almost a reverse of Nero, is described by Pliny as so powerful that he was the object of unrestrained female sexual desire.[8] The very presence of an emperor altered the lives of not just the aristocracy, but also the rest of the people of Rome, right down to the lowest of the low – even they could partake in the new imperial world of pleasure.

THE POWER AND THE GLORY

There is a seldom-noticed aside in Juvenal's famous denunciation of the city of Rome in *Satire* 3 on the availability of pleasure outside its walls: 'all the towns (*oppida*, i.e. not Rome) now stage gladiatorial shows (*munera*).' Over half of all the examples of theatres and amphitheatres from Italy were built in the first

1. Fresco of a maritime villa from Stabiae, Italy.
Museo Archeologico Nazionale, Naples. Erich Lessing/Art Resource NY.

2. Fresco of sex scene from Pompeii.
Museo Archeologico Nazionale, Naples. Erich Lessing/Art Resource NY.

3. Dining scene from the House of the Chaste Lovers in Pompeii.
Author's photograph.

4. The blinding of the Cyclops by Odysseus. *Author's photograph.*

5. The Getty Villa at Malibu with carefully positioned copies of the six peploi from the Villa of the Papyri. *Author's photograph.*

6. The Laocoon group. Roman copy perhaps after Agesander, Athenodorus, and Polydorus of Rhodes. *Museo Pio Clementino, Vatican Museums. Timothy McCarthy/Art Resource NY.*

The amphitheatre at Alba Fucens.

century CE.[9] We see a proliferation of purpose-built venues for the holding of gladiatorial games and the viewing of spectacles on the stage accompanied by aural sensations. The benefactors for these events were the elite, who had access to new resources of wealth from beyond the agricultural hinterlands of their own towns. For example, the amphitheatre at Alba Fucens was constructed by the prefect of the praetorian guard, Q. Naevius Cordus Sutorius Macro.[10] Important and powerful in Rome, he may have appeared locally to display the qualities found in an emperor. He could provide pleasure for others, had the finances to build facilities that replicated the experience of pleasure in the capital, and could be seen to be far wealthier and far more powerful than anyone else locally. Men such as Macro had experience of the emperor's desires and had seen how the ruler gave pleasure to his people – they watched and copied the great man, hoping to emulate his achievements in the towns of Italy outside Rome (the latter was the emperor's domain). Moreover, the residents in the cities of Italy expected and even demanded that the elite should provide entertainment – the people of the city of Pollentia in northern Italy prevented the burial of a leading veteran with a demand that games be provided as part of his funeral.[11] The peak in amphitheatre and theatre construction across Italy was accompanied by a similar increase in the building of bathing establishments.[12] It is also possible to see an expansion in the construction of market buildings or *macella* in this same period, suggesting that the supply of provisions was regarded as a matter of public interest.[13] What we are seeing in these basic statistics is a pattern of change: the local elite were building far fewer temples and structures for the defence of their city and were instead lavishing their wealth on buildings that created the same material conditions for the delivery of pleasure, copying the actions of the emperors who had recreated Rome as a city of gleaming marble. No longer were these structures confined to Rome and the cities to the south in Latium and Campania; over the course of the first century these monuments would be built in the major towns on the roads leading from Rome right way across the peninsula of Italy.[14] The first century created a new infrastructure for the delivery of pleasure to the inhabitants in many of the towns of Italy.

The pattern of change found in Italy was observed by Tacitus, in the reign of the emperor Nerva (97–8 CE), to be at the heart of Rome's successful conquest of Britain. Under the Flavian emperors, Tacitus' father-in-law, Julius Agricola, had encouraged the Britons to build temples, forums and Roman-style houses. However, there soon followed facilities for bathing, colonnades (perhaps luxury villas) and banquets – features that were easily identified with the culture of pleasure created by Rome.[15] Interestingly, amphitheatres and theatres and their attendant pantomimes are not mentioned – the former only appear in Britain in the second century and the latter made little impact on these new towns of the provincials in Britain – the Britons were not ready for these novel art forms. What Tacitus suggests lies at the very heart of town foundation was a desire to engage with the culture of Roman pleasure.[16] The kings of Iron-Age Britain (like other client kings of Rome) had adopted a repertoire of Augustan imagery on their coinage, and had access to and experience of Roman commodities, including (importantly) wine.[17] Hence, it should come as little surprise that we can identify the adoption of features of the culture of pleasure as part of a Roman package that Britons understood as 'civilization'.[18] In short, it was pleasure that conquered barbarians as much as it was the actions of the legions commanded by their governor. The rebel Boudicca, in contrast, was provided with a speech by the Greek historian, Cassius Dio, that rejected the whole package: bathing in warm water, eating delicacies, drinking unmixed wine, the use of perfumes, sleeping on soft beds (with boys rather than women), and being enslaved to their emperor – Nero the lyre player.[19] Fittingly, Boudicca would destroy three Roman towns: London, Colchester and St Albans – the very places that Tacitus saw as providing the Britons with a gateway to the Roman way of life.[20]

PLEASURE AND CHANGE

Tacitus portrayed a picture of a new golden age dawning under the emperor Nerva at the end of the century – an age that would combine monarchy and concepts of freedom that were previously incompatible.[21] But this is clearly rhetoric; no doubt many said before that Caligula's, Nero's and even Domitian's accessions were all new ages, and much would be elaborated by Pliny in his *Panegyric* praising the emperor Trajan.[22] At stake for the speakers of these words about their present age was an idea that the past was corrupt and the present would be better under the current ruler. It is a theme that politicians in Western democracies embrace at elections – recently Barack Obama and Tony Blair – a rhetoric followed by disillusionment as change is not delivered and the locations of power continue as before. Fascinatingly, in the political realm human beings buy into the rhetoric of difference between past, present and future – whether living in a twenty-first-century democracy or under Rome's emperors. Looked at objectively, Nero's 'unacceptable' public promotion of Greek culture in first century CE is not so different from Hadrian's 'acceptable' public promotion of Greek culture in the second century CE. The parallel between the 'bad' Nero and the 'good' Hadrian can be taken further; both Nero and Hadrian had male lovers. Both Hadrian's love for Antinous and Nero's desire for Sporus were displayed for all to see and it seems clear that Antinous became a popular figure, whereas Sporus did not.[23] What we might be seeing here though is a shift in Roman culture; writers of the age of Nerva and Trajan could condemn Nero (after all, they knew he was bad) for the very engagement with pleasure that might have appealed to a future emperor and his people. This is the obvious danger of rhetoric; it is possible to denounce a pursuit of a past emperor only to discover later that it appeals in private to the current ruler; a situation that requires determining which pleasures were acceptable to the Romans, and which were not is subject to interpretation.[24]

What is clear is that with the Roman emperors came a new way of viewing the pleasure pursuits of an individual. While alive, an imperial leader was to be watched both in the public realm of politics (*negotium*) and in the private or semi-private realm of pleasure (*otium*). This was different from the Republic of the 50s BCE, where there were multiple models of how to live, from Lucullus in his gardens, Crassus accumulating wealth, Pompey seeking recognition in love with his new wife, Caesar fighting the Gauls and committing adultery, through to the more austere characters – Cicero and Cato, who were isolated from the new interest in pleasure. Now, in the first century CE, the emperor was known as a trendsetter, and the pleasures of the emperor would seem to have become those of the aristocracy, and subsequently provided to his people. There is an interesting link between pleasure and power at work here – the more powerful the man was, the greater the range of enjoyments he has access to. This causes all emperors to be associated with stories of excess when viewed from the secure position of knowing that they are dead. Even so, some pleasures continued after death – Poppaea, Nero's wife, was still associated with a type of perfume long after her demise.[25] Each new reign is associated with a quite different set of leisure pursuits and it is logical that the Roman aristocracy, or at least significant sections of it, adjusted their cultural horizons with reference to each accession.[26]

So change truly characterized the landscape of Roman pleasure. By the end of the century, food tasted different and there was a greater variety available; more people drank wine, which was produced in many different places; the baths were full of light rather than shadowy, if not dark; the cities abounded with places to watch spectacles (gladiatorial combats and pantomimes); the pleasure palaces of the rich had become more elaborate, and people even smelled different, with a greater emphasis on perfumes. But how did people react to change? We saw that a woman, who would have been in her 30s during Nero's golden age of pantomime, even into her old age had a group of freed slaves specializing in pantomime living in her house.[27] Her enjoyment of this form of entertainment had not diminished and she continued to fund public performances, even in the reign of Trajan, when Pliny would have us believe that taste had changed. Perhaps what we are seeing here is the long-term effect of the cultural changes brought about by the emperors, and it is notable that other Romans in later life under Trajan were not adverse to a stage performance to accompany their dinner.[28] These are all examples of the old living in the past.[29] It is just such older men who were often willing to condemn the actions of the young – interestingly under the emperor Domitian even the old men were silent, a sign of their oppression.[30] Tacitus looked forward to his old age and the opportunity to write a history of his own times under Nerva and Trajan.[31] Young men by contrast tended to be attracted to new trends; they were expected to indulge in pleasure and embrace the freedom that they gained at the end of their childhood; as such it is not surprising, at least to the ancients, that younger emperors sought such experiences to perhaps even greater excess.[32] The old could compare the present with times past, but, like the past, the old were marginal to the interests of the present. Those living at the end of the century who remembered experiences of pleasure from the first half of the century were a minority – those over the age of 60 probably constituted as few as 7 per cent of the population.[33] However, it was this group of the population who had the leisure to write the philosophical works that ultimately formed the basis for Stoic philosophy and a critique of the Roman culture, particularly of the actions of younger men.[34] The point is that in a context of rapid change over the century, young men at different points in time experienced a quite different range of pursuits, which they adopted, cherished or repudiated in later life.

JUVENAL DEFINES THE CENTURY

To sum up the first century of pleasure, Juvenal's *Satires*, written as the century reached its close, are the perfect guide. The works were written for entertainment, yet still paint a vivid picture of what the writer sees as the excesses of pleasure of the recent past. Women in *Satire* 6 are revealed to conceal their true selves through the use of clothing, jewellery, make-up and perfumes.[35] Vast colonnades, shady groves, tracts of land or palaces near the forum could conceal a bad man.[36] Caetronius, an otherwise unknown individual, is recreated to represent the pleasure derived from building vast villas on the Bay of Gaieta, in the hills near Tivoli (Tibur) and Palestrina (Praeneste) with its walls clad in imported marble from Greece. These had in view the creation of structures to rival the famous sanctuaries of Fortuna at Palestrina and of Hercules at Tivoli.[37] Equally, the gourmand who could identify the origin of an oyster from the very first bite was revealed to be a man who had had experience of Nero's banquets, in which Falernian wine rekindled the flagging partygoers late into the night.[38] And Juvenal does not simply mention the pleasure of eating oysters, but includes their origins: off mount Circeii (on the Bay of Gaieta); from Baiae or even from Richborough (on the Kent coast) – a mixture of locations associated with luxury and exoticism. Importantly, Juvenal reveals pleasure as the means to differentiate the status of people: a client invited to dinner is presented in *Satire* 5 with positively repulsive food (the equivalent of serving guests cat food today) and drink served on poor pottery; while his host lords it over him sipping the finest wine and served the tastiest food on jewel-encrusted dishes. Stage performers and gladiators become the objects of desire in *Satire* 6, revealing a connection between the pleasures found in the theatre and in private performances at home; this culminates in a female fan being transformed into a gladiator.[39] The hiring or purchase of commodities for display is represented as the cause of a fall from riches into poverty, and a similar slippery slope to poverty is revealed in relation to the consumption of food at dinner.[40] Listening to or reading the *Satires* was of course a pleasure, but what Juvenal reveals to his audience is the nature of pleasure in the first century CE: an expensive passing distraction in which all attempted to dabble, but which could in turn place them on the very edge of self-destruction.

PLEASURE – IT'S THE ECONOMY, STUPID

There is a resonance between the Rome of Juvenal and the present: in many ways, our newspapers enjoy the voyeuristic spectacle of seeing a wealthy and famous person on the brink of self-destruction through overindulgence in pleasure or consumption. However, we should resist the idea that the Roman Empire self-destructed through its engagement with pleasure. What we find instead in the first century CE is a sense of how the power of consumption (as much as the use of power) might lead to a person's demise, regardless of whether he was an emperor or a wealthy member of the elite. This causes the reader to see pleasure as dangerous, due to its fleeting sensations and lack of long-term satisfaction (the

Villa of the Quintilii close to the Via Appia.

difference between consuming a *cornetto* and a *panino* in Rome, as discussed in the Introduction). It has to be said, of course, that it was the super-rich whose villas and houses constructed the view of the Roman landscape for others and it was the super-rich who fully engaged with pleasure. Nevertheless, as we have seen, emperors and local patrons were at pains to create a culture of pleasure for the population (at least of cities) through donations, gifts and the staging of performances. The plebs had access to Rome's culture of pleasure, but had little actual power to choose the nature of pleasure on offer to them.

The culture of consumption that developed over the course of the first century CE fuelled a desire for new products and new built environments in which to experience pleasure. Public architecture at Rome and in the cities of Italy was not built on the cheap.[41] It incorporated numerous innovations: glazed windows in the baths, glazed windows in temples to display art collections, new vault technologies that included the use of iron ribs, to name just three.[42] The point is that technological innovations of these types cost money, they are not cheap, and inscriptions that refer to the costs of construction do this to demonstrate the expense of construction and the quality of the building.[43] With increases in the demand for buildings, not just in Rome but also in the rest of Italy, bricks replaced the irregular stone facings that characterized earlier buildings. The reasons behind this change were that economies could be made in the speed of construction.[44] Similarly, in the use of repetitive forms – think of arches in aqueducts, theatres or amphitheatres – there is a saving in time and the number of skills required for construction.[45] The replacement of one building technology with another can be seen today if you visit both Pompeii destroyed in 79 CE and Ostia rebuilt in brick-faced concrete in the second century CE.

What we are seeing at these sites is a phenomenon related to demand, and that demand again related to the available labour force as much as to economic forces associated directly with cost. The use of these techniques, put simply, allowed Roman society to produce more buildings at a faster rate in the first century CE than it would have been possible in the middle of the first century BCE. At the same time, the demand for greater decoration (often using imported marbles) and more sophisticated architectural forms caused the economic cost of public buildings to rise.[46] The demand for more sophisticated or more prestigious buildings built faster at a higher cost was an economic driving force. This is a measurable manifestation of how the culture of pleasure drove the Roman economy in the first century CE.[47] Some of these changes were driven by the benefactions of an emperor, but these alone cannot account for the replication of the built forms of the capital across Italy, in vast numbers of theatres and amphitheatres constructed using very similar techniques. What this discussion of technological innovation within the Roman building industry indicates is that the desire for pleasure drives the economy in quite different ways from those that place an emphasis upon cost or price alone. This was not just true of the built forms that survive in the archaeological record, but was also true of other forms of production: the demand for pleasure redrew the monetary economy. It was driven as much by the emperor's desire to provide ever more sophisticated benefactions, as by the demand of the plebs for the consumption of items otherwise beyond their economic reach. Equally, the desire of Roman aristocrats to follow the emperor's lead allowed for the spread of this economic phenomenon beyond Rome to the other cities of Italy and into parts of the provinces of the Empire.

At the same time, there is a mass culture of consumption in the first century CE that affected all aspects of the culture of the Roman Empire. In some ways, the Roman Empire was the first global economy with cheap products (such as wine) being produced in the provinces for consumption in the capital. The reach of Rome's global economy stretched beyond the boundaries of the Empire into places as far away as the mint towns of India. The trade with India had started as early as the second century BCE but it is in the first century CE that a peak in the consumption patterns of Roman goods can be found.[48] The patterns of consumption across the space of the Empire were quite diverse with a greater intensity towards its centre.[49] They are difficult to identify with any clarity; more telling perhaps are the patterns of production, especially those of metals in the first century CE. Rome had access to all the copper, silver and gold deposits to be found in Europe and the Mediterranean, of which roughly a quarter were actively mined.[50] The level of production of metal over the course of human history has been established in relation to atmospheric pollution at the time of the formation of the ice in Greenland. Cores from the Greenland ice cap reveal a peak in atmospheric pollution in antiquity occurring about 2,000 years ago, in other words from the beginning of the first century CE.[51] This may not be surprising in itself, but what is astonishing is that the level of production needed to produce this amount of atmospheric pollution – the production of 50–80,000 tonnes of lead per annum; 15,000 tonnes of copper per annum and 10,000 tonnes of zinc per annum – was not seen again in Europe until 1820 and the industrial revolution.[52] The evidence from the Greenland ice cores has been confirmed through the analysis of lake sediments in Sweden, Switzerland and Croatia, as well as analysis of marshes in south-west France and peat bogs in Britain.[53] This evidence for atmospheric pollution from metalworking points to an efficiency of metal extraction: the Roman Empire, comprising a mere 60 million people, was producing as much metal as Europe did in 1820 with a population of well over 200 million people and on a rather more advanced technological basis.[54] Driving the exploitation of metals in the first century CE was not so much the need to provide for larger and larger armies as the desire to utilize metals in the service of pleasure. Consumption of metal was everywhere: the production of coinage, water pipes, iron reinforcements for buildings, drinking cups or dinner plates – but is impossible to quantify. What we do find in this very same period with its peak in metal production is a peak in finds of shipwrecks across the

Mediterranean, further suggesting that the first century CE was a time of the greatest economic expansion in Europe prior to the industrial revolution.[55] Driving the economy was a desire within Roman society to buy into a culture of pleasure, in which those who could built, consumed and magnaminously gave money to enable the masses to experience pleasure. This economic impulse or cultural catalyst, including the pleasure derived from giving pleasure or gifts of pleasure to others, continued into the second century CE – but by the following century it was no longer economically sustainable or seen to be culturally desirable in the face of political and military uncertainty. New priorities in the fourth century CE reshaped Roman culture towards a less public display of wealth, a limitation of public benefactions apart from those related to church building and a recasting of the first century CE as a past to be avoided. Underlying the new cultural priorities of the fourth century lay the critiques of pleasure found among the Stoic authors of the first century CE, who were quoted and reinvented within a new Christian critique of the past and its association with excess. The culture of pleasure found in the first century CE did not survive into the later Roman Empire, but what did remain was an idea of a culture driven by the passionate enjoyment of pleasure – an idea that has passed down to us in the twenty-first century. Yet the symbols of pleasure found in Rome of the first century CE remain those that we value in the twenty-first century. These values are revealed by any view of the lives of the rich and famous in celebrity magazines, newspapers and TV programmes: property, food and drink, collectibles, the body beautiful and an intersection with entertainment for the masses, whether in film, in sport or royal spectacles. In both ancient and modern contexts, pleasure flourishes and emphasizes the inequalities within society, and the use of pleasure by the famous becomes a spectacle for others, regardless of whether they might approve or criticize the activity of those more famous (or at least more wealthy) than themselves. No one was more famous or more wealthy than a Roman emperor; the emperor's use of pleasure was to be enjoyed by others and emulated by some aristocrats, but could not be challenged or competed with. By the end of the second century, the emperor was no longer seen at Rome for long periods of time, war had replaced peace, the mining of metals had significantly decreased, the population had been decimated by a smallpox pandemic and we might conclude that the Roman age of pleasure had come to a close.[56] Looked at in the long term, the culture of pleasure at Rome was short-lived – a fleeting sensation in the course of human history – but its impact as an idea and a cultural phenomenon has survived to this day.

Timeline

753 BCE	Foundation of Rome
509 BCE	Expulsion of kings of Rome – the Republic is established
390 BCE	Gauls sack Rome
362 BCE	First known theatre games (*ludi scaenici*)
264 BCE	First known gladiatorial fights held at Rome
167 BCE	Greece and Macedonia conquered by Rome – as a result, taxation of Roman citizens is suspended
146 BCE	Rome destroys the cities of Carthage and Corinth
63 BCE	Lucullus retires from public life and lives in his gardens (*horti*) in Rome
55 BCE	Dedication of Pompey's theatre in Rome
49 BCE	Julius Caesar crosses the Rubicon and begins the civil war with Pompey
46 BCE	Julius Caesar appointed dictator for ten years
44 BCE	Assassination of Julius Caesar
43 BCE	Proscription and killing of Cicero
31 BCE	Battle of Actium: Octavian defeats Anthony and Cleopatra. Results in the conquest of Egypt
29 BCE	Dedication of first stone amphitheatre in Rome, built by Statilius Taurus
28 BCE	Octavian restores 82 temples in Rome Work begins on Octavian's mausoleum in Rome
27 BCE	Octavian 'restores' the Republic and takes the name Augustus, marking the beginning of imperial rule
25 BCE	Dedication of the original Pantheon
19 BCE	Completion of the baths of Agrippa
13 BCE	Dedication of the theatre of Marcellus. Dedication of the theatre of Balbus

12 BCE	Death of Agrippa: he leaves his gardens and baths to the Roman people for their use
9 BCE	Dedication of the Altar of Peace (*Ara Pacis*) in Rome
7 BCE	City of Rome divided into 14 regions
2 BCE	Completion of the Forum of Augustus
14 CE	Death of Augustus and succession of his adopted son Tiberius. Deification of Augustus: building of the temple of the Divine Augustus commences – completed in reign of Caligula. Election of magistrates is transferred from the people of Rome to the senate
15 CE	Sejanus is the commander of the Praetorian Guard
26 CE	Tiberius withdraws to Campania
31 CE	Sejanus is deposed and executed
37 CE	Death of Tiberius and accession of Caligula
41 CE	Murder of Caligula and accession of Claudius
43 CE	Conquest of Britain
56 CE	Death of Claudius and accession of Nero (his adopted son). Deification of Claudius; his wife Agrippina begins building temple to Claudius – completed under Vespasian
57 CE	Wooden amphitheatre constructed on the Campus Martius
60 CE	Neronia festival celebrated. Opening of Nero's baths
64 CE	Great Fire of Rome. Nero supervises the rebuilding of the city and constructs the Golden House
65 CE	Suicide of Seneca
66 CE	Jewish Revolt begins. Suicide of Petronius
68 CE	Suicide of Nero
69 CE	Civil War: the 'year of the four Emperors', Galba, Otho, Vitellius and Vespasian
70 CE	Capture of Jerusaleum; end of Jewish Revolt
75 CE	Dedication of the Temple of Peace
79 CE	Death of Vespasian and accession of Titus (his son). Building of the temple of Vespasian commences – completed in the reign of Domitian and called the

	temple of Vespasian and Titus. Eruption of Vesuvius and destruction of Pompeii and Herculaneum. Death of Pliny the Elder
80 CE	Dedication of the Colosseum. Major fire in Rome, resulting in the destruction of much of the city. Death of Titus and accession of his brother Domitian. Deification of Titus
96 CE	Murder of Domitian and accession of Nerva
97 CE	Dedication of Nerva's Forum (*Forum transitorium*)
98 CE	Death of Nerva and accession of his adopted son Trajan
112 CE	Dedication of Trajan's Forum
117 CE	Death of Trajan and accession of Hadrian. Deification of Trajan
118 CE	Work begins on Hadrian's Villa at Tivoli

Glossary

Agricola — Senator, governor of Britain and father-in-law of Tacitus, who wrote a biography of Agricola's life (40–93 CE).

Agrippa — Right hand man of Augustus, was involved in construction of major projects in the development of the Campus Martius (c. 64–12 BCE).

Agrippina — Mother of Nero, granddaughter of Antonia (c. 15–59 CE).

Anio — 120 km- (75 mile-) long river forms part of the border between Latin and Sabine territory, joins the river Tiber north of Rome. Was the source of the flow over the Anio Vetus (built 272 BCE) and Anio Novus (built 52 CE) aqueducts.

Antonia — Daughter of Mark Antony, mother of the emperor Claudius and grandmother of emperor Caligula; wife of emperor Claudius (c. 36 BCE–37 CE).

Apicius — Name given to creators of new dishes, the recipes of Apicius come from a fourth-century CE writer of this name.

Appian — Greek historian who wrote works of Roman history in the second century CE.

Apuleius — Writer and orator from North Africa, author of the *Golden Ass* (born c. 125 CE).

ASBO — Anti-Social Behaviour Order issued in the UK in twenty-first century to young delinquents to prevent them from performing anti-social acts.

Ass — Lowest denomination of Roman coinage.

Atella	A town in Campania from which a genre of theatre performance gains it name: Atellan farces.
Athenaeus	Late second-century CE writer.
Atrium	The central covered courtyard of the Roman house, a place into which visitors were welcomed.
Attis	Young lover of Cybele in mythology, whose self-castration creates a model for the priests of Cybele.
Baiae	Resort town on the Bay of Naples associated with thermal springs.
Berenice	Daughter of Herod Agrippa (biblical figure), openly lived with the future emperor Titus when she visited Rome in 75 CE (b. 28 CE).
Boudicca	Led revolt of the Iceni and Trinovantes (60–61 CE), destroyed cities of Verulamium (St Albans); Camulodunum (Colchester) and Londinium (London), prior to defeat by Suetonius Paulinus' army; she committed suicide by taking poison.
Caecuban	A very high quality wine of the first century CE.
Caldarium	The hottest room in the Roman baths.
Campus Martius	Originally the Field of Mars where the young trained for military service, by the first century CE this area close to the Tiber was developed as a new monumental centre within Rome.
Capitol	Alternative name for the Capitoline Hill.
Capitoline Hill	Location of Rome's major temple dedicated to Jupiter Optimus Maximus (509 BCE), it was the destination of triumphal processions.
Cassius Dio	Senator from Greece, wrote an 80-book history of Rome in Greek, but using a Latin grammatical word order (c. 164–230 CE).
Cato the Elder	Paragon of virtue from Rome's past, famous for his prescient insistence that Carthage should be destroyed ('*Carthargo delenda est*') (234–149 BCE).
Cato the Younger	Great-grandson of the elder Cato, famous for his failed opposition to Julius Caesar, and his

subsequent suicide at Utica; a model of resistance to autocracy for the first century CE (c. 95–46 BCE).

Catullus	Writer of love poetry (c. 84–54 BCE).
Celsus	Wrote an encyclopedia in early first century CE, of which only the section on medicine survives.
Chiusi	A town north-east of Rome.
Cicero	Politician and prolific author (106–43 BCE).
Cinaedus	Literally, a dancing boy; in reality a passive male who was more female than male, often regarded as the giver of pleasure to others who sexually penetrated his body.
Circus of Flaminius	A public area rather than a circus with tiers of seating for the holding of games; constructed in 221 BCE on the Campus Martius, it was the location of public meetings in the Republic.
Circus Maximus	Rome's major chariot-racing arena, said to have been founded by Romulus, enlarged by Julius Caesar, repaired after fire damage by Caligula and restored after fire again by Trajan.
Cithara	Lyre, musical stringed instrument.
Clement of Alexandria	Convert to Christianity and ordained, wrote extensively on the nature of Roman religion and education (c. 150–216 CE).
Clodia	Confusingly, three sisters of Clodius had this name, one of whom (Clodia Metelli) was probably the lover of the poet Catullus; she features in his poems under the name Lesbia (95–45 BCE).
Clodius	Political opponent of both Cicero and Pompey, who used popular support of the urban plebs to gain political power in the late republic (92–52 BCE).
Collegium	A club or guild, associated with group activity. Many were associated with specific trades or the worship of a specific god. Their main activities were the holding of dinners and providing funerals/burials for members.

Columella	Writer of a manual on agricultural practices (b. 50 CE).
Consul	Traditionally the highest annually elected magistrate in Rome with two elected per annum, under the Empire four were elected per annum.
Corpus Inscriptionum Latinarum	Publication of Latin inscriptions begun in the nineteenth century under the direction of Theodor Mommsen; continues to be updated today.
Crassus	A key player in the 60s and 50s BCE and the disintegration of the Roman Republic, a rival to Pompey, he died leading his forces at the Battle of Carrhae – Rome's greatest defeat by the Parthians.
Cubiculum	A bedroom, a place of privacy or even secrecy.
Cumae	City on the Bay of Naples, originally a Greek colony (740 BCE), but from 180 BCE used Latin as its official language.
Cybele	The great mother goddess brought to Rome from modern Turkey during the crisis of the second Punic War (205–204 BCE), and served by eunuch priests at her temple on the Palatine Hill.
Dionysus	Greek god of wine, equivalent to the Italian/Roman god Bacchus.
Esquiline Hill	A region of Rome associated with *horti* (gardens).
Etruria	Region of Italy adjacent to Mediterranean coast north of Rome, associated with the Etruscan language and the people associated with that language – the Etruscans.
Eutropius	Fourth-century CE historian.
Falernian	A high-quality Campanian wine.
Fortuna	Roman goddess of fortune, responsible in eyes of Romans of raising individuals up, such as Sejanus, only to cast them down again.
Forum Romanum	Refers to the Forum established in the republic to distinguish it from the fora built by Julius Caesar, Augustus, Nerva and Trajan.

Frigidarium	The coldest room in the Roman baths.
Ganymede	Beautiful Trojan prince in mythology who was abducted by Jupiter and taken to Mount Olympus; he became wine-waiter to the gods, with all the sexual connotations associated with this role.
Garum	Fish paste.
Gaul	Roman province with a geographical equivalence to modern France.
Gellius	Wrote the *Attic Nights* in the second century CE, a collection of what appears to be unrelated themes – the stuff to pass long winter evenings in Athens – yet retains an underlying educational purpose.
Gemonian Steps	Led from the Mamertine prison to the summit of the Capitoline Hill; on the steps the bodies of criminals were exposed for public torment in full view of the crowds gathered below in the Forum Romanum.
Hannibal	Successful Carthaginian general who defeated Rome's armies in battle in Italy during the second Punic War fought between 219 and 202 BCE.
Homer	Earliest known Greek poet (8th century BCE).
Horace	Poet, son of a freed slave (65–8 BCE).
Hortensius	Politician and orator, a skilled rival of Cicero in the late republic (c. 114–49 BCE).
Inscriptiones Latinae Selectae	Publication of a selection of the most significant Latin inscriptions.
Josephus	Greek historian captured in Jewish War who became an advocate of Flavian rule of the empire and Roman rule over Judaea; he later became a Roman citizen (b. 37 CE).
Juvenal	Roman satirist (late 1st and early 2nd century CE).
L'Année Epigraphique	Annual journal that contains all recently reported finds of inscriptions.
Laelius	Closest friend of Scipio Aemilianus, famous for his wisdom (c. 190–129 BCE).

Laurentum	Region of coastal villa construction to south of Ostia, within easy reach of Rome.
Lepidus	Third member of the triumvirate with Antony and Octavian, isolated by the other two members at an early stage.
Liquamen	Fish sauce.
Livia	Second wife of the emperor Augustus (c. 58 BCE–29 CE).
Livy	Wrote *Ab Urbe Condita* or 'From the Time the City was Founded' – a history of Rome down to his own time (59 BCE–17 CE).
Lucullus	A successful and able general who became politically inactive and retired to his pleasure gardens to pursue an Epicurean lifestyle (d.57/56 BCE).
Lucan	Prolific writer (c. 39–65 CE).
Lucania	Region of southern Italy.
Lucian	A lawyer and later an itinerant speaker on philosophy; a number of his works survive (b. 120 CE).
Lucilius	Roman satirist whose work only survives in fragments (born c. 180 BCE).
Macrobius	Senator and writer (5th century CE).
Maecenas	Adviser to Octavian and patron of the poets of the Augustan age.
Mamertine Prison	Located on the slope between the Forum Romanum and the Capitoline Hill. The lower chamber was entered by a shaft and is of circular form with a radius of 3.5m.
Martial	Writer of epigrams from Spain, lived in Rome but returned to Spain later in his life (c. 38–104 CE).
Messalina	Great-granddaughter of Augustus' sister Octavia – married to the emperor Claudius, mother of his children: Octavia and Brittanicus (c. 20–48 CE).
Musonius Rufus	Stoic philosopher, sent into exile by both Nero and Vespasian (c. 30–80 CE).

Negotium	Broadly defined as business of any nature, including duties, public offices, attendance to needs of tenants, etc.
Nomentum	A town to the north-east of Rome.
Ostia	A city at mouth of the Tiber; today most of the standing remains date from the early second century CE.
Otium	Broadly defined as leisure that might include everything within this book, as well as intellectual discussion, the study of literature and other more academic pursuits.
Ovid	Writer of poetry, especially love poetry (c. 43 BCE–17 CE).
Palaestra	Rectilinear area with colonnades, associated with bath buildings, but also found to exist as public buildings in their own right (e.g. the Palaestra Grande at Pompeii).
Palatine Hill	Location of Romulus' legendary foundation of the city; in the first century CE it was gradually taken over as the imperial palace expanded from the houses of Augustus and Livia.
Pannonia	Roman province in the Balkans.
Parthia	Country with a geographical equivalent to modern Iraq and Iran, a major empire that was at peace and at war with Rome over the course of the first century CE.
Paterfamilias	The head of the household, or father of the family who in law had complete autonomy over members of his family; yet in practice his role was associated with affection rather than tyranny over the lives of his children. However, he was the one to be active in the arrangement of marriages and other major life changes of members of the family.
Peristyle	A courtyard of a Roman house larger than the atrium and most commonly positioned to the rear of the house. Often the peristyle could contain

	gardens, fountains, outdoor dining rooms or adjacent dining rooms.
Persius	Neronian satirist (c. 34–62 CE).
Petronius	Neronian novelist, whose only surviving work, the *Satyrica*, provides the basis for much information on dining. Petronius might have been the pleasure-loving courtier of the same name examined by Tacitus (*Annals*: 16.17–20).
Phlegon of Tralles	Freedman of Hadrian, author of a number of works including that on wondrous events.
Picenum	A region of Italy bordering on the Adriatic sea.
Pliny the Elder	Senator and writer of the vast work the *Natural History* (c. 23–79 CE). Died during the eruption of Vesuvius while at Stabiae.
Pliny the Younger	Senator and nephew of Pliny the Elder, wrote *Letters* for publication and also the *Panegyric* in praise of the emperor Trajan (c. 61–112 CE).
Plutarch	Greek philospher and biographer; sadly his biographies of emperors are lost apart from the lives of Galba and Otho (c. 50–120 CE).
Polemo	Physiognomist and orator whose public performances of both arts drew crowds and rivals (88–144 CE).
Pompey the Great	Roman general and statesman who famously cleared the Mediterranean of pirates (c. 106–48 BCE).
Porticus	Difficult to categorize; it can refer to structures similar to that of a basilica or Greek *stoa*, but would also seem to refer to any sort of collonade whether found at a villa or enclosing a temple complex.
Portus	An artificial harbour to the north of the estuary of the Tiber constructed initially by the emperor Claudius, but further work was undertaken by Nero and Trajan. This created the first secure harbour in the vicinity of Rome in which the grain fleet and other larger vessels could dock.

Puteoli	Greek city colonized by Rome in 194 BCE, it became the major port for Rome until the establishment of Portus in the mid first century BCE. Modern town of Pozzuoli is built over this ancient city 12 km from Naples.
Pylades	The greatest pantomime innovator of the Augustan age.
Quintilian	Lawyer and authority on the nature of rhetoric (c. 35–94 CE).
Sallust	Politician and later historian (c. 86–35 BCE).
Scipio Aemilianus	Adopted son of Scipio Africanus, successful general and politician; also destroyer of the Spanish town of Numantia (c. 185–129 BCE).
Scipio Africanus	The hero of Rome's struggle against the armies of Carthage, led by Hannibal; embroiled in political and financial scandals in the 180s BCE, he retired to his villa in Campania to avoid standing trial (236–184 BCE).
Sejanus	Sole prefect of the praetorian guard 23–31 CE; later killed on the orders of Tiberius.
Sempronia	Aristocratic supporter of Catiline and associated with the Catilinarian conspiracy foiled by Cicero in 63 BCE.
Senator	Member of the Roman senate with landed wealth of more than 1 million *sesterces*.
Seneca the Elder	Writer of history and on declamation, from Spain (c. 50 BCE–40 CE).
Seneca the Younger	Son of the elder Seneca, a wealthy senator, tutor and adviser to the emperor Nero, a strong critic of pleasure and a Stoic philosopher (c. 4 BCE–65 CE).
Sentius	Successful career politician under the emperor Augustus.
Sesterces (plural form)	Roman coin valued at 2½ *asses* or a ¼ of a *denarius*. A legionary earned 900 *sesterces* per annum; a person needed wealth to the value of 1 million

sesterces to qualify for membership of the senate, 400,000 *sesterces* to be a Roman knight and 100,000 *sesterces* to serve on a local town council.

Sigillaria	Region of Rome associated with the making and selling of gift items.
Spartacus	Former Roman auxiliary soldier, Thracian gladiator, and leader of a slave revolt from 73–71 BCE.
Statius	A poet from Naples who participated in poetry competitions as part of the games given under Domitian (45–96 CE).
Strabo	From Amaesia in modern Turkey, writer of the geography that described the world at the beginning of the first century CE (c. 64 BCE–21 CE).
Strigil	Bronze implement used to scrape the body clean at the baths.
Suetonius	Biographer of the lives of emperors (c. 70–130 CE).
Tacitus	Senator and historian of the first century CE and biographer of Agricola, he also wrote a surviving treatise on *Germania* (c. 56–118).
Tarpeian Rock	Not so much a rock but a cliff edge of the Capitoline Hill from which victims of the Roman state were hurled to their deaths.
Tepidarium	The warm room in the Roman baths.
Tertullian	A lawyer who provided a written defence of early Christianity (c. 160–240 CE).
Theophrastus	Fourth/third century BCE philosopher.
Thermae	Latin term for the larger and more complex baths, it can be interchanged with the word *balneum* or bathhouse.
Triclinium	Dining room of a Roman house, often identified by the remains of masonry couches found in the houses and gardens of Pompeii, Herculaneum and other Roman cities.
Umbria	Geographical region in central Italy.
Varro	Extremely prolific author who sought to systematize

	knowledge of the Latin language; also wrote a surviving treatise on agricultural practices (c. 116–27 BCE).
Vergil	Writer of poetry (c. 70–19 BCE).
Vitruvius	His *On Architecture* is the only surviving treatise on the subject from antiquity, composed in the later years of Augustus' reign.

Further Reading

Any list for further reading is both a personal one and a provisional one. I have kept the list short and apologize to all scholars whom I have omitted – this has more to do with conciseness than my feelings about the quality of their work. Choices have to be made (think about which book you would recommend on gladiators for example). I have chosen books (and in absence of books, articles in journals or chapters in books) on the basis of what I see as attractive for readers new to the subject and those I have enjoyed. For readers of this list, especially students, the works mentioned are the next step and attention should also be paid to the bibliography at the end of this book.

INTRODUCTION

Key to understanding the writing of pleasure are the introductions by Oswyn Murray to two volumes edited by him in the 1990s that include papers by an international cast: *Sympotica: A Symposium on the Symposion* published in 1990 and *In Vino Veritas*, edited with M. Tecuşan and published in 1995. Recently, historians of more modern periods have examined the sensory realms in the analysis of the early modern metropolis undergoing change; see papers in A. Cowan and J. Steward, *The City and the Senses: Urban Culture Since 1500.*

1 INTO THE WORLD OF ROMAN PLEASURE

For the connection between the products of the provinces and their consumption, Andrew Dalby sets out the full range of products in *Empires of Pleasure: Luxury and Indulgence in the Roman World.* Underpinning much of this chapter lies

Martial's last two books of *Epigrams*; the best translation available of these is that by R. Shackleton Bailey in the *Loeb Classical Library* series, which provides parallel Latin text and translation. The Saturnalia was the subject of some discussion on TV in Tony Robinson's *Worst Xmas Jobs in History* (Spire Productions) that will no doubt be broadcast regularly in our own festive season. For images of vomiting in Roman art, see John Clarke's very well-illustrated *Looking at Laughter: Humour, Power, and Transgression in Roman Visual Culture, 100 BC – AD 250* or his *Art in the Lives of Ordinary Romans*.

2 THE EMPEROR'S PLEASURES

Inevitably, any discussion of the emperor's pleasures rests on the biographies of Suetonius. Numerous English translations of this work are available. On his methods and interests, Andrew Wallace-Hadrill's study simply entitled *Suetonius* offers a full study of the author and his subject. The judgement of the emperors' actions by others is a theme pursued by a number of authors, perhaps most effectively in Catharine Edwards' *The Politics of Immorality in Ancient Rome*. Caroline Vout's recent examination of the connection, *Power and Eroticism in Imperial Rome*, deals with the sexualization of the emperors. There are numerous biographies of the emperors; by far the most effective is Edward Champlin's *Nero*, which reveals much about the politics of pleasure.

3 THE AESTHETICS OF THE CITY

The importance of the image of the city to the new regime of Augustus is discussed extensively by Paul Zanker in his *The Power of Images in the Age of Augustus*, and also by Diane Favro in her *The Urban Image of Augustan Rome*. There is far less discussion of the role of later emperors in print. Edward Champlin's study *Nero* has the city of Rome as its central focus and is particularly good on the reaction of Nero to the fire of 64 CE. R. H. Darwall-Smith provides a book-length study of the rebuilding of Rome after this fire in his *Emperors and Architecture: A Study of Flavian Rome*.

4 A LITTLE PLACE IN THE COUNTRY

For the reinterpretation of villa architecture in the literature of the late first century CE, see N. K. Zeiner's *Nothing Ordinary Here: Statius as Creator of Distinction in the Silvae*. Bettina Bergmann connects the vision of the villa in text with its physical setting in her essay 'Painted Perspectives of a Villa Visit: Landscape as Status and Metaphor' (in E. K. Gazda (ed.) *Roman Art in the Private Sphere: New Perspectives on the Architecture and Decor of the Domus, Villa and Insula*, Ann Arbor, pp. 49–70). Eleanor Leach provides a fuller account of visual representation in her book: *The Social Life of Painting in Ancient Rome and on the Bay of Naples*. Sadly, there is no full survey of archaeological remains in English. X. Lafon's *Villa Maritima: Recherches sur les villas littorales de l'Italie romaine* has a full and well-illustrated survey of maritime villas; see also H. Mielsch, *La Villa Romana* for further examples.

5 THE ROMAN BODY AT THE BATHS

Garrett Fagan's study *Bathing in Public in the Roman World* provides a very full study of the activity and the building of new bathhouses in the first century CE. For analysis of architecture and plans of bath buildings see Inge Nielsen's *Thermae et Balnea: The Architecture and Cultural History of Roman Public Baths*. This book and F. Yegül's *Baths and Bathing in Classical Antiquity* have much to say about how Romans bathed. Many of the thoughts that lie behind this chapter draw on those of Asa Eger and can be found in his paper: 'Queered Space in the Roman Bathhouse', (in M. Harlow and R. Laurence (eds) *Age and Ageing in the Roman Empire*, Portsmouth, RI, pp. 131–51).

6 ROMAN EROTICS

Antonio Varrone provides a guide to the sexualized graffiti in his *Erotica Pompeiana: Love Inscriptions on the Walls of Pompeii*. There is a full study of the visualization of sex in John Clarke's revealing *Looking at Lovemaking: Constructions of Sexuality in Roman Art 100 BC – AD 250*. Tom McGinn has undertaken a very thorough study of prostitution: *The Economy of Prostitution in the Roman World*. There is still considerable disagreement over the nature of the customers of prostitutes. For my own current view, see the second edition of *Roman Pompeii: Space and Society*. The arguments for the existence of Roman homosexuality can be found in two articles: the first by Amy Richlin 'Not before Homosexuality: The Materiality of the Cinaedus in the Roman Law against Love between Men' (*Journal of the History of Sexuality*, 3: 523–73) and the second by R. Taylor, 'Two Pathic Subcultures in Ancient Rome' (*Journal of the History of Sexuality*, 7: 319–71).

7 DINING

Lying behind so much of the modern study of Roman dining is the work of the late John D'Arms. These studies are published in journals and edited volumes, but are well worth tracking down: 'The Roman *Convivium* and the Idea of Equality' (in O. Murray (ed.) *Sympotica: A Symposium on the Symposion*, Oxford, pp. 308–20); 'Control, Companionship and Clientela: Some Social Functions of the Roman Communal Meal' (*Echos du Monde Classique*, 28: 327–48); 'Slaves at the Roman *Convivia*' (in W. J. Slater (ed.) *Dining in a Classical Context*, Ann Arbor, pp. 171–84); and 'Performing Culture: Roman Spectacle and the Banquets of the Powerful' (in B. Bergmann and C. Kondoleon (eds) *The Art of Ancient Spectacle*, New Haven, pp. 283–300). See in addition: Matthew Roller, *Dining Posture in Ancient Rome: Bodies, Values and Status*. For the representation of dining in wall painting, see K. Dunbabin, *The Roman Banquet: Images of Conviviality*.

8 FOOD AND WINE

It is difficult to get away from the text of Apicius with its various recipes for Roman dishes. The text (or translation) should be consulted with Andrew Dalby's *Food in the Ancient World from A to Z* to hand for explanation of technical terms and for a wider understanding of any single ingredient or its combination with another ingredient. There are now numerous books that provide recipes that seek to replicate or at least have a stab at creating the sensation of Roman tastes. Sally Grainger's *Cooking Apicius: Roman Recipes for Today* provides a useful guide to how we might envisage a recreation of a Roman dish for a modern palate. Emily Gowers discusses the representation and meaning of food in various genres of Latin literature in *The Loaded Table: Representations of Food in Literature* in what is now a classic study. For drinking, there is not a book-length study of the subject in English: A. Tchernia's *Le Vin de l'Italie romaine* is fundamental. However, there are excellent articles in English by Nicholas Purcell on the wine trade: 'Wine and Wealth in Ancient Italy' (*Journal of Roman Studies*, 75: 1–19) and by John D'Arms on heavy drinking: 'Heavy Drinking and Drunkenness in the Roman World: Four Questions for Historians' (in O. Murray and M. Tecuşan (eds) *In Vino Veritas*, London, pp. 304–17).

9 A GREAT SONG AND DANCE

Nicholas Horsfall in his 2003 book, *The Culture of the Roman Plebs*, drew scholars' attention to the centrality of song in the creation of cultural memory in Roman society. Hence, his work is fundamental to this subject. To date, there is no single volume that deals with this subject and readers need to hunt down articles in journals and edited books. The recent discoveries of musical notation and their interpretation are discussed by W. A. Johnson in two articles 'New Instrumental Music from Graeco-Roman Egypt' (*Bulletin of the American Association of Papyrologists*, 37: 17–36) and 'Musical Evenings in the Early Empire: New Evidence from a Greek Papyrus with Musical Notation' (*Journal of Hellenic Studies*, 120: 57–85). The role of pantomime as a cultural genre is very thoroughly discussed by E. J. Jory in a series of articles: 'The Literary Evidence for the Beginnings of Imperial Pantomime' (*Bulletin of the Institute of Classical Studies*, 28: 147–61); 'The Early Pantomime Riots' (in A. Moffatt (ed.) *Maistor: Classical, Byzantine and Renaissance Studies for Robert Browning*, Canberra, pp. 57–66); and 'The Drama of the Dance: Prolegomena to an Iconography of Imperial Pantomime' (in W. J. Slater (ed.) *Roman Theater and Society*, Ann Arbor, pp. 1–28). For Nero on stage, see the biography by Edward Champlin. On the spread of Roman theatres, see Frank Sear's architectural study: *Roman Theatres: An Architectural Survey*.

10 VIOLENCE

Richard Saller draws a distinction between domestic violence meted out to
slaves and the corporal punishment that children were subjected to in his
book *Patriarchy, Property and Death in the Roman Family*. Keith Bradley sets
out the evidence for the punishment of slaves in his book *Masters and Slaves
in the Roman Empire: A Study in Social Control*. The watching of violence at
the amphitheatre is discussed in numerous modern studies, but *Emperors
and Gladiators* by the late Thomas Wiedemann continues to lead the pack. K.
Coleman provides a full discussion of Martial's work *On Spectacles* that includes
the choreographed violence at the opening of the Colosseum in her book *M.
Valerii Martialis Liber Spectaculorum*. There is no full survey in English of
amphitheatres, similar to J.-C. Golvin's *L'Amphithéâtre romain*, but see now
Katherine Welch's *The Roman Amphitheatre from its Origins to the Colosseum* for
a survey of Italian amphitheatres.

11 COLLECTORS AND COLLECTIONS

Although this subject might be less well known to readers, there is a book-length
study of the subject by A. Bounia – *The Nature of Classical Collecting: Collectors
and Collections, 100 BCE –100 CE*. Barbara Kellum sets out the structure of the
first well-lit collection in Rome in her paper: 'The City Adorned: Programmatic
Display at the *Aedes Concordiae*' in K. A. Raaflaub and M. Toher's volume
Between Republic and Empire: Interpretations of Augustus and His Principate.
The role of art in society in the first century CE is discussed in J. Isager, *Pliny on
Art and Society: The Elder Pliny's Chapters on the History of Art*. Robert Garland's
In the Eye of the Beholder provides an overview of the ancient understanding of
human birth abnormalities.

12 PLEASURE TRANSFORMS ROMAN CULTURE

The work of Oswyn Murray referred to above under 'Introduction' is fundamental. Caroline Vout extends our understanding of the dynamics of pleasure

from the first century CE into the second century in her book: *Power and Eroticism in Imperial Rome*. Her work builds on some important observations to be found in Natalie Kampen's end piece to A. O. Koloski-Ostrow and C. L. Lyons' book *Naked Truths: Women, Sexuality and Gender in Classical Art and Archaeology*.

Notes

Notes to the Introduction: Roman Passions

1   Murray, 1995: 6.
2   Murray, 1995: 5.
3   Murray, 1995: 6.
4   Drawing on Veblen, 1970; see Murray 1995: 7–9.
5   Murray, 1995: 11.

Notes to Chapter 1: Into the World of Roman Pleasure

1   Seneca, *On the Happy Life*: 7.7.
2   Seneca, *On the Happy Life*: 12.3.
3   Seneca, *On the Happy Life*: 17.1–2.
4   Martial, *Epigrams*: 4.53.
5   Martial, *Epigrams*: 14.1.
6   Martial, *Epigrams*: 13.3.
7   Martial, *Epigrams*: 13.4; 13.5; 13.7.
8   Martial, *Epigrams*: 13.6.
9   Compare earlier listing from beginning of the first century CE found in Horace, *Satires*: 2.4; see Gowers 1993: 135–61.
10 Martial, *Epigrams*: 13.1; 13.6.
11 Martial, *Epigrams*: 13.127; 6.80.
12 Martial, *Epigrams*: 13.34.
13 Martial, *Epigrams*: 13.26.

14 Martial, *Epigrams*: 13.34.

15 Statius, *Silva*: 1.6.82.

16 Martial, *Epigrams*: 4.88; 5.18; 5.19; 5.42.

17 Martial, *Epigrams*: 5.59

18 Martial, *Epigrams*: 4.46.

19 Lucian, *Saturnalia*.

20 Seneca, *Letters*: 18.

21 Atkinson 1914.

22 Curtis 1985: 215 calculates a ratio of 29% imported to 71% local production.

23 Martial, *Epigrams*: 4.28.

24 Seneca, *Letters*: 12.3.

25 For example a chariot constructed entirely from silver; Suetonius, *Life of Claudius*:16.

26 Gellius, *Attic Nights*: 2.3.5; 5.4.

27 Martial, *Epigrams*: 14.122.

28 Pliny, *Natural History*: 14.145–6.

29 Pliny, *Natural History*: 19.85, 20.34–5.

30 Pliny, *Natural History*: 20.12.4, 22.132.

31 Columella, *On Agriculture*: 1.3.19.

32 Cicero, *Letters to Atticus*: 13.52.

33 Martial, *Epigrams*: 6.24.

34 Suetonius, *Life of Vespasian*: 19.

35 Martial, *Epigrams*: 5.84.

36 Martial, *Epigrams*: 5.2.

37 Plautus, *Miles Gloriosus*: 691.

38 Tibullus, Elegies: 3.1.1–5.

39 Tertullian, *De Idolataria*: 14.6.

40 Suetonius, *Life of Titus*: 8.

41 Suetonius, *Life of Augustus*: 57.

42 Suetonius , *Life of Titus*: 7.

43 Tacitus, *Annals*: 15.35–7; Cassius Dio, *History of Rome*: 62.15.1–6.

44 Champlin 2003: 150–6.

Notes to Chapter 2: The Emperor's Pleasures

1   Suetonius, *Life of Augustus*: 26.
2   e.g. Suetonius, *Life of Augustus*: 13, 15, 16, 17, 19, 27.
3   Suetonius, *Life of Augustus*: 28.
4   For all these details see *Res Gestae Divi Augusti: The Achievements of the Divine Augustus* edited by P. A. Brunt and J. M. Moore; also Suetonius, *Life of Augustus*: 20–2; 29–30; 41; 43; 47.
5   See *Res Gestae Divi Augusti: The Achievements of The Divine Augustus* edited by P. A. Brunt and J. M. Moore, also Suetonius, *Life of Augustus*: 52–3, 57–8.
6   Wallace-Hadrill 1982 discusses the author and his subject.
7   Suetonius, *Life of Augustus*: 72–3.
8   Suetonius, *Life of Augustus*: 65; Cassius Dio, *History of Rome*: 55.10.12 reports that his daughter partied in the forum and on the very rostra from which Augustus made his moralistic speeches.
9   Macrobius, *Saturnalia*: 2.5.8.
10   Suetonius, *Life of Augustus*: 69.
11   Suetonius, *Life of Augustus*: 71.
12   Suetonius, *Life of Augustus*: 74, 76, 77.
13   Suetonius, *Life of Augustus*: 74.
14   Suetonius, *Life of Augustus*: 51.
15   Suetonius, *Life of Augustus*: 11, 15.
16   Suetonius, *Life of Tiberius*: 42.
17   Suetonius , *Life of Tiberius*: 38.
18   Suetonius, *Life of Tiberius*: 42.
19   Suetonius, *Life of Tiberius*: 45.
20   Suetonius, *Life of Tiberius*: 41–2.
21   Suetonius, *Life of Tiberius*: 43–4.
22   Suetonius, *Life of Tiberius*: 72.
23   Suetonius, *Life of Tiberius*: 60–2.
24   Suetonius, *Life of Caligula*: 10–11.
25   Suetonius, *Life of Caligula*: 13.
26   Suetonius, *Life of Caligula*: 17.
27   Suetonius, *Life of Caligula*: 18.
28   Suetonius, *Life of Caligula* : 22.

29 Suetonius, *Life of Caligula*: 24–6.

30 Suetonius, *Life of Caligula*: 29.

31 Suetonius, *Life of Claudius*: 5.

32 Suetonius, *Life of Claudius*: 8.

33 Suetonius, *Life of Claudius*: 17–21.

34 Suetonius, *Life of Claudius*: 22–3.

35 Suetonius, *Life of Claudius*: 26.

36 Suetonius, *Life of Claudius*: 23.

37 Suetonius, *Life of Vespasian*: 4–5, 7.

38 Suetonius, *Life of Vespasian*: 3.

39 Suetonius, *Life of Vespasian*: 21–3.

40 Suetonius, *Life of Titus*: 3.

41 Suetonius, *Life of Titus*: 7.

42 Suetonius, *Life of Titus*: 7.

43 Suetonius, *Life of Domitian*: 1.3.

44 Suetonius, *Life of Domitian*: 11.

45 Suetonius, *Life of Domitian*: 12.

46 Suetonius, *Life of Domitian*: 21.

47 Suetonius, *Life of Domitian*: 22.

48 Wallace-Hadrill 1988: 171 note 41 for references to sources.

49 Bartsch 1994 reveals these matters at greater length.

50 Pliny, *Panegyric*: 2.

51 Pliny, *Panegyric*: 81.

52 Pliny, *Panegyric*: 49.

53 Pliny, *Panegyric*: 51.

54 See Edwards 1993: 173–206 for full discussion.

Notes to Chapter 3: The Aesthetics of the City

1 Plutarch, *Life of Pompey*: 42.

2 Cicero, *Pro Sestio*: 106; *Letters to Atticus*: 14.3.3; *Letters to Friends*: 8.2.1.

3 Plutarch, *Life of Pompey*: 52; Seneca, *On the Shortness of Life*: 13.6–7; Pliny, *Natural History*: 7.19–21; 7.158; 8.53; 8.64; 8.70; 8.84; Cassius Dio, *History of Rome*: 39.38.

4   Seneca, *To Marcia on Consolation*: 20.4; Velleius Paterculus, *History of Rome*: 2.48.

5   Velleius Paterculus, *History of Rome*: 2.29; Bell 2004: 12.

6   Pliny, *Natural History*: 7.34.

7   Pliny, *Natural History*: 7.98; 36.41.

8   Cassius Dio, *History of Rome*: 39.38.

9   Suetonius, *Life of Caesar*: 44; Cicero, *Letters to Atticus*: 13.33a.

10   Appian, *Civil Wars*: 2.102.

11   Ovid, *Art of Love*: 1.81.

12   Cassius Dio, *History of Rome*: 43.22.

13   Pliny, *Natural History*: 35.26.

14   See Zanker 1988 for discussion of monuments and style.

15   Seneca, *On Benefits*: 3.32.4.

16   Cassius Dio, *History of Rome*: 55.8.3–4.

17   Cassius Dio, *History of Rome*: 66.24.2.

18   Cassius Dio, *History of Rome*: 53.27.

19   Pliny, *Natural History*: 34.13; 36.38.

20   *Tabulae Pompeiane Sulpiciorum*: 27.

21   Suetonius, *Life of Augustus*: 29.

22   Pliny, *Natural History*: 7.91–2; Caesar, *Civil Wars*: 1.9.2.

23   Vitruvius, *On Architecture* 1 preface; Augustus, *Res Gestae*: 34.

24   Augustus, *Res Gestae*: 21.

25   Suetonius, *Life of Augustus*: 28.

26   Tacitus, *Histories*: 1.5.

27   Tacitus, *Annals*: 15.38–43.

28   Champlin 2003: 206; Panella 2001 for the topography of the area.

29   Pliny, *Natural History*: 34.84; Griffin 1984: 138–41; Darwall-Smith 1996: 37–8.

30   Pliny, *Natural History*: 36.163.

31   Moormann 1998; Ball 2003.

32   Pausanias, *Description of Greece*: 10.27.3–5; Pliny, *Natural History*: 34.84.

33   Pliny, *Natural History*: 36.37.

34   Beard and Henderson 2001: 65–74 for discussion of the impact of this find.

35   Cassius Dio, *History of Rome*: 66.10.4–5.

36   See Beard 1998: 30.

37   Beagon 2005: 6–20.

38 Martial, *On Spectacles*: 1.
39 Cassius Dio, *History of Rome*: 66.25; Martial, *On Spectacles*; see Chapter 10 for discussion.
40 Suetonius, *Life of Titus*: 8.
41 Coleman 2006: lxv–lxxii; *Corpus Inscriptionum Latinarum*: 6.40454a.
42 Pliny, *Natural History*: 36.102.
43 Darwall-Smith 1996: 59.
44 Darwall-Smith 1996: 65.
45 Pliny, *Natural History*: 36.27.
46 *Corpus Inscriptionum Latinarum*: 6.2065.
47 Suetonius, *Life of Vespasian*: 8; Cassius Dio, *History of Rome*: 65.10; Tacitus, *Histories*: 4–53; Darwall-Smith 1996: 41–7.
48 Cassius Dio, *History of Rome*: 66.24.
49 Suetonius, *Life of Titus*: 8.
50 Suetonius, *Life of Domitian*: 5.
51 Darwall-Smith 1996: 256 explores the role of fire in the provision of redevelopment opportunities.
52 Suetonius, *Life of Julius Caesar*: 10; Pliny, *Natural History*: 33.53; Cassius Dio, *History of Rome*: 37.8.2.
53 Scobie 1986; Morley 1996; Scheidel 2003; compare Laurence 1997.
54 A view developed from Purcell 1987: 187.
55 A theme pursued by Favro 1996.

Notes to Chapter 4: A Little Place in the Country

1 Lafon 2001 and Mielsch 1990 provide full accounts of the material evidence for villas.
2 For the archaeology of villas close to Rome see papers in Santillo Frizell and Klynne 2005.
3 Statius, *Silvae*: 1.3.
4 Statius, *Silvae*: 1.3.
5 Zeiner 2005: 82–97.
6 Pliny, *Letters*: 2.17; Lafon 2001: 279–85; Leach 2004: 173; Elsner 1995: 80–2; Pavlovskis 1973: 26–32; Sherwin-White 1966: 28–31 on chronology.

7   See Pliny, *Letters*: 5.6.

8   Expressed in Pliny, *Natural History*: 36.48–50; Leach 2004: 57, 169–70.

9   Pliny, *Natural History*: 35.116–7; Vitruvius, *On Architecture*: 7.5.2; Schefold 1960; Ling 1977; Bergmann 1991; Clarke 1996; compare Purcell 1987, 1995 on views across the landscapes of villas found in texts and/or discovered by archaeology.

10   Bergmann 1991: 50.

11   Statius, *Silvae*: 2.2; Russo 2004; van Dam 1984: 187–280; Bergmann 1991; Pavlovskis 1973: 13–16.

12   Parslow 1995: 177–89.

13   Pliny, *Natural History*: 3.70; Vitruvius, *On Architecture*: 6.5.3; D'Arms 1970: 126.

14   Pliny, *Letters*: 3.1; Sherwin-White 1966: 206–10; Syme 1991: 540–50.

15   *Inscriptiones Latinae Selectae*: 6030; Pliny *Letters*: 1.3.1, 2.17.14, 5.6.17.

16   A similar structure is known from Pliny's own villa, *Letters*: 5.6.33.

17   Plutarch, *Life of Lucullus*: 39.2–3.

18   Pliny, *Natural History*: 36.109–10.

19   Edwards 1993: 137–72 is particularly revealing on these issues.

20   Seneca, *Controversiae*: 2.1.13.

21   Horace, *Carmina*: 2.15.1–5.

22   Seneca, *Letters*: 89.21.

23   Plutarch, *Life of Lucullus*: 39.2–3.

24   Pliny, *Natural History*: 19.50–9; Wallace-Hadrill 1998; see Grimal 1969 for old but full description of gardens in Rome.

25   Broise and Jolivet 1998; Coarelli 1983.

26   See papers in Cima and La Rocca 1986 for a full study of the evidence.

27   Jashemski 1993 provides a catalogue of garden paintings; Dawson 1944 provides a catalogue of mythological landscape paintings; see Clarke 1996 for a catalogue of landscape paintings in the villa of Oplontis.

28   Cicero, *Letters to Atticus*: 13.33.4; La Rocca 1995: 5; Cicero, *Letters to Atticus*: 12.25.

29   Cicero, *On Duties*: 1.138; Pliny, *Natural History*: 36.103; Cicero, *Letters to Friends*: 5.6.2.

30   A visit to the Villa of the Quintilii on the Via Appia would also be rewarding; see Ashby 1910 and Ricci 1998 for descriptions of the standing remains.

31   Plutarch, *Life of Lucullus*: 38–42.

32   Cicero, *On Laws*: 2.2.

33 Cicero, *On the Republic*, see Harlow and Laurence 2009.

34 Boatwright 1998.

35 Hong et al 1994 and 1996.

36 Asconius, *On the Pro Milone*: 37; Plutarch, *Life of Pompey*: 44.

37 As set out by D'Arms 1998, on which much of this section depends.

38 Varro, *On Rustic Things*: 3.2.16.

39 Pliny, *Natural History*: 14.97; D'Arms 1998: 38.

40 Plutarch, *Life of Caesar*: 55.4; Pliny, *Natural History*: 9.171, 14.97; see D'Arms 1998: 38–9. Beard 2007: 259–61 identifies these features of mass dining as innovations of Caesar's triumphs.

41 Cassius Dio, *History of Rome*: 43.42.1.

42 Cicero, *Letters to Friends*: 7.26; Suetonius, *Life of Julius Caesar*: 43.

43 Boatwright 1998; also papers in di Pasquale and Paolucci 2007.

Notes to Chapter 5: The Roman Body at the Baths

1 On the bedroom see the next chapter, delineation of privacy see Riggsby 1997. On social mixing at the baths see Hallett 2005: 61–101; Scobie 1986: 429; Nielsen 1990: 140–2. Note also the role of communal urination and defecation in Roman toilets; see articles by Jansen 1997, 2000, 2001, 2007.

2 Tacitus, *Life of Agricola*: 20–2.

3 See papers in Classen 2005 for sensations of the skin and touch; for bathing as a social experience Fagan 1999a: 3–4 delineates the territory.

4 Eger 2007 develops the theme further.

5 Nielsen 1990; and Yegül 1992 provide extensive surveys of the surviving remains of Roman bathing establishments and their usage.

6 Hallett 2005: 78–83.

7 See discussion in Hallett 2005: 71–6.

8 Hallett 2005: 83–7.

9 Cassius Dio, *History of Rome*: 58.2.4.

10 Eger 2007 explores the distinctions.

11 Martial, *Epigrams*: 10.48.3; Nielsen 1990: 135–8.

12 Seneca, *On the Happy Life*: 6–7.

13 Seneca, *Letters*: 86.

14 Seneca, *On the Happy Life*: 7.7.

15 Seneca, *Letters*: 122.6.

16 Seneca, *Letters*: 86; 90.25; compare Pliny, *Natural History*: 33.153, 36.121, 36.189.

17 Seneca, *Letters*: 56.

18 Seneca, *On the Shortness of Life*: 12.7.

19 Seneca, *Letters*: 108.16.

20 Seneca, *Moral Letters*: 90.19; Fagan 1999b: 52 note 42.

21 Petronius, *Satyrica*: 26–8.

22 Eger 2007: 146–7.

23 Augustine, *Confessions*: 2.3.

24 Cicero, *On Oratory*: 2.224, *On Duties*: 1.129.

25 Goldhill 2002 for further discussion.

26 Williams 1999: 119–24; Eger 2007: 134.

27 Stewart 1994.

28 Petronius, *Satyrica*: 87 – see Eger 2007: 135.

29 A factor highlighted by Eger 2007 in his cross-cultural study of bathing practices and pleasure.

30 Gleason 1995 for discussion of this subject and a work which provides the basis for the discussion of physiognomy in this book.

31 Polemo, *Physiognomy*: 1.1.118–20F; translated in Gleason 1995: 41.

32 Gleason 1995: 55.

33 Clement of Alexandria, *Paidagogos*: 3.11.73–4; Gleason 1995: 61–2.

34 Soranus, *Gynaecology*: 2.32; Gleason 1995: 70–3.

35 Gleason 1995: 63.

36 Quintilian, *Institutes*: 11.3.69–83, 11.3.128–9.

37 Gleason 1995: 64–5 for definition.

38 Gleason 1995: 76–81.

39 Gleason 1995: 68–9.

40 Clement of Alexandria, *Paidagogos*: 3.1.27–31; Seneca, *Letters*: 56.

41 Discussed by Gleason 1995: 74–6.

42 Gleason 1995: 76–81.

43 Persius, *Satires*: 4.33–41; Hallett 2005: 80–1.

44 Seneca, *On the Shortness of Life*: 13, *Moral Letters*: 86.

45 Galen, *Hygiene*: 2.3 [K.6.745–47]; Gleason 1995: 86.

46 Hallett 2005, especially 282–95.

47 Stevenson 1995.

48 Suetonius, *Life of Domitian*: 7; Cassius Dio, *History of Rome*: 67.2.3; law re-enacted by emperor Nerva, Cassius Dio, *History of Rome*: 68.2.4.

49 Bullough 2002; Hopkins 1978.

50 Apuleius, *The Golden Ass*: 35; see Lightfoot 2002; for other references of a similar nature see Hales 2002 note 27 and discussion by Beard 1994; Stevenson 1995.

51 Skinner 1997: 138–9.

52 Bullough and Bullough 1993.

53 Fagan 1999a reviews evidence for slaves bathing.

54 Statius, *Silvae*: 3.4.65–77.

55 Fagan 1999b: 12–39 provides a longer analysis of this subject.

56 Martial, *Epigrams*: 6.42; Statius, *Silvae*: 1.5.

57 Martial, *Epigrams*: 1.59, 2.14.

58 Martial, *Epigrams*: 6.42; Statius, *Silvae*: 1.5.

59 Martial, *Epigrams*: 1.23, 3.3, 3.51, 3.68, 3.72, 6.93, 9.33, 11.22, 11.51, 11.63, 12.83.

60 Martial, *Epigrams*: 9.33, 7.82; see also Juvenal, *Satires*: 9.33–7; Cassius Dio, *History of Rome*: 80.4–5; Taylor 1997: 363–5.

61 Ovid, *Art of Love*: 3.638–41; Pliny, *Natural History*: 33.153; Quintilian, *Institutes*: 5.9.14; see Fagan 1999b: 26–7 for discussion.

62 Martial, *Epigrams*: 2.52, 6.93.

63 Martial, *Epigrams*: 7.35, 3.68.

64 Martial, *Epigrams*: 7.34; Eger 2007: 141.

65 Fagan 1999b: 34–5.

66 Petronius, *Satyrica*: 91 with Eger 2007: 137.

67 Strabo, *Geography*: 5.4.5; Cassius Dio, *Roman History*: 48.51.2.

68 Sallust, *Catilinarian Conspiracy*; Horace, *Carmen*: 3.1.33–46, 3.24.4.

69 D'Arms 2003: 57–68.

70 Suetonius, *Life of Augustus*: 64.

71 Pliny, *Panegyricus*: 82.

72 Ovid, *Art of Love*: 1.283; Martial, *Epigrams*: 1.62; Propertius, *Elegies*: 1.11.30.

73 Seneca, *Letters*: 51.

74 Strabo, *Geography*: 5.4.7.

75 D'Arms 2003: 120.

76   Seneca, *Letters*: 51.

77   e.g. Martial, *Epigrams*: 6.42; Statius, *Silvae*: 1.5.60–4.

Notes to Chapter 6: Roman Erotics

1   See papers in Larmour et al 1997.

2   Clarke 1998, 2007.

3   Compare the analysis of Williams 1999 and Richelin 1992: 81–3.

4   Langlands 2006 for discussion of morality and sexuality in high culture.

5   See Clarke 1998: 212–40; 2007: 194–212 for discussion and full illustration; compare McGinn 2004: 112–33.

6   Clarke 2007.

7   Clarke 1998: 61–72 for visual analysis.

8   See examples in Clarke 1998.

9   Clarke 1998: 224.

10   Compare the use of mirrors by Hostius Quadra – Seneca, *Natural Questions*: 1.16.

11   Ovid, *Art of Love*: 3.768–808 with additions from *Corpus Inscriptionum Latinarum*: 4.3951, 8473; Gibson 2003: 390–6.

12   Parker 1997 succinctly describes the language; see Adams 1982: 118–38 for a fuller treatment of sexual vocabulary and sexual allusion.

13   See Varrone 2002 for a manual of sexual graffiti.

14   *Corpus Inscriptionum Latinarum*: 4.2175; *Corpus Inscriptionum Latinarum*: 4.10232a.

15   *Corpus Inscriptionum Latinarum*: 4.2319b; *Corpus Inscriptionum Latinarum*: 4.9027; *Corpus Inscriptionum Latinarum*: 4.4264.

16   For text of Galen, see C. G. Kuhn's 1965 edition *Clandii Galeni Opera Omnia*: 12.249 Hildesheim; Martial, *Epigrams*: 6.26, 11.25, 11.47, 11.50.

17   Varrone 2002: 77 note 114.

18   See index of *Corpus Inscriptionum Latinarum*: 4 supplement 1 for overview.

19   McKeown 2007 for a review of the evidence; see also Richelin 1992: 34–44.

20   Seager 1974.

21   Martial, *Epigrams*: 3.69; McGinn 2004: 124–5.

22   McKeown 2007.

23 Martial, *Epigrams*: 2.47, 4.42, 9.22, 11.8, 11.22, 11.23, 11.26, 11.43, 11.63, 11.70, 11.78, 11.87, 12.86, 12.96; Petronius, *Satyrica*: 28.4, 64.6–12, 74.8–17.

24 Clarke 1998: 196–206.

25 *Corpus Inscriptionum Latinarum*: 4.5408, 1969, 3999, 8940; McGinn 2004: 40–55 on prices.

26 *Corpus Inscriptionum Latinarum*: 4.1751.

27 *Corpus Inscriptionum Latinarum*: 4.7339.

28 *Corpus Inscriptionum Latinarum*: 4.8356.

29 *Corpus Inscriptionum Latinarum*: 4.2450.

30 McGinn 2004: 295–302.

31 Parker 1997 for discussion.

32 The exact number of brothels in Pompeii is the subject of debate, see Laurence 2007 for my own view and discussion of the views of others.

33 McGinn 2004: 295–302.

34 Clarke 1998.

35 Martial, *Epigrams*: 3.71: 'When your slave boy has an aching cock, Naevolus, and you an aching arse, I need be no seer to guess what you do.'

36 Margolis 2004 for discussion.

37 But see Rousselle 1988: 27–9, 39, 71 for discussion of medical anatomy of the female orgasm.

38 E.g. Ovid, *Art of Love*: 2.703–32, 3.769–88.

39 *Corpus Inscriptionum Latinarum*: 4.2066.

40 Lucretius: 4.1192; Ovid, *Amores*: 1.4.66, *Art of Love*: 2.685–90, 3.769–88; Martial, *Epigrams*: 11.29, 11.60; Apuleius, *Metamorphoses*: 11.29.3.

41 See discussion by Henderson 2006 and Parker 1992.

42 *Corpus Inscriptionum Latinarum*: 4.4239, 2248.

43 Rousselle 1988.

44 King 2004: 84–5.

45 Horace, *Sermiones*: 1.2.116–9.

46 *Corpus Inscriptionum Latinarum*: 4.2066; compare Martial, *Epigrams*: 9.22, 9.41; *Corpus Inscriptionum Latinarum*: 4.1863 on the cook.

47 Clarke 2007: 188–9 with plate 22 for position of fountain.

48 For examples see Clarke 2007: 92–3.

49 Richelin 1993: 537.

50 Summed up in Catullus, *Poems*: 61; Richelin 1993: 534.

51 Eger 2007.

52 Richelin 1993: 544–5.

53 Compare with Catiline in the Republic, see Cicero, *Against Catiline*: 2.23.

54 Taylor 1997 exposes the power relations at work.

55 See for example Seneca, *Letters*: 47.7.

56 Taylor 1997: 327–8.

57 *Appendix Vergiliana*: 13, a pattern repeated in other authors e.g. Taylor 1997: 329–30.

58 Bullough and Bullough 1993.

59 Taylor 1997: 344–5.

Notes to Chapter 7: Dining

1 Nutton 1995; Garnsey 1999.

2 See Purcell 2005 and Wilkins 2005.

3 See examples in D'Arms 1984.

4 Cicero, *Letters to Friends*: 9.24.

5 Tacitus, *Life of Agricola*: 21; Cassius Dio, *History of Rome*: 62.6.4.

6 E.g. *Satires*: 5.24 – discussed by Gowers 1993: 188–219; Pliny, *Letters*: 2.6 with D'Arms 1990.

7 Suetonius, *Life of Claudius*: 32, *Life of Titus*: 2 ; Tacitus, *Annals*: 13.16; Roller 2006: 159–69, 170–1; Booth 1991; Jashemski 1979: 90; Bradley 1998a: 46; but note Sigismund-Nielsen 1998: 58–9.

8 Quintilian, *Institutes*: 1.2.8; Bradley 1998a: 44.

9 Valerius Maximus: 2.1.2.

10 Roller 2005.

11 Cicero, *Letters to Atticus*: 5.1; Roller 2005: 70.

12 Roller 2005.

13 E.g. Suetonius, *Life of Augustus*: 69, *Life of Caligula*: 25.

14 Valerius Maximus: 2.1.5; Pliny, *The Natural History*: 14.141; Seneca, *Letters*: 85.20; Pliny, *Natural History*: 14.137–42.

15 Gowers 1993: 4; Bradley 1998a: 42–3; Roller 2006: 164.

16 Clement of Alexandria, *Paedagogus*: 2.13, 2.31, 2.55, 2.60.

17 Corbeill 1997.

18   Suetonius, *Life of Nero*: 31; Bek 1983.

19   Plutarch, *Moralia*: 619B–F.

20   Plutarch, *Moralia*: 619E–F.

21   Fredrick's 2003: 317 discussion of Plutarch, *Moralia* on this subject.

22   Graham 2005.

23   Varro, *apud Nonius*: 117.

24   Vitruvius, *On Architecture*: 6.3.

25   Jashemski 1979: 89–94 surveys the evidence from Pompeii.

26   Bek 1983: 84.

27   Pliny, *Letters*: 2.17; Bek 1983: 100.

28   *Sunday Times*: 5 June 2005.

29   Although there is some connection in Latin literature between dining and sex, see Gowers 1993: 37; Adams 1982: 138–9.

30   Dunbabin 2003: 52–63; Roller 2005: 61–5, 82–7; 2006: 45–83.

31   Dunbabin 2003: 56–7.

32   Fredrick 2003: 327–37 on erotic paintings and dining rooms.

33   Edwards 2007: 162–3; D'Arms 1984: 341.

34   Compare Seneca, *Letters*: 47.8.

35   Petronius, *Satyrica*: 27–77; Courtney 2001: 72–126; Sullivan 1968: 56–9; Conte 1996: 104–39.

36   Petronius, *Satyrica*: 39.

37   Plutarch, *Moralia*: 528b; D'Arms 1999: 301.

38   Macrobius, *Saturnalia*: 7.5.32.

39   Seneca, *On the Happy Life*: 11.4; D'Arms 1999: 303; 1991 on role of slaves at dinner.

40   Gowers 1993: 17.

41   Seneca, *Letters*: 114.

42   Gellius, *Attic Nights*: 6.22.4; Plutarch, *Life of Cato the Elder*: 9; Gowers 1993: 13.

43   Livy, *History of Rome*: 39.6.7–9.

44   Tacitus, *Annals*: 3.53–5.

45   Gowers 1993: 16–17 for discussion.

46   Seneca, *Letters*: 95.

47   Pliny, *Natural History*: 15.105.

48   Pliny, *Natural History*: 8.170, 10.45.

49   Pliny, *Natural History*: 8.211.

50 Suetonius, *Life of Vitellius*: 1–7.

51 Suetonius, *Life of Vitellius*: 13; Gowers 1993: 20.

52 Suetonius, *Life of Vitellius*: 17, see Chapter 11 for discussion of this incident.

53 Moormann 2000.

54 Rodriguez-Almeida 2000.

55 Liebeschuetz 2000.

56 Jansen 2000.

57 See also Martial, *Epigrams*: 3.82, 6.89; Bradley 1998a: 44.

58 Celsus, *On Medicine*: 1.3.17; Gowers 1993: 19.

59 Cicero, *Letters to Friends*: 7.26.

60 Patterson 2006: 252–63; Donahue 2004: 84–9, 128–36.

61 Pliny, *Letters*: 10.33–4.

62 *Corpus Inscriptionum Latinarum*: 14.2112.

63 *Digest of Justininian*: 3.4.1.

64 Hermansen 1982: 55–90.

65 Varro, *Rustic Things*: 3.2.16.

66 Hermansen 1982: 62–3.

67 See Donahue 2004: 85–9 for text, translation and commentary on the law.

68 Donahue 2004: 88–9.

69 Donahue 2004: 265 cites Philo, *Special Laws*: 2.145–6 to support this idea.

70 Cassius Dio, *History of Rome*: 54.2.

71 Donahue 2004: 37–8.

72 Patterson 2006: 169–76.

73 *Corpus Inscriptionum Latinarum*: 9.2962, 9.3160, 10.688, 14.2112.

Notes to Chapter 8: Food and Wine

1 Pliny, *Natural History*: 14.5.

2 Tertullian, *Apologeticus*: 3.6.

3 Dalby 2003: 16–18 for ancient sources.

4 Apicius: 1.6–1.28.

5 E.g. Grant 1999 or Grainger 2006.

6 Grainger 2006: 11.

7 Grainger 2006: 20.

8   Martial, *Epigrams*: 7.31; Juvenal, *Satires*: 5.104–6.

9   Dalby 2000: 213–14.

10 De Ruyt 1983: 341–50.

11 Varro, *Menippean Satires*: 316; Martial, *Epigrams*: 1.103; Horace, *Satires*: 2.6.63–76.

12 Martial, *Epigrams*: 1.41, 12.57 sets out some of the dynamics of the economics of street trading at Rome – see now Morley 2007.

13 Martial, *Epigrams*: 13.32; Horace, *Satires*: 2.3.227–8; Martial, *Epigrams*: 11.27.

14 Classen et al 1994: 13–50 investigate the smells of antiquity; see also papers in Drobnick 2006 on the analysis of smells in cultures.

15 Propertius, *Elegies*: 3.10; Dalby 2000: 245.

16 Martial, *Epigrams*: 9.60; Horace, *Odes*:1.36.15–16; Classen 1993: 17–20.

17 Horace, *Odes*: 1.38.6–8.

18 Ovid, *Fasti*: 5.331–46.

19 Pliny, *Natural History*: 13.20–23, see Vons 1999 for full discussion of exotic essences in Pliny and see also Faure 1987.

20 Pliny, *Natural History*: 13.26; Athenaeus, *Deipnosophitae*: 688E–692C; Mattingly 1990.

21 Pliny, *Natural History*: 13.22; Athenaeus, *Deipnosophitae*: 553A–B, 689E–F.

22 Theophrastus, *De Causis Plantarum*: 6 makes this clear.

23 Grocock and Grainger 2006: 8.

24 Apicius: 8.2.1.

25 Thurmond 2006: 263.

26 Miller 1968.

27 Miller 1968: 23–5 provides the data and analysis.

28 Pliny, *Natural History*: 6.101, 12.84; Tacitus, *Annals*: 3.53; Miller 1968: 222–32.

29 Pliny, *Natural History*: 9.62–3.

30 Martial, *Epigrams*: 14.220.

31 Juvenal, *Satires*: 9.107–19.

32 Pliny, *Natural History*: 9.67.

33 Curtis 1991.

34 Grainger 2006: 27–9 for expert discussion and definition; Rawson and Li 2004 explain the science behind flavours; Lucretius, *De Rerum Natura*: 4.617–72 on sensation of taste.

35 Grainger 2006: 29.

36   Grant 1999: 29–30.
37   Grainger 2006: 45–6.
38   Apicius: 2.2.9.
39   Apicius: 3.7; Grainger 2006: 56.
40   Apicius: 4.1.2; Grainger 2006: 50–1.
41   Grainger 2006: 98; Apicius: 4.2.36.
42   Apicius: 4.3.6; Grainger 2006: 82–3 for the modern recipe.
43   Apicius: 6.2.22; on use of sauces see Solomon 1995.
44   Pliny, *Natural History*: 10.133; Seneca, *Letters*: 110.12; Suetonius, *Life of Vitellius*: 13.
45   Apicius: 7.14.1.
46   Apicius: 9.1.2, 9.1.3, 9.7.
47   See Edwards 1984, Grant 1999, Grainger 2006 or Kaufman 2006.
48   Solomon 1995: 127.
49   Purcell 1994: 191.
50   See Carver 2001 for discussion of export to Britain; Tchernia 1984 for the Italian context.
51   *Corpus Inscriptionum Latinarum*: 4.1679.
52   Purcell 1994: 198 and D'Arms 1995: 308–12 discuss abstinence in childhood.
53   Pliny, *Natural History*: 14.89–90; Valerius Maximus, *Memorable Deeds and Sayings*: 6.3; Aulus Gellius, *Attic Nights*: 10.23.4–5; Bettini 1995 and Purcell 1994 for discussion.
54   Purcell 1994: 200; D'Arms 1995: 308–12.
55   Plutarch, *Roman Questions*: 6, 20; Macrobius, *Saturnalia*: 1.12.25; Purcell 1994: 200.
56   See Dunbabin 2003.
57   Suetonius, *Life of Augustus*: 65.
58   Murray 1995 comes close to articulating a theory of pleasure in his discussion of wine, but see Chapter 1 above.
59   D'Arms 1995: 304–6.
60   See Villard 1988 for discussion.
61   Purcell 1985.
62   Suetonius, *Life of Domitian*: 7.2, this may have been a means to prevent further consumption as Purcell 1985 argues with reference to Levick 1982: 66–73 on the interpretation of this passage.

63 Purcell 1985: 13–15.

64 Pliny, *Natural History*: 14.8.

65 Pliny, *Natural History*: 14.4, see Purcell 1985: 17–18 for other examples.

66 Pliny, *Natural History*: 14.38–39.

67 Columella, *On Agriculture*: 3.3.

68 Pliny, *Natural History*: 14.48–52; Columella, *On Agriculture*: 3.3.

69 Tchernia 1986: 11–21.

70 Pliny, *Natural History*: 14.55–57.

71 Pliny, *Natural History*: 14.59–97; Tchernia 1995: 299; 1986: 28–39, 201–3; Brun 2004.

72 *Corpus Inscriptionum Latinarum*: 4.1679.

73 Pliny, *Natural History*: 14.71–2; see Tchernia 1984: 321–44 Appendix 2 for other references to the *grands crus*.

74 Pliny, *Letters*: 2.6.

75 See review by Heath in Douglas 1987: 46.

76 Seneca, *Letters*: 83.11; see D'Arms 1995 on heavy drinking.

77 D'Arms 1995 on basis of *Digest*: 21.1.4.2, 14.4, 25.6; also Pliny, *Natural History*: 14.147–50.

78 Suetonius, *Life of Tiberius*: 42; Seneca, *Letters*: 83.14–15.

Notes to Chapter 9: A Great Song and Dance

1 Cassius Dio, *History of Rome*: 57.18.3.

2 Horsfall 2003 cleverly draws our attention to the significances of music and song for the creation of collective oral memory at Rome.

3 Persius, *Satires*: 3.18.

4 Horsfall 2003: 11–20 sets out these examples and much more.

5 Statius, *Silvae*: 1.2.

6 Pseudo-Vergil, *Copa*; Sallust, *Catilinarian Conspiracy*: 25.2.

7 Macrobius, *Saturnalia*: 3.14.5.

8 Horsfall 2003: 35 based on Macrobius, *Saturnalia*: 3.14.4.

9 Cicero, *Against Catiline*: 2.23.

10 Cicero, *Laws*: 2.39; *Brutus*: 75; *Tusculan Disputations*: 1.3, 4.3; Valerius Maximus, *Deeds and Sayings*: 2.1.10; Zorzetti 1990.

11 Macrobius, *Saturnalia*: 3.14.7.

12 Lucilius fragment: 33 [Warmington].

13 Johnson 2000a, 2000b for full discussion.

14 You can hear this piece on the internet at http://classics.uc.edu/music/michigan.

15 Johnson 2000a: 30.

16 Letters 1969.

17 Suetonius, *Life of Nero*: 20, Landels 1999: 200–2; also attempted by the emperor Hadrian, *Life of Hadrian*: 15.9.

18 Pliny, *Letters*: 7.4.9.

19 Landels 1999: 172–90 on the tradition of music at Rome.

20 Sear 2006 for full survey of remains including indication of dating.

21 Vitruvius, *On Architecture*: 5.3.1.

22 Vitruvius, *On Architecture*: 5.3.3; discussed by Landels 1999: 189–95.

23 On theories of harmony, see Barker 1989.

24 Jory 1981 reviews the evidence, see now Lada-Richards 2007: 22–5, also Jory 1996.

25 Athenaeus, *Deipnosophistae*: 1.20.

26 See also Macrobius, *Saturnalia*: 2.7.18.

27 Seneca, *Controversiae*: 3 Preface 10; see Jory 1981 for dissemination of pantomime and cultural change in first century CE.

28 Tacitus, *Annals*: 1.77; Valerius Maximus, *Memorable Deeds and Sayings*: 2.4; compare rioting in previous year in Tacitus, *Annals*: 1.54.2; Cassius Dio, *History of Rome*: 56.47.2.

29 Cassius Dio, *History of Rome*: 57.21.3; Tacitus, *Annals*: 4.14.3; Suetonius, *Life of Tiberius*: 37.

30 Cassius Dio, *History of Rome*: 60.28.3–5, on destruction of Mnester's lover Poppaea see Tacitus, *Annals*: 11.4 and Mnester's demise at Tacitus, *Annals*: 11.36

31 Cassius Dio, *History of Rome*: 59.5.5; Suetonius, *Life of Caligula*: 54, 58; Josephus, *Jewish Antiquities*: 19.94, 104.

32 Jory 1984: 63–5.

33 See Lada-Richards 2005 for discussion of this passage; compare Jory 1984 highlighting other passages of Lucian's *Saltatio*.

34 Seneca, *Natural Questions*: 7.32.

35 Cassius Dio, *History of Rome*: 61.19; Suetonius, *Life of Nero*: 11.

36 Suetonius, *Life of Nero*: 23.

37 Suetonius, *Life of Nero*: 20.

38 Celsus, *On Medicine*: 7.25.1–2; Martial, *Epigrams*: 7.82.1; 11.75; 14.215; Juvenal, *Satires*: 6.379; Jackson 2005 for discussion of the procedure.

39 Cassius Dio, *History of Rome*: 62.20.

40 Suetonius, *Life of Nero*: 21; Cassius Dio, *History of Rome*: 62.20.

41 Suetonius, *Life of Nero*: 54.

42 Edwards 1994.

43 For the chronological development and content see Champlin 2003: 68–83.

44 Cassius Dio, *History of Rome*: 62.20.

45 See Champlin 2003: 84–111 on use of mythology for justification of political ends.

46 Champlin 2003: 82.

47 Pliny, *Letters*: 3.1.

48 Pliny, *Letters*: 7.24.

49 Sherwin-White 1966: 431–2.

50 Harlow and Laurence 2002: 129.

51 Ramage 1983: 69–70.

52 Horace, *Odes*: 3.29; Martial, *Epigrams*: 12.18, 12.57; Pliny, *Letters*: 1.9.7.

53 Statius, *Silvae*: 1.1.63–65.

54 Martial, *Epigrams*: 10.74.

55 Juvenal, *Satires*: 3.23; Pliny, *Natural History*: 26.111; Quintilian, *Institutes*: 9.4.12.

56 Compare Horace, *Satires*: 1.4; and Martial, *Epigrams*: 3.44.

57 Martial, *Epigrams*: 1.41.6–10, 6.64.21, 14.233.

58 Loane 1938: 149.

59 *Digest of Justinian*: 14.2.5.4; 19.5.20.2; Seneca, *On Benefits*: 6.38.3; Ovid, *Art of Love*: 1.421–2.

60 Horsfall 2003: 57, 98–9.

61 Martial, *Epigrams*: 7.61.

62 Loane 1938: 113–56 remains the most thorough treatment of urban distribution; see Morley 2007 for a more recent macro-scale approach.

63 Horsfall 2003: 43–5 for examples.

Notes to Chapter 10: Violence

1   Syme 1961 for discussion of Vedius' identity and now Capponi 2002.
2   For versions of the story: Seneca, *On Anger*: 3.40, Pliny, *Natural History*: 9.77; Cassius Dio, *History of Rome*: 54.23.1–5.
3   Seneca, *On Clemency*: 1.18.2; on his view of slavery see Griffin 1976: 256–85.
4   See discussion by Africa 1995 for interpretations of the incident.
5   Seneca, *Letters*: 47.3; *On Anger*: 3.24–5.
6   Saller 1991: 158; Bradley 1984: 119–20.
7   Seneca, *Letters*: 122.15.
8   Seneca, *Letters*: 14.6.
9   Bradley 1984: 118–23 provides a survey of examples.
10 Wiseman 1985: 5–10.
11 Gellius, *Attic Nights*: 10.3.2–17.
12 Parker 1989: 240.
13 *L'Année Epigraphique* 1971 no. 88.
14 For example at neighbouring Cumae, *L'Année Epigraphique* 1971 no. 89, translated in Gardner and Wiedemann 1991 no. 22.
15 Tacitus, *Annals*: 14.42–5.
16 Bradley 1984: 131 suggests cremation was the punishment on basis of *Digest of Justinian* 48.19.28.11.
17 Kajanto 1969; Tacitus, *Annals*: 13.32 on extension of law to freed slaves.
18 Seneca, *Letters*: 12.3.
19 Saller 1994: 151.
20 Cahn 2006 for a perspective on children as witnesses and victims of the violence inflicted on others.
21 Pliny, *Natural History*: 36.163, 8.197; Cassius Dio, *History of Rome*: 58.7 following Wiedemann 1996: 213–21; Seager 2005: 151–88, 227–30, for discussion of Sejanus' rise and fall.
22 Tacitus, *Annals*: 4.3.
23 Seager 2005: 155–6, 227–8.
24 Levick 1999: 168–79.
25 Tacitus, *Annals*: 6.24.
26 Cassius Dio, *History of Rome*: 58.11.6; see Plass 1995: 7; Bargagli and Grosso 1997: 24 for text from *Fasti Ostiensis*.

27 Levick 1999: 201–7.

28 Saller 1994 for references, but see now Laes 2005.

29 Seneca, *On Firmness*: 12.3, similar modes of thinking can be found in Plutarch's *De Liberis Educandis.*

30 Plutarch, *Life of Cato*: 5, 20, 21.

31 Seneca, *On Clemency*: 1.14.1, 1.16.3; Saller 1991.

32 Cassius Dio, *History of Rome*: 61.9; Tacitus, *Annals*: 13.25; Suetonius, *Life of Nero*: 26, 28: Champlin 2003: 164–5 for discussion.

33 Barker 2005 discusses the phenomenon.

34 Golvin 1988 for full survey; Wiedemann 1992 on identity and the amphitheatre.

35 Coleman 1990: 46–7.

36 Coleman 2006 for full discussion of the text.

37 Martial, *On Spectacles*: 15 and 27; see Wiedemann 1992: 178–9; Coleman 2006: 140–7; 235–43.

38 *On Spectacles*: 7; Wiedemann 1992: 84–5.

39 Coleman 1990; 2006: 62–8 for full discussion.

40 *On Spectacles*: 8; Coleman 2006: 97–100.

41 *On Spectacles*: 22 and 23; Coleman 2006: 186–94.

42 *On Spectacles*: 17.

43 Seneca, *On Anger*: 1.1.6.

44 Seneca, *On the Shortness of Life*: 13.3–7; Pliny, *Natural History*: 8.21; Bell 2004: 170ff for discussion.

45 Pliny, *Natural History*: 8.17; Beagon 1992: 125; Bell 2004: 163–4.

46 Fulford and Wallace-Hadrill 1999; Bradley 1998a: 545–56.

47 Fitzgerald 2005.

48 Beagon 1992: 147.

49 Cassius Dio, *History of Rome*: 66.25; Hopkins 1983: 8–10 discusses the scale of the games.

50 Josephus, *Jewish War*: 7.37–8; 7.39–40.

51 Beard 2007 on the discussion of the historical veracity of accounts of triumphs.

52 Josephus, *Jewish War*: 7.137–48; Flory 1998 identifies a role for women as viewers of the triumph.

53 Josephus, *Jewish War*: 7.153–7; Versnel 1970: 388–93.

54 Jacobelli 2003.

55 Pliny, *Natural History*: 35.52.

56 *Corpus Inscriptionum Latinarum*: 4.4342, 4353; Hopkins 1983; Wiedemann 1992: 30–5; and more recently Kyle 1998: 79–90.

57 Wistrand 1990 for full discussion.

58 Kyle 1998: 3–4; Wiedemann 1992: 128–60 exposes the absence of opposition.

59 Compare Kyle 1998: 265.

60 On the issues of violence in the wake of 9/11 see essays in Castelli and Jakobsen 2004.

61 See Wiedemann 1992: 71–2 for a pre-9/11 view.

62 Seneca, *On Anger*: 2.32.

63 For example Appian's *Civil Wars* written in the second century; Plass 1995: 144–7 for discussion of orgiastic violence; see Tacitus, *Histories*: 3.33 and Suetonius, *Life of Vitellius*: 17 for examples; Seneca, *On Anger*: 3.2 creates a pastiche of violent civil conflict.

64 Tacitus, *Annals*: 1.1–6.

65 Seneca, *Letters*: 47.19–21.

66 Suetonius, *Life of Domitian*: 21; *Scriptores Historiae Augustae, Life of Avidius Cassius*: 2.4 assigns the saying to Hadrian; see Laurence and Paterson 1999.

67 Tacitus, *Annals*: 3.65; Plass 1995: 113–15 on the comparison.

68 Levick 1999: 180–99.

69 Seneca, *On Anger*: 3.19; Cassius Dio, *History of Rome*: 59.19.7–8.

70 Bauman 1996: 66–70.

71 Eutropius: 7.15; Champlin 2003: 5.

72 Suetonius, *Life of Caligula*: 20.

Notes to Chapter 11: Collectors and Collections

1 Getty 1976: 268–75.

2 Getty 1966: 9.

3 Suetonius, *Life of Augustus*: 70.

4 Pollitt 1978: 161–2; Pliny, *Natural History*: 33.147, 35.130. Pliny the Elder records a relatively poor woman purchasing rock-crystal cups for the aristocratic fortune of 150,000 *sesterces* (*Natural History*: 37.29).

5 Getty 1976: 276–8.

6 Pliny, *Natural History*: 36.27, 36.195.

7   Pliny, *Natural History*: 37.18–20.

8   Pliny, *Natural History*: 35.26.

9   Pollitt 1978; Isager 1991: 70–3; Tanner 2006: 235–76 on wider issues in Pliny's history of art in Greece. On moral crisis: Pliny, *Natural History*: 33.147–150, 34.14, 34.34, 37.12–14; compare slightly earlier Livy, *History of Rome*: 25.40.1–3, 39.6.7, and later Plutarch, *Life of Marcellus*: 21.5.

10 Bounia 2004: 202; Isager 1991: 83–4.

11 Tanner 2006: 255–60.

12 Martial, *Epigrams*: 9.43; Suetonius, *Life of Julius Caesar*: 47.

13 Pliny, *Natural History*: 34.16–17; Isager 1991: 85–6.

14 Suetonius, *Life of Augustus*: 72; Pliny, *Natural History*: 9.4.9–11 on dead Nereids washed up on shores of Gaul in the reign of Augustus.

15 Cassius Dio, *History of Rome*: 76.21–23.

16 Phlegon of Tralles, *Book of Marvels*: 14.

17 Phlegon of Tralles, *Book of Marvels*: 14.

18 Phlegon of Tralles, *Book of Marvels*: 15.

19 Pliny, *Natural History*: 7.3.35; Phlegon of Tralles, *Book of Marvels*: 34.

20 The Phoenix was a bird thought to regenerate itself every 540 years. A maggot was said to form on the decaying body of the Phoenix; in time the maggot was transformed into a Phoenix. It is also a symbol of eternity – see Evans 2003 for discussion. Most authors at the time were sceptical of its authenticity: Tacitus, *Annals*: 6.28; Pliny, *Natural History*: 10.2.5; Cassius Dio, *History of Rome*: 58.27.1; Aurelius Victor, *Caesars*: 4.

21 Plutarch, *Life of Sulla*: 27; Pausanias, *Geography of Greece*: 9.20–1.

22 Isager 1991: 157–68; Strong 1994 on the tradition of display.

23 Kellum 1990: 276; see Gaspari 1979 for architectural study; Cassius Dio, *History of Rome*: 55.1, 55.8, 56.25 for dating of construction.

24 Becatti 1973–1974 for full discussion and the speculation of location of art works by Kellum 1990.

25 On the use of white and coloured marble see Bradley 2005–2006; Kellum 1990: 277.

26 Kellum 1990 for recent discussion.

27 Pliny, *Natural Hisory*: 34.77, 34.90, 34.89, 34.73, 34.80.

28 Pliny, *Natural History*: 35.131, 35.144; Isager 1991: 159–60 for summary in English; also Bounia 2004: 184–5.

29   Pliny, *Natural History*: 36.33–4, 7.30.7; Isager 1991: 163–6; Becatti 1956; Suetonius, *Life of Julius Caesar*: 44; Cicero, *Letters to Atticus*: 4.16; Bounia 2004: 188–9.

30   Isager 1991: 160–2; Bounia 2004: 186–7.

31   Pliny, *Natural History*: 35.24–6.

32   De Caro 1987 for full description.

33   De Caro 1987 for full descriptions and illustrations of the sculptures.

34   Mattusch and Lie 2005: 155–7.

35   De Caro 1987: 100.

36   De Caro 1987: 129; Pliny, *Natural History*: 34.18.

37   Cicero, *Letters to Atticus*: 1.1, 1.6.2, 1.9.2, 1.10.3.

38   Mattusch and Lie 2005 for full catalogue and study of the sculpture from the villa.

39   Mattusch and Lie 2005: 15; Bartman 1991: 71.

40   Suetonius, *Life of Tiberius*: 39; Tacitus, *Annals*: 4.59.

41   Carey 2002.

42   Stewart 1977: 85–7.

43   Pliny, *Natural History*: 13.91–5.

44   Ulrich 2007: 213–14; Mols 1999.

45   Ulrich 2007: 224; Cicero, *Against Verres*: 4.35; Varro, *On the Latin Language*: 5.126.

46   Mols and Moormann 1993–1994.

47   Painter 2001 for modern study; Maiuri 1933 for original publication.

48   Painter 2001: 26; Seneca, *Dialogues*: 9.1.7; Pliny, *Natural History*: 33. 53–5, 154; Martial, *Epigrams*: 3.40, 4.39.

49   For discussion see Cirillo and Casale 2004.

50   Mastroroberto 2006a and 2006b; AAVV 2006; for wider context AAVV 1991; compare for bronze vessels Tassinari 1993.

51   Kuttner 1995; Clarke 1998: 61–72.

52   Painter 2001: 28.

53   Pliny, *Natural History*: 34.11.

54   Pliny, *Natural History*: 7.75.

55   Seneca, *Letters*: 50.

56   Ripley 1977; Adams 2001: 1–2.

57   Martial, *Epigrams*: 8.13; Plutarch, *Moralia*: 520C; Quintilian, *Institutes*: 2.5.11.

58   Garland 1995: 46–8; Ernst 2006 on the development of normal and abnormal in modern thought.

59 Stevenson et al 1993: vii.

60 Petronius, *Satyricon*: 1.28.

61 Suetonius, *Life of Augustus*: 83; *Life of Tiberius*: 61; *Life of Domitian*: 4; Tacitus, *Annals*: 15.34; Juvenal, *Satires*: 4.113–22; Garland 1995: 48–50.

62 Compare Ravenscroft 2006 on the liminal position of dwarfs in the Hapsburg court in early modern Spain.

63 Garland 1995: 67–70; Stevenson 1993: 7.

64 Compare Mitchell 2006 on shift in meaning of conjoined twins in the nineteenth century.

65 Suetonius, *Life of Augustus*: 43.

66 The evidence is discussed by Burnet 2002.

67 Pliny, *Natural History*: 7.75.

Notes to Chapter 12: Pleasure Transforms Roman Culture

1 Zanker 1988; Galinsky 1996.

2 See essays in Habinek and Schiesaro 1997.

3 Vout 2007 links eroticism to power in first-century Rome.

4 For the development of the academic study of sensory perception see papers in the following volumes: Classen 1993; 2005; Classen et al 1994; Bull and Black 2003; Drobnick 2006; Korsmeyer 2005.

5 For example Plutarch, *Life of Pompey*: 24; see De Souza 2008: 92–3 for other textual references.

6 Edwards 2007: 113–43.

7 As Nero did; see Champlin 2003.

8 Pliny, *Panegyricus*: 22.3; Kampen 1997: 271–2; discussed by Vout 2007: 20.

9 Jouffroy 1986: 326.

10 *L'Année Epigraphique*: 1957: 250; see Patterson 2006: 134–5 for further examples.

11 Suetonius, *Life of Tiberius*: 37.

12 Patterson 2006: 148–60.

13 Patterson 2006: 161–9.

14 See Patterson 2006: 125–60 with Sear 2006: 118–85 for theatres.

15 Tacitus, *Life of Agricola*: 21.

16   On the relationship between identity and consumption/consumer choice in the archaeological record, see Ray 2006; Monteil 2004; Martins 2003; Fincham 2002.

17   See Creighton 2000.

18   See Creighton 2006 for development of towns in Britain.

19   Cassius Dio, *History of Rome*: 62.7.4.

20   Tacitus, *Annals of Imperial Rome*: 14.33.

21   Tacitus, *Agricola*: 3.

22   See Seneca, *On Mercy*: 1.6; Bartsch 1994 on Pliny's *Panegyric*.

23   Vout 2007: 66–7.

24   See Bartsch 1994 for discussion of rhetoric under Trajan.

25   Juvenal, *Satires*: 6.462.

26   Tacitus, *Life of Agricola*: 3 alludes to the adjustment to life under Nerva from life under Domitian.

27   Pliny, *Letters*: 7.24.

28   Pliny, *Letters*: 3.1; Harlow and Laurence 2002: 123–30.

29   See Cokayne 2003: 81–3; Parkin 2003: 239–47 on marginality of the old.

30   Tacitus, *Life of Agricola*: 3.

31   Tacitus, *The Histories*: 1.1.

32   Eyben 1993:19–23; 31–41; Parkin in press.

33   Parkin 1993: 36–56 for the demography of old age.

34   See Rudich 1993, 1997 for studies of opposition to the rule of pleasure.

35   Gold 1998: 372.

36   Juvenal, *Satire*: 4.5–10.

37   Juvenal, *Satire*: 14.86–95.

38   Juvenal, *Satire*: 4.135–43.

39   Juvenal, *Satire*: 6.67–133.

40   Juvenal, *Satire*: 11.1–11.

41   DeLaine 2006; compare Wilson 2006.

42   Seen most clearly in the renewal of bath buildings in Italy, see DeLaine 1999: 70–3.

43   Duncan-Jones 1990: 177–8 for costs; DeLaine 2006 for discussion.

44   Wilson 2006 follows DeLaine 2000 on this.

45   Wilson 2006: 229.

46   DeLaine 2006: 244.

47 DeLaine 1992 for discussion of change in design of bath buildings in this period, an urban terrain in which technological refinements can be measured and documented.

48 Suresh 2004: 101–2; also papers in Cimino 1994.

49 Hopkins' 2002 restatement of his position in 1980 continues to provide a model for the economy; see Saller 2002 for discussion.

50 Shepherd 1993 for a full listing, see Nriagu 1983 for sources of lead.

51 Nriagu 1996, 1998; Hong et al 1994, 1996; Boutron 1995; Rosman et al 1997.

52 I do not in any way wish to stress that lead poisoning caused the fall of the Roman Empire – Nriagu 1983 provides an overview of the concept, but I find his conclusions less than compelling. As he says there were many reasons for the fall of the Roman Empire.

53 Renberg et al 1994, 2000, 2002; Miko et al 2005; Alfonso et al 2001; Le Roux et al 2004.

54 For study of technology of Roman iron working see Sim and Ridge 2002; Wilson 2002 discusses recent debates and draws together the evidence for mining in the Roman period.

55 De Calataÿ 2005 discusses the evidence for long-term change that he sees ending in c. 300 CE, see also Wilson 2002.

56 Duncan-Jones 1996; Scheidel 2002 for effects of the smallpox pandemic known as the Antonine Plague. Wilson 2002: 29 suggests that many of the problems can be traced back to a cessation of production at key mining sites of precious metals.

Select Bibliography

AAVV (1991) *L'argento dei Romani: Vasellame da Tavola e d'apparato* (Rome).

——(2006) *Argenti a Pompei* (Naples).

Adams, J.N. (1982) *The Latin Sexual Vocabulary* (London).

Adams, R. (2001) *Freaks and the American Cultural Imagination* (Chicago).

Africa, T.W. (1995) 'Adam Smith, the wicked knight and the use of anecdotes'. *Greece and Rome*, 42: 70–5.

Alfonso, S., Grousset, F., Massée, L. and Tastet, J.-P. (2001) 'A European lead isotope signal recorded from 6000–300 Years BP in coastal marshes (SW France)'. *Atmospheric Environment*, 35: 3595–605.

Ashby, T. (1910) 'La Villa dei Quintilii'. *Ausonia*, 4: 2–42.

Ball, L.F. (2003) *The Domus Aurea and the Roman Architectural Revolution* (Cambridge).

Bargagli, B. and Grosso, C. (1997) *I Fasti Ostiensis: documento della storia di Ostia* (Rome).

Barker, A. (1989) *Greek Musical Writings Volume II: Harmonic and Acoustic Theory* (Cambridge).

Barker, G.T. (2005) *Dying to be Men* (London).

Bartman, E. (1991) 'Sculptural collecting and display in the private realm', in E.K. Gazda (ed.) *Roman Art in the Private Sphere* (Ann Arbor) pp. 71–88.

Bartsch, S. (1994) *Actors in the Audience: Theatricality and Doublespeak from Nero to Hadrian* (Cambridge MA)

Bauman, R.A. (1996) *Crime and Punishment in Ancient Rome* (London).

Beagon, M. (1992) *Roman Nature: The Thought of Pliny the Elder* (Oxford).

——(2005) *The Elder Pliny on the Human Animal* (Oxford).

Beard, M. (1994) 'The Roman and the foreign: The cult of the "Great Mother" in Imperial Rome', in N. Thomas and C. Humphrey (eds) *Shamanism, History, and the State* (Ann Arbor) pp. 164–90.

——(1998) 'Imaginary *Horti*: or up the garden path', in M. Cima and E. La Rocca (eds) *Horti Romani* (Rome) pp. 23–32.

Beard, M. and Henderson, J. (2001) *Classical Art: From Greece to Rome* (Oxford).

Becatti, G. (1956) 'Letture pliniane: le opere d'arte nei Monumenta Asini Pollionis e negli Horti Serviliani', in *Studi in Onore di Calderini e Paribeni* volume 3 (Milan) pp. 199–210.

——(1973–1974) 'Opere d'arte Greca nella Roman di Tiberio'. *Archeologia Classica*, 25–26: 18–53.

Bek, L. (1983) 'Questiones conviviales: The idea of the triclinium and the staging of convivial ceremony from Rome to Byzantium'. *Analecta Romana Instituti Danici*, 12: 81–107.

Bell, A. (2004) *Spectacular Power in the Greek and Roman City* (Oxford).

Bergmann, B. (1991) 'Painted perspectives of a villa visit: landscape as status and metaphor', in E.K. Gazda (ed.) *Roman Art in the Private Sphere: New Perspectives on the Architecture and Decor of the Domus, Villa and Insula* (Ann Arbor) pp. 49–70.

Bettini, M. '*In Vino Stuprum*', in O. Murray and M. Tecuşan (eds) *In Vino Veritas* (London) pp. 224–35.

Bloomer, W.M. (1997) 'Schooling in persona: Imagination and subordination in Roman education'. *Classical Antiquity*, 16: 57–78.

Boatwright, M.T. (1998) 'Luxuriant gardens and extravagant women: The *horti* of Rome from Republic to Empire', in M. Cima and E. La Rocca (eds) *Horti Romani* (Rome) pp. 71–82.

Bodel, J. (1999) 'The *Cena Trimalchionis*', in H. Hofmann (ed.) *Latin Fiction: The Latin Novel in Context* (London).

Booth, A. (1991) 'The age for reclining and its attendant perils', in W.J. Slater (ed.) *Dining in a Classical Context* (Ann Arbor) pp. 105–20.

Bounia, A. (2004) *The Nature of Classical Collecting: Collectors and Collections, 100 BCE – 100 CE* (Aldershot).

Boutron, C.F. (1995) 'Historical reconstruction of the earth's past atmospheric environment from Greenland and Antarctic snow and ice cores'. *Environmental Reviews*, 3.1: 1–28.

Bradley, K.R. (1984) *Masters and Slaves in the Roman Empire: A Study in Social Control* (Oxford).

——(1998a) 'The sentimental education of the Roman child: The role of pet-keeping'. *Latomus*, 57: 523–57.

——(1998b) 'The Roman family at dinner', in I. Nielsen and H. Sigismund-Nielsen (eds) *Meals in a Social Context: Aspects of the Communal Meal in the Hellenistic and Roman World* (Aarhus) pp. 36–55.

Bradley, M. (2005–2006) 'Colour and marble in early Imperial Rome'. *Cambridge Classical Journal*, 52: 1–22.

Broise, H. and Jolivet, V. (1998) 'Il giardino e l'acqua: l'esempio degli *Horti Lucullani*', in M. Cima and E. La Rocca (eds) *Horti Romani* (Rome) pp. 189–202.

Brun, J.-P. (2004) *Archéologie du vin et de l'huile dans l'Empire Romain* (Paris).

Bull, M. and Black, L. (2003) *The Auditory Culture Reader* (Oxford).

Bullough, V.L. (2002) 'Eunuchs in history and society', in S. Tougher (ed.) *Eunuchs in Antiquity and Beyond* (London) pp. 1–18.

Bullough, V.L. and Bullough, B. (1993) *Cross Dressing, Sex and Gender* (Philadelphia).

Burnet, S. (2002) 'Dwarf athletes in the Roman Empire'. *The Ancient History Bulletin*, 17: 17–32.

Cahn, N. (2006) 'Child witnessing of domestic violence', in N.E. Dowd, D.G. Singer and R.F. Wilson (eds) *Handbook of Children, Culture and Violence* (London) pp. 3–20.

Capponi, L. (2002) 'Maecenas and Pollio'. *Zeitschrift für Papyrologie und Epigraphik*, 140: 181–4.

Carey, S. (2002) 'A tradition of adventures in the imperial grotto'. *Greece and Rome*, 49: 44–61.

Carosella, A. (1996) *Gli Scavi di Stabia: Giornale di scavo* (Rome).

Carver, E. (2001) *The Visibility of Imported Wine and its Associated Accoutrements in Later Iron Age Britain* (BAR British Series 325), (Oxford).

Castelli, E.A. and Jakobsen, J.R. (2004) *Interventions: Activists and Academics Respond to Violence* (New York).

Champlin, E. (2003) *Nero* (Cambridge, MA).

Cima, M. and La Rocca, E. (1986) *Le tranquile dimore degli dei: La residenza imperiale degli Horti Lamiani* (Venice).

——(1998) *Horti Romani* (Rome).

Cimino, R.M. (1994) *Ancient Rome and India: Commercial and Cultural Contacts between the Roman World and India* (Delhi).

Cirillo, A. and Casale, A. (2004) *Il Tesoro di Boscoreale e il suo scopritore: la vera storia rcostruita dell'epoca* (Pompeii).

Clarke, J.R. (1996) 'Landscape paintings in the Villa of Oplontis'. *Journal of Roman Archaeology*, 9: 81–107.

——(1998) *Looking at Lovemaking: Constructions of Sexuality in Roman Art 100 BC – AD 250* (Berkeley).

——(2003a) 'Representations of male to female love making', in M. Golden and P. Toohey (eds) *Sex and Difference in Ancient Greece and Rome* (Edinburgh): 221–38.

——(2003b) *Art in the Lives of Ordinary Romans: Visual Representation and Non-Elite Viewers in Italy 100 BC – AD 315* (Berkeley).

——(2007) *Looking at Laughter. Humour, Power, and Transgression in Roman Visual Culture, 100 BC – AD 250* (Berkeley).

Classen, C. (1993) *Worlds of Sense: Exploring the Senses in History and across Cultures* (London).

——(2005) *The Book of Touch* (Oxford).

Classen, C., Howes, D. and Synnott, A. (1994) *Aroma: The Cultural History of Smell* (London).

Coarelli, F. (1983) 'Architettura sacra e architecttura privata nella tarda republicca', in P. Gros (ed.) *Architecture et société: de l'archaïse Grec à la fin de la répulique romaine* (Rome) pp. 191–217.

——(2001) 'L'armamento e le classi dei gladiatori', in A. La Regina (ed.) *Sangue e Arena* (Rome) pp. 153–74.

Cokayne, K. (2003) *Experiencing Old Age in Ancient Rome* (London).

Coleman, K.M. (1990) 'Fatal charades: Roman executions staged as mythological enactments'. *Journal of Roman Studies*, 80: 44–73.

——(2006) *M. Valerii Martialis Liber Spectaculorum* (Oxford).

Conte, G.B. (1996) *The Hidden Author: An Interpretation of Petronius' Satyricon* (Berkeley).

Cooley, A. and Cooley, M. (2004) *Pompeii: A Sourcebook* (London).

Corbeill, A. (1997) 'Dining deviants in Roman political invective', in J. Hallett and M. Skinner (eds) *Roman Sexualities* (Princeton) pp. 99–128.

Courtney, E. (2001) *A Companion to Petronius* (Oxford).

Cowan, A. and Steward, J. (2007) *The City and the Senses: Urban Culture Since 1500* (Basingstoke).

Creighton, J. (2000) *Coins and Power in Late Iron Age Britain* (Cambridge).

——(2006) *Britannia: The Creation of a Roman Province* (London).

Curtis, R.I. (1991) *Garum and Salsamenta: Production and Commerce in Materia Medica* (Leiden).

Dalby, A. (2000) *Empires of Pleasures: Luxury and Indulgence in the Roman World* (London).

——(2003) *Food in the Ancient World from A to Z* (London).

Dam, H.-J. van (1984) *P. Papinius Statius Silvae Book II: A Commentary* (*Mnemosyne Supplement* 82), (Leiden).

D'Arms, J.H. (1970) *Romans on the Bay of Naples* (Cambridge, MA).

——(1981) *Commerce and Social Standing in Ancient Rome* (Cambridge, MA).

——(1984) 'Control, companionship and clientela: Some social functions of the Roman communal meal'. *Echos du Monde Classique*, 28: 327–48.

——(1990) 'The Roman *Convivium* and the idea of equality', in O. Murray (ed.) *Sympotica: A Symposium on the Symposion* (Oxford) pp. 308–20.

——(1991) 'Slaves at the Roman *Convivia*', in W.J. Slater (ed.) *Dining in a Classical Context* (Ann Arbor) pp. 171–84.

——(1995) 'Heavy drinking and drunkenness in the Roman world: Four questions for historians', in O. Murray and M. Tecuşan (eds) *In Vino Veritas* (London) pp. 304–17.

——(1998) 'Between public and private: The *Epulum Publicum* and Caesar's *Horti Trans Tiberim*', in M. Cima and E. La Rocca (eds) *Horti Romani* (Rome) pp. 33–43.

——(1999) 'Performing culture: Roman spectacle and the banquets of the powerful', in B. Bergmann and C. Kondoleon (eds) *The Art of Ancient Spectacle* (New Haven) pp. 283–300.

——(2003) *Romans on the Bay of Naples and Other Essays on Roman Campania* (Bari).

Darwall-Smith, R.H. (1996) *Emperors and Architecture: A Study of Flavian Rome* (Brussels).

Dawson, C.M. (1944) *The Romano-Campanian Mythological Landscape Painting* (*Yale Classical Studies* 9), (New Haven).

De Callataÿ, F. (2005) 'The Graeco-Roman economy in the super long-run: Lead, copper and shipwrecks'. *Journal of Roman Archaeology*, 18: 361–72.

De Caro, S. (1987) 'The Sculptures of the Villa of Poppaea at Oplontis: A preliminary report', in E.B. Macdougall *Ancient Roman Villa Gardens* (Dumbarton Oaks Colloquium on the History of Landscape Architecture 10), (Washington, DC) pp. 77–134.

DeLaine, J. (1992) 'New models, old models: Continuity and change in the design of public baths', in H.-J. Schalles, H. von Hesberg and P. Zanker (eds) *Die Römische*

Stadt im 2. Jahrhundert n. Chr.: Der Funktionswandel des öffentlichen Raumes (Cologne) pp. 257–76.

——(1999) 'Benefactions and urban renewal: Bath buildings in Roman Italy', in J. DeLaine and D.E. Johnston (eds) *Roman Baths and Bathing* (Portsmouth, RI) pp. 67–74.

——(2000) 'Bricks and mortar: Exploring the economics of building techniques at Rome and Ostia', in D.J. Mattingly and J. Salmon (eds) *Economies beyond Agriculture in the Classical World* (London) pp. 271–96.

——(2006) 'The cost of creation: Technology at the service of construction', in E. Lo Cascio (ed.) *Innovazione Tecnica e Progresso Economico nel Mondo Romano* (Bari) pp. 227–52.

De Souza, P. (2008) 'Rome's contribution to the development of piracy', in R.L. Hohlfelder (ed.) *The Maritime World of Ancient Rome* (Memoirs of the American Academy in Rome Supplement VI) pp. 71–96.

Donahue, J.F. (2004) *The Roman Community at Table during the Principate* (Ann Arbor).

Douglas, M. (1987) *Constructive Drinking: Perspectives on Drink from Anthropology* (Cambridge).

Drobnick, J. (2006) *The Smell Culture Reader* (Oxford).

Dunbabin, K.M.D. (2003) *The Roman Banquet: Images of Conviviality* (Cambridge).

Duncan-Jones, R. (1982) *The Roman Economy: Quantitative Studies* (Cambridge).

——(1990) *Structure and Scale in the Roman Economy* (Cambridge).

——(1996) 'The impact of the Antonine plague'. *Journal of Roman Archaeology,* 9: 108–36.

Edwards, C. (1993) *The Politics of Immorality in Ancient Rome* (Cambridge).

——(1994) 'Beware of imitations: Theatre and the subversion of imperial identity', in J. Elsner and J. Masters (eds) *Reflections of Nero: Culture, History and Representation* (London) pp. 83–97.

——(2007) *Death in Ancient Rome* (New Haven).

Edwards, J. (1984) *The Roman Cookery of Apicius* (Washington).

Eger, A.A. (2007) 'Queered space in the Roman bath-house', in M. Harlow and R. Laurence (eds) *Age and Ageing in the Roman Empire* (Portsmouth, RI) pp. 131–51.

Elsner, J. (1994) 'Constructing decadence: The representation of Nero as imperial builder', in J. Elsner and J. Masters (eds) *Reflections of Nero: Culture, History and Representation* (London) pp. 112–30.

——(1995) *Art and the Roman Viewer: The Transformation of Art from the Pagan World to Christianity* (Cambridge).

Ernst, W. (2006) 'The normal and the abnormal: Reflections on norms and normativity', in W. Ernst (ed.) *Histories of the Normal and Abnormal: Social and Cultural Histories of Norms and Normativity* (London) pp. 1–25.

Evans, R. (2003) 'Searching for Paradise: Landscape, Utopia and Rome'. *Arethusa*, 36: 285–307.

Eyben, E. (1993) *Restless Youth in Ancient Rome* (London).

Fagan, G. (1999a) 'Interpreting the evidence: Did slaves bathe in the baths?', in J. DeLaine and D.E. Johnston (eds) *Roman Baths and Bathing Part 1: Bathing and Society* (Portsmouth, RI) pp. 25–34.

——(1999b) *Bathing in Public in the Roman World* (Ann Arbor).

Faure, P. (1987) *Parfums et aromates de l'antiquité* (Paris).

Favro, D. (1996) *The Urban Image of Augustan Rome* (Cambridge).

Feingold, M. and Pashayan, H. (1983) *Genetics and Birth Defects in Clinical Practice* (Boston).

Fincham, G. (2002) 'Consumer theory and Roman North Africa: A post-colonial approach to the ancient economy', in M. Carruthers, C. van Driel-Murray, A. Gardner, J. Lucas, L. Revell and E. Swift (eds) *TRAC 2001. Proceedings of the Eleventh Annual Theoretical Roman Archaeology Conference* (Oxford) pp. 34–44.

Fitzgerald, A. (2005) *Animal Abuse and Family Violence. Researching the Interrelationships of Abusive Power* (Lewiston, NY).

Flory, M.B. (1998) 'The integration of women into the Roman triumph'. *Historia*, 47: 489–94.

Foucault, M. (1978) *The History of Sexuality Volume 1: An Introduction.* (Harmandsworth).

——(1984a) *The History of Sexuality Volume 3: The Care of the Self* (Harmandsworth).

——(1984b) 'Space, knowledge and power' in P. Rabinow (ed.) *The Foucault Reader* (New York) pp. 239–56

Fredrick, D. (2003) 'Grasping the Pangolin: Sensuous ambiguity in Roman dining'. *Arethusa*, 36: 309–44.

Fulford, M. and Wallace-Hadrill, A. (1999) 'Towards a history of pre-Roman Pompeii: Excavations beneath the House of Amarantus'. *Papers of the British School at Rome*, 67: 37–144.

Galinsky, K. (1996) *Augustan Culture: An Interpretative Introduction* (Princeton).

Gardner, J.F. and Wiedemann, T. (1991) *The Roman Household: A Sourcebook* (London).

Garland, R. (1995) *In the Eye of the Beholder: Deformity and Disability in the Graeco-Roman World* (London).

Garnsey, P. (1999) *Food and Society in Classical Antiquity* (Cambridge).

Garthwaite, J. (1984) 'Statius *Silvae* 3.4: On the fate of Earinus', in H. Temporini and W. Haase (eds) *Aufstieg und Niedergang der Römischen Welt*, II.32.1: 111–24.

Gaspari, C. (1979) *Aedes Concordiae Augustae* (Rome).

Getty, J.P. (1966) *The Joys of Collecting* (London).

——(1976) *As I See it: The Autobiography of J. Paul Getty* (London).

Gibson, R. (2003) *Ovid: Ars Amatoria Book 3* (Cambridge).

Gigante, M. (1979) *Civiltà delle forme letterarie nell'antica Pompei* (Naples).

Gleason, M. (1995) *Making Men: Sophists and Self-presentation in Ancient Rome* (Princeton).

Gold, B.K. (1998) 'Women's bodies in Juvenal's *Satires*'. *Arethusa*, 31: 369–86.

Goldhill, S. (2002) 'The erotic experience of looking: Cultural conflict and the gaze in empire culture', in M.C. Nussbaum and J. Sihvola (eds) *The Sleep of Reason: Erotic Experience and Sexual Ethics in Ancient Greece and Rome* (Chicago) pp. 374–99.

Golvin, J.-C. (1988) *L'Amphithéâtre romain* (Paris).

Gowers, E. (1993) *The Loaded Table: Representations of Food in Literature* (Oxford).

Graham, E.-J. (2005) 'Dining al fresco with the living and the dead in Roman Italy', in M. Carroll, D. Hadley and H. Wilmott (eds) *Consuming Passions: Dining from Antiquity to the Eighteenth Century* (Stroud) pp. 49–66.

Grainger, S. (2006) *Cooking Apicius: Roman Recipes for Today* (Totnes).

Grant, M. (1999) *Roman Cookery: Ancient Recipes for Modern Kitchens* (Totnes).

Griffin, M. (1976) *Seneca: A Philosopher in Politics* (Oxford).

——(1984) *Nero* (London).

Grocock, C. and Grainger, S. (2006) *Apicius: A Critical Edition with an Introduction and an English Translation of the Latin Recipe Text Apicius* (Totnes).

Habinek, T. (2005) *The World of Roman Song: From Ritualized Speech to Social Order* (Baltimore)

Habinek, T. and A. Schiesaro (1997) *The Roman Cultural Revolution* (Cambridge).

Hales, S. (2002) 'Looking for eunuchs: The *Galli* and Attis in Roman art', in S. Tougher (ed.) *Eunuchs in Antiquity and Beyond* (London) pp. 87–102.

Hallett, C.H. (2005) *The Roman Nude: Heroic Statuary 200 BC – AD 300* (Oxford).

Harlow, M. and Laurence, R. (2009) 'De amicitia: The role of age', in *Passages from Antiquity to the Middle Ages III: De Amicitia (Acta Instituti Romani Finlandiae)*.

Henderson, J. (2006) 'In Ovid with bed', in R. Gibson, S. Green and A. Sharrock (eds) *The Art of Love: Bimillennial Essays on Ovid's Ars Amatoria annd Remedia Amoris* (Oxford) pp. 77–95.

Hermansen, G. (1982) *Ostia: Aspects of Roman City Life* (Edmonton).

Hong, S., Candelone, J. P., Patterson, C.C. and Boutron, C.F. (1994) 'Greenland ice evidence of hemispheric pollution two millennia ago by Greek and Roman civilizations'. *Science*, 265: 1841–3.

——(1996) 'History of ancient copper smelting pollution during Roman and medieval times recorded in Greenland ice'. *Science*, 272: 246–9.

Hopkins, K. (1978) *Conquerors and Slaves: Sociological Studies in Roman History 1* (Cambridge).

——(1980) 'Taxes and trade in the Roman empire, 200 BC – AD 400'. *Journal of Roman Studies*, 70: 101–25.

——(1983) *Death and Renewal: Sociological Studies in Roman History 2* (Cambridge).

——(2002) 'Rome, taxes, rents and trade', in W. Scheidel and S. von Reden (eds) *The Ancient Economy* (Edinburgh) pp. 190–230.

Horsfall, N. (2003) *The Culture of the Roman Plebs* (London).

Isager, J. (1991) *Pliny on Art and Society: The Elder Pliny's Chapters on the History of Art* (London).

Jackson, R. (2005) 'Circumcision and self-image: Celsus's "Operation on the Penis"', in A. Hopkins and M. Wyke (eds) *Roman Bodies: Antiquity to the Eighteenth Century,* British School at Rome (London) pp. 23–32.

Jacobelli, L. (2003) *Gladiators at Pompeii* (Los Angeles).

Jansen, G.E.M. (1997) 'Private toilets at Pompeii: Appearance and operation', in S.E. Bon and R. Jones (eds) *Sequence and Space in Pompeii* (Oxford) pp. 121–34.

——(2000) 'Systems for the Disposal of waste and excreta in Roman cities: The situation at Pompeii, Herculaneum and Ostia', in X. Dupré Raventós and J.-A. Remolà (eds) *Sordes Urbis: La Eliminación de Risiduos en la Ciudad Romana* (Rome) pp. 37–50.

——(2001) 'Water-pipe systems in the houses of Pompeii: Distribution and use', in A.O. Koloski-Ostrow (ed.) *Water, Use, and Hydraulics in the Roman City* (Boston) pp. 27–40.

——(2003) 'Social distinctions and issues of privacy in the toilets of Hadrian's villa'. *Journal of Roman Archaeology*, 16: 137–52.

——(2007) 'Toilets with a view: The luxurious toilets of the Emperor Hadrian at his villa near Tivoli'. *Babesch*, 82: 165–82.

Jashemski, W.F. (1979) *The Gardens of Pompeii, Herculaneum and the Villas Destroyed by Vesuvius* (New Rochelle, NY).

——(1987) 'Recently excavated gardens and cultivated land of the Villas at Boscoreale and Oplontis', in E.B. Macdougall (ed.) *Ancient Roman Villa Gardens* (Dumbarton Oaks Colloquium on the History of Landscape Architecture 10), (Washington, DC) pp. 30–75.

——(1993) *The Gardens of Pompeii, Herculaneum and the Villas destroyed by Vesuvius. Volume II, Appendices* (New Rochelle, NY).

Johnson, W.A. (2000a) 'New instrumental music from Graeco-Roman Egypt'. *Bulletin of the American Association of Papyrologists*, 37: 17–36.

——(2000b) 'Musical evenings in the early empire: New evidence from a Greek papyrus with musical notation'. *Journal of Hellenic Studies*, 120: 57–85.

Jory, E.J. (1981) 'The literary evidence for the beginnings of imperial pantomime'. *Bulletin of the Institute of Classical Studies*, 28: 147–61.

——(1984) 'The early pantomime riots', in A. Moffatt (ed.) *Maistor: Classical, Byzantine and Renaissance Studies for Robert Browning* (Canberra) pp. 57–66.

——(1996) 'The drama of the dance: Prolegomena to an iconography of imperial pantomime', in W.J. Slater (ed.) *Roman theater and society* (Ann Arbor) pp. 1–28.

Jouffroy, H. (1986) *La Construction publique en Italie et dans l'Afrique Romaine* (Strasburg).

Kajanto, I. (1969) 'Tacitus and the slaves: An interpretation of the annals XIV, 42–45'. *Arctos*, 6: 43–60.

Kampen, N. (1997) 'Epilogue: Gender and desire', in A.O. Koloski-Ostrow and C.L. Lyons (eds) *Naked Truths: Women, Sexuality and Gender in Classical Art and Archaeology* (London) pp. 267–78.

Kaufman, C.K. (2006) *Cooking in Ancient Civilisations* (London).

Kellum, B. (1990) 'The city adorned: Programmatic display at the *Aedes Concordiae*', in K.A. Raaflaub and M. Toher (eds) *Between Republic and Empire: Interpretations of Augustus and His Principate* (Berkeley) pp. 276–307.

Kennedy, G.A. (1987) 'The history of Latin education'. *Helios*, 14 (2): 7–16.

King, H. (2004) *The Disease of Virgins: Green Sickness, Chlorosis and the Problems of Puberty* (London).

Kirsch, S.J. (2006) *Children, Adolescents and Media Violence: A Critical Look at the Research* (London).

Korsmeyer, C. (2005) *The Taste Culture Reader: Experiencing Food and Drink* (Oxford).

Kuttner, A.L. (1995) *Dynasty and Empire in the Age of Augustus: The Case of the Boscoreale Cups* (Berkeley).

Kyle, D.G. (1998) *Spectacles of Death in Ancient Rome* (London).

Lada-Richards, I. (2005) 'In the mirror of the dance: A Lucianic metaphor in its performative and ethical contexts'. *Mnemosyne*, 58: 335–57.

——(2007) *Silent Eloquence: Lucian and Pantomime Dancing* (London).

Laes, C. (2005) 'Childbeating in antiquity: Some reconsiderations', in K. Mustakallio, J. Hanska, H.-L. Sainio and V. Vuolanto (eds) *Hoping for Continuity: Childhood, Education and Death in Antiquity and the Middle Ages* (Rome) pp. 75–90.

Lafon, X. (2001) *Villa maritima: Recherches sur les villas littorales de l'Italie romaine* (Rome).

Landels, J.G. (1999) *Music in Ancient Greece and Rome* (London).

Langlands, R. (2006) *Sexual Morality in Ancient Rome* (Cambridge).

Larmour, D., Miller, P.A. and Platter, C. (1997) *Rethinking Sexuality: Foucault and Classical Antiquity* (Princeton).

La Rocca, E. (1986) 'Il lusso come espressione di potere', in M. Cima and E. La Rocca (eds) *Le tranquille dimore degli dei: La residenza imperiale degli Horti Lamiani* (Venice) pp. 3–36.

Laurence R. (1997) 'Writing the Roman metropolis', in H. Parkins (ed.) *Roman Urbanism: Beyond the Consumer Model* (London) pp. 1–20.

Laurence R. and Paterson J. (1999) 'Power and laughter: Imperial *Dicta*'. *Papers of the British School at Rome*, 67: 183–97.

Leach, E.W. (1997) 'Horace and the material culture of Augustan Rome', in T. Habinek and A. Schiesaro (eds) *The Roman Cultural Revolution* (Cambridge) pp. 105–21.

——(2004) *The Social Life of Painting in Ancient Rome and on the Bay of Naples* (Cambridge).

Le Roux, G., Weiss, D., Grattan, J., Grivelet, N., Krachler, M., Cheburkin, A., Rausch, N., Kober, B. and Shotyk, W. (2004) 'Identifying the sources and timing of ancient

and medieval atmospheric pollution in England using a peat profile from Lindow
Bog, Manchester'. *Journal of Environmental Monitoring*, 6: 502–10.

Letters, R.J. (1969) 'The scales of some surviving Auloi'. *Classical Quarterly*, 19:
266–8.

Le Vane, D. and Getty, J.P. (1955) *Collector's Choice: The Chronicle of an Artistic
Odyssey through Europe* (London).

Levick, B. (1982) 'Domitian and the provinces'. *Latomus*, 41: 50–73.

——(1999) *Tiberius the Politician* (London).

Liebeschuetz, W. (2000) 'Rubbish disposal in Greek and Roman cities', in X. Dupré
Raventós and J.-A. Remolà (eds) *Sordes Urbes: La Eliminación de Residuos en la
Ciudad Romana* (Rome) pp. 51–62.

Lightfoot, J.L. (2002) 'Sacred eunuchism in the cult of the Syrian goddess', in
S. Tougher (ed.) *Eunuchs in Antiquity and Beyond* (London): 71–86.

Ling, R. (1977) 'Studius and the beginnings of Roman landscape painting'. *Journal of
Roman Studies*, 67: 1–16.

Loane, H.J. (1938) *Industry and Commerce of The City of Rome (50 BC – AD 200)*,
(Baltimore).

Maiuri, A. (1933) *La Casa del Menandro e il suo tesoro di aregenteria* (Rome).

Margolis, J. (2004) *O: The Intimate History of the Orgasm* (London).

Martins, C. (2003) 'Becoming consumers: Looking beyond wealth as an explanation
for villa variability', in G. Carr, E. Swift and J. Weekes (eds) *TRAC 2002. Proceedings
of the Twelfth Annual Theoretical Roman Archaeology Conference* (Oxford)
pp. 84–100.

Mastroroberto, M. (2006a) 'Il tesoro di Moregine e le "coppe della riconciliazione"',
in *Aregenti a Pompei* (Naples) pp. 31–45.

——(2006b) 'Il tesoro di Moregine', in *Aregenti a Pompei* (Naples) pp. 224–37.

Mattingly, D. (1990) 'Paintings, presses and perfume production at Pompeii'. *Oxford
Journal of Archaeology*, 9: 71–90.

Mattusch, C.C. and Lie, H. (2005) *The Villa dei Papiri at Herculaneum: Life and
Afterlife of a Sculpture Collection* (Los Angeles).

McGinn, T. (2004) *The Economy of Prostitution in the Roman World* (Ann Arbor).

McKeown, N. (2007) 'Had they no shame? Martial, Statius, and Roman sexual
attitudes towards slave children', in S. Crawford and G. Shepherd (eds) *Children,
Childhood and Society*, BAR Int. Ser. 1696 (Oxford) pp. 57–62.

Mielsch, H. (1990) *La Villa Romana* (Florence).

Miko, S., Mesić, S., Šparcia-Miko, M. and Prohić, E. (2005) 'Isotropic trends and enrichment of atmospheric lead during the past two millennia in Lake Vrana on Cres Island (Croatia)'. *RMZ – Materials and Geoenvironment*, 52: 95–7.

Miller, J.I. (1968) *The Spice Trade of the Roman Empire 29 BC to AD 641* (Oxford).

Mitchell, S. (2006) 'From "monstrous" to "abnormal": The case of conjoined twins in the nineteenth century', in W. Ernst (ed.) *Histories of the Normal and Abnormal. Social and Cultural Histories of Norms and Normativity* (London) pp. 53–72.

Mols, S.T.A.M. (1999) *Wooden Furniture in Herculaneum* (Amsterdam).

Mols, S.T.A.M. and Moormann, E.M. (1993–1994) '*Ex parvo crevit*. Proposta per una lettura iconografia della Tomba di Vestorius Priscus fuori Porta Vesuvio a Pompei'. *Rivista di Studi Pompeiane*, 6: 15–52.

Monteil, G. (2004) 'Samian and consumer choice in Roman London', in B. Coxford, H. Eckardt, J. Meade and J. Weekes (eds) *TRAC 2003. Proceedings of the Thirteenth Annual Theoretical Roman Archaeology Conference* (Oxford) pp. 1–15.

Moormann, E.M. (1998) '"Vivere come un uomo": L'uso dello spazio nella Domus Aurea', in M. Cima and E. La Rocca (eds) *Horti Romani* (Rome) pp. 345–61.

——(2000) 'La Bellezza dell'Immondezza: Raffigurazioni di Rifiuti nell'Arte Ellenistica e Romana', in X. Dupré Raventós and J.-A. Remolà (eds) *Sordes Urbes: La Eliminación de Residuos en la Ciudad Romana* (Rome) pp. 75–94.

Morley, N. (1996) *Metropolis and Hinterland: the City of Rome and the Italian Economy 200 BC – AD 200* (Cambridge).

——(2007) 'The early Roman Empire: Distribution', in W. Scheidel, I. Morris, and R. Saller (eds) *The Cambridge Economic History of the Greco-Roman World* (Cambridge) pp. 570–91.

Murray, O. (1990) 'Sympotic history', in O. Murray (ed.) *Sympotica: A Symposium on the Symposion* (Oxford) pp. 3–13.

——(1995) 'Histories of Pleasure', in O. Murray and M. Tecuşan (eds) *In Vino Veritas* (London) pp. 3–17.

Newland, C.E. (2002) *Statius' Silvae and the Poetics of Empire* (Cambridge).

Noy, D. (2000) *Foreigners at Rome: Citizens and Strangers* (London).

Nriagu, J.O. (1983) *Lead and Lead Poisoning in Antiquity* (New York).

——(1996) 'A history of global metal pollution'. *Science*, 272: 223–4.

——(1998) 'Tales told in lead'. *Science*, 281: 1622–3.

Nutton, V. (1995) 'Galen and the traveller's fare', in J. Wilkins, D. Harvey and M. Dobson (eds) *Food in Antiquity* (Exeter) pp. 359–70.

Painter, K.S. (2001) *The Insula of the Menander at Pompeii Volume IV: The Silver Treasure* (Oxford).

Panella, C. (2001) 'La valle del Colosseo prima del Colosseo e la Meta Sudans', in A. La Regina (ed.) *Sangue e Arena* (Rome) pp. 49–68.

Parker, H. (1989) 'Crucially funny or Tranio on the couch: The *servus callidus* and jokes about torture'. *Transactions of the American Philological Association*, 119: 233–46.

——(1992) 'Love's body anatomized: The ancient erotic handbooks and the rhetoric of sexuality', in A. Richlin (ed.) *Pornography and Representation in Greece and Rome* (New York).

——(1997) 'The tetratogenic grid', in J.P. Hallett and M.B. Skinner (eds) *Roman Sexualities* (Princeton) pp. 47–65.

Parkin, T. (2003) *Old Age in the Roman World: A Cultural and Social History* (Baltimore).

——(in press) 'The elderly children of Greece and Rome'.

Parslow, C.C. (1995) *Rediscovering Antiquity: Karl Weber and the Excavation of Herculaneum, Pompeii, and Stabiae* (Cambridge).

Di Pasquale, G. and Paolucci, F. (2007) *Il giardino antico da Babilonia a Roma* (Florence).

Patterson, J. (2006) *Landscapes and Cities: Rural Settlement and Civic Transformation in Early Imperial Italy* (Oxford).

Pavlovskis, Z. (1973) *Man in an Artificial Landscape: The Marvels of Civilization in Imperial Roman Literature* (*Mnemosyne Supplement 25*), (Leiden).

Pisapia, M.S. (1989) *Mosaici Antichi in Italia, Regione Prima: Stabiae* (Rome).

Plass, P. (1995) *The Game of Death in Ancient Rome: Arena Sport and Political Suicide* (London).

Plaza, M. (2000) *Laughter and Derision in Petronius' Satyrica* (Stockholm).

Pollitt, J.J. (1978) 'The impact of Greek art on Rome'. *Transactions of the American Philological Association*, 108: 155–74.

Purcell, N. (1985) 'Wine and wealth in ancient Italy'. *Journal of Roman Studies*, 75: 1–19.

——(1987) 'Town in country and country in town', in W.F. Jashemski (ed.) *Ancient Roman Villa Gardens* (Washington) pp. 185–203.

——(1994) 'Women and wine in ancient Rome', in M. McDonald (ed.) *Gender, Drink and Drugs* (Oxford)

——(1995) 'The Roman villa and the landscape of production', in T. Cornell and K. Lomas (eds) *Urban Society in Roman Italy* (London) pp.151–80.

——(1995b) 'Eating fish: The paradoxes of seafood', in J. Wilkins, D. Harvey and M. Dobson (eds) *Food in Antiquity* (Exeter) pp. 132–48.

——(1996) 'Rome and its development under Augustus and his successors', in A.K. Bowman, E. Champlin, and A. Lintott (eds) *The Cambridge Ancient History X: The Augustan Empire 43 BC – AD 69* (Cambridge) pp. 782–811.

——(2005) 'The way we used to eat, community and history at Rome', in B.K. Gold and J.F. Donahue (eds) *Roman Dining* (A Special Issue of *American Journal of Philology*), (Baltimore) pp. 1–30.

Ramage, E.S. (1983) 'Urban problems in ancient Rome', in R.T. Marchese (ed.) *Aspects of Graeco-Roman Urbanism: Essays on the Classical City,* BAR Int. Ser. 188 (Oxford) pp. 61–92.

Ravenscroft, J. (2006) 'Invisible friends: Questioning the representation of the court dwarf in Hapsburg Spain', in W. Ernst (ed.) *Histories of the Normal and Abnormal: Social and Cultural Histories of Norms and Normativity* (London) pp. 26–52.

Rawson, E. (1987) *'Discrimina Ordinum*: The *Lex Julia Theatralis'. Papers of the British School at Rome,* 55: 83–114.

Rawson, N. and Li, X. (2004) 'The cellular basis of flavour perception: Taste and aroma', in A.J. Taylor and D.D. Roberts (eds) *Flavour Perception* (Oxford) pp. 56–85.

Ray, N. (2006) 'Consumption and Roman archaeology: Beyond Pompeii', in B. Croxford, H. Goodchild, J. Lucas and N. Ray (eds) *TRAC 2005. Proceedings of the Ffiteenth Annual Theoretical Roman Archaeology Conference* (Oxford) pp. 25–41.

Renberg, I., Brännvall, M.-L., Bindler, R. and Emteryd, O. (2000) 'Atmospheric lead pollution history during four millennia (2000 BC to 2000 AD) in Sweden'. *Ambio,* 29: 150–56.

——(2002) 'Stable isotope and lake sediments – a useful combination for the study of atmospheric lead pollution'. *The Science of the Total Environment,* 292: 45–54.

Renberg, I., Persson, M.W. and Emteryd, O. (1994) 'Pre-industrial atmospheric lead contamination detected in Swedish lake sediments'. *Nature,* 368: 323–6.

Ricci, A. (1998) *La Villa dei Quintili: Fonti scritti e fonti figurate* (Rome).

Richelin, A. (1992) *The Garden of Priapus: Sexuality and Aggression in Roman Humour (Revised Edition)*, (New York).

——(1993) 'Not before homosexuality: The materiality of the Cinaedus in the Roman law against love between men'. *Journal of the History of Sexuality,* 3: 523–73.

Riggsby, A.M. (1997) 'Public and private in Roman culture: The case of the *Cubiculum*'. *Journal of Roman Archaeology*, 10: 36–56.

Ripley, R.L. (1977) *Ripley's Believe it or not! Human oddities* (New York).

Rodriguez-Almeida, E. (2000) 'Roma, una Città "self-cleaning"?', in X. Dupré Raventos and J.-A. Remolà (eds) *Sordes Urbes: La Eliminación de Residuos en la Ciudad Romana* (Rome) pp. 123–7.

Roller, M. (2005) 'Horizontal women: Posture and sex in the Roman *Convivium*', in B.K. Gold and J.F. Donahue (eds) *Roman Dining* (A Special Issue of *American Journal of Philology*), Baltimore: 49–94.

——(2006) *Dining Posture in Ancient Rome: Bodies, Values and Status* (Princeton).

Rosman, K.J.R., Chisholm, W., Hong, S., Candelone, J.-P. and Boutron, C.F. (1997) 'Lead from Carthaginian and Roman Spanish mines isotopically identified in Greenland ice dated from 600 BC to 300 AD'. *Environmental Science and Technology*, 31: 3413–16.

Rousselle, A. (1988) *Porneia: On Desire and the Body in Antiquity* (Oxford).

Rudich, V. (1993) *Political Dissidence under Nero* (London).

——(1997) *Dissidence and Literature under Nero* (London).

Russell, D.A. (1989) 'Arts and sciences in ancient education'. *Greece and Rome*, 36: 210–25.

Russo, M. (2004) 'Alla ricerca della villa sorrentina di Pollio Felice nella baia di Puolo', in F. Senatore (ed.) *Pompei, Capri e La Pernisola Sorrentina* (Capri) pp. 103–78.

Saller, R.P. (2002) 'Framing the debate over growth in the ancient economy', in W. Scheidel and S. von Reden (eds) *The Ancient Economy* (Edinburgh) pp. 251–69.

Santillo Frizell, B. and Klynne, A. (2005) *Roman Villas around the Urbs: Interaction with Landscape and Environment* (Rome).

Schefold, K. (1960) 'Origins of Roman landscape painting'. *The Art Bulletin*, 43: 87–96.

Scheidel, W. (2002) 'A model of demographic and economic change in Roman Egypt after the Antonine plague'. *Journal of Roman Archaeology*, 15: 97–113.

——(2003) 'Germs for Rome', in C. Edwards and G. Woolf (eds) *Rome the Cosmopolis* (Cambridge) pp. 158–76.

Scobie, A. (1986) 'Slums, sanitation and mortality in the Roman world'. *Klio*, 68: 399–433.

Seager, R. (1974) '*Venustus, Lepidus, Bellus, Salsus:* Notes on the language of Catullus'. *Latomus*, 33: 891–4.

——(2005) *Tiberius*, 2nd edition (Oxford).

Sear, F. (2006) *Roman Theatres: An Architectural Survey* (Oxford).

Shepherd, R. (1993) *Ancient Mining* (London).

Sherwin-White, A.N. (1966) *The Letters of Pliny: A Historical and Social Commentary* (Oxford).

Siegel, R.E. (1970) *Galen on Sense Perception* (New York).

Sigismund-Nielsen, H. (1998) 'Roman children at mealtimes', in I. Nielsen and H. Sigismund-Nielsen (eds) *Meals in a Social Context: Aspects of the Communal Meal in the Hellenistic and Roman World* (Aarhus) pp. 56–66.

Sim, D. and Ridge, I. (2002) *Iron for the Eagles: The Iron Industry of Roman Britain* (Stroud).

Skinner, M. (1997) '*Ego mulier:* The construction of male sexuality in Catullus', in J. Hallett and M. Skinner (eds) *Roman Sexualities* (Princeton): 129–50.

Solomon, J. (1995) 'The Apician Sauce: *Ius Apicianum*', in J. Wilkins, D. Harvey and M. Dobson (eds) *Food in Antiquity* (Exeter) pp. 115–31.

Squire, M. (2003) 'Giant questions: Dining with Polyphemus at Sperlonga and Baiae'. *Apollo* (July): 29–37.

Stevenson, R.E. (1993) 'Causes of human anomalies: An overview and historical perspective', in Stevenson, R. E., Hall, J.G. and Goodman, R.M. (eds) *Human Malformations and Related Anomalies* (Oxford) pp. 3–20.

Stevenson, R.J. and Boakes, R.A. (2004) 'Sweet and sour smells: Learned syncrethesia between senses of taste and smell', in G.A. Calvert, L. Spence and B.E. Stein (eds) *The Handbook of Multi-Sensory Processes* (Cambridge, MA) pp. 69–84.

Stevenson, W. (1995) 'The rise of eunuchs in Greco-Roman antiquity'. *Journal of the History of Sexuality*, 5: 495–511.

Stewart, A.F. (1977) 'To entertain an emperor: Sperlonga, Laokoon and Tiberius at the dinner-table'. *Journal of Roman Studies*, 67: 76–90.

Stewart, R. (1994) 'Domitian and Roman religion: Juvenal, *Satires* Two and Four'. *Transactions of the American Philological Association*, 124: 309–32.

Strong, D. (1994) *Roman Museums: Selected Papers on Roman Art and Architecture* (London).

Sullivan, J.P. (1968) *The Satyricon of Petronius: A Literary Study* (London).

Suresh, S. (2004) *Symbols of Trade: Roman and Pseudo-Roman Objects found in India* (Delhi).

Syme, R. (1961) 'Who was Vedius Pollio?'. *Journal of Roman Studies*, 51: 23–30.

——(1989) 'Diet on Capri'. *Athenaeum*, 67: 263–72.

——(1991) *Roman Papers VII* (Oxford).

Tanner, J. (2006) *The Invention of Art History in Ancient Greece: Religion, Society, and Artistic Rationalism* (Cambridge).

Tassinari, S. (1993) *Il vasellame bronzeo di Pompei* (Rome).

Taylor, R. (1997) 'Two Pathic subcultures in ancient Rome'. *Journal of the History of Sexuality*, 7: 319–71.

Tchernia, A. (1984) *Le Vin de l'Italie romaine* (Rome).

——(1995) 'Le Vin et l'honneur', in O. Murray and M. Tecuşan (eds) *In Vino Veritas* (London) pp. 297–303.

Thurmond, D.L. (2006) *A Handbook of Food Processing in Classical Rome – For Her Bounty No Winter* (Leiden).

Ulrich, R.B. (2007) *Roman Woodworking* (New Haven).

Varrone, A. (2002) *Erotica Pompeiana: Love Inscriptions on the Walls of Pompeii* (Rome).

Veblen, T. (1970) *The Theory of the Leisure Class* (London).

Versnel, H.S. (1970) *Triumphus: An Inquiry into the Origin, Development and Meaning of the Roman Triumph* (Leiden).

Veyne, P. (2003) *Seneca: The Life of a Stoic* (London).

Villard, P. (1988) 'Le Mélange et ses problèmes'. *Revue des Études Anciennes*, 90: 19–33.

Vons, J. (1999) '"Il est des parfums sauvages comme l'odeur du desert": Étude du vocabulaire des parfums chez Pline l'Ancien'. *Latomus*, 58: 820–38.

Vout, C. (2007) *Power and Eroticism in Imperial Rome* (Cambridge).

Wallace-Hadrill, A. (1982) *Suetonius* (London).

——(1998) '*Horti* and Hellenization', in M. Cima and E. La Rocca (eds) *Horti Romani* (Rome) pp. 1–12.

Walters, J. (1998) 'Making a spectacle: Deviant men, invective and pleasure'. *Arethusa*, 31: 355–67.

Welch, K. (2008) *The Roman Amphiteatre from its Origins to the Colosseum* (Cambridge).

Wiedemann, T. (1992) *Emperors and Gladiators* (London).

——(1996) 'Tiberius to Nero', in A.K. Bowman, E. Champlin and A. Lintott (eds) *The Cambridge Ancient History, Volume 10: The Augustan Empire 43 BC – AD 69*, second edition (Cambridge) pp. 198–255.

Wilkins, J. (2005) 'Land and sea: Italy and the Mediterranean in the Roman discourse of dining', in B.K. Gold and J.F. Donahue (eds) *Roman Dining* (A Special Issue of *American Journal of Philology*), (Baltimore): 31–48.

Williams, C. (1999) *Roman Homosexuality: Ideologies of Masculinity in Classical Antiquity* (New York).

Wilson, A. (2002) 'Machines, power and the ancient economy'. *Journal of Roman Studies*, 92: 1–32.

——(2006) 'The economic impact of technological advances in the Roman construction industry', in E. Lo Cascio (ed.) *Innovazione Tecnica e Progresso Economico nel Mondo Romano* (Bari) pp. 225–36.

Wiseman, T.P. (1985) *Catullus and his World: A reappraisal* (Cambridge).

Wistrand, M. (1990) 'Violence and entertainment in Seneca the younger'. *Eranos*, 88: 31–46.

Younger, J.G. (2005) *Sex in the Ancient World from A to Z* (London).

Zanker, P. (1988) *The Power of Images in the Age of Augustus* (Ann Arbor).

Zeiner, N.K. (2005) *Nothing Ordinary Here: Statius as Creator of Distinction in the Silvae* (New York).

Zorzetti, N. (1990) 'The *Carmina Convivialia*', in O. Murray (ed.) *Sympotica: A Symposium on the Symposion* (Oxford) pp. 289–307.

Index